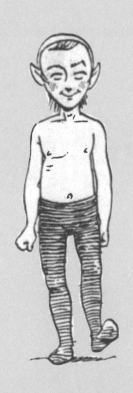

YOU

The Owner's Manual for Teens

A Guide to a Healthy Body and Happy Life

MICHAEL F. ROIZEN, MD
MEHMET C. OZ, MD
AND ELLEN ROME, MD, MPH

with Ted Spiker, Craig Wynett,
Zoe Oz, and Linda G. Kahn, MPH

ILLUSTRATIONS BY GARY HALLGREN

FREE PRESS
NEW YORK   LONDON   TORONTO   SYDNEY

Free Press
A Division of Simon & Schuster, Inc.
1230 Avenue of the Americas
New York, NY 10020

First Free Press hardcover edition June 2011

FREE PRESS and colophon are trademarks of Simon & Schuster, Inc.

For information about special discounts for bulk purchases,
please contact Simon & Schuster Special Sales at
1-866-506-1949 or business@simonandschuster.com.

The Simon & Schuster Speakers Bureau can bring authors to your live event. For
more information or to book an event contact the Simon & Schuster Speakers Bureau
at 1-866-248-3049 or visit our website at www.simonspeakers.com.

Manufactured in the United States of America

3   5   7   9   10   8   6   4   2

Library of Congress Cataloging-in-Publication Data

Roizen, Michael F.
You, the owner's manual for teens / Michael F. Roizen, Mehmet C. Oz, and Ellen Rome ;
with Ted Spiker . . . [et al.] ; illustrations by Gary Hallgren.
    p.   cm.
1. Teenagers—Health and hygiene.   2. Adolescent psychology.   I. Oz, Mehmet, 1960–
    II. Rome, Ellen.   III. Title.
    RA777.R64   2011
613'.0433—dc22   2011009184

ISBN 978-0-7432-9258-0
ISBN 978-0-7432-9259-7 (ebook)

For teens everywhere—
you are the future and always will be.

Note to Readers

This publication contains the opinions and ideas of its authors. It is intended to provide helpful and informative material on the subjects addressed in the publication. It is sold with the understanding that the authors and publisher are not engaged in rendering medical, health, or any other kind of personal professional services in the book. The reader should consult his or her medical, health, or other competent professional before adopting any of the suggestions in this book or drawing inferences from it.

The authors and publisher specifically disclaim all responsibility for any liability, loss, or risk, personal or otherwise, which is incurred as a consequence, directly or indirectly, of the use and application of any of the contents of this book.

Contents

Introduction

If we gave you three minutes to scribble down a list of the most important things in your life, we suspect you'd pop in your earbuds, dial up some of your favorite music, and scratch down a few answers that look something like this:

Your friends and family

The boy or girl you like

Having cool clothes

School

Making it through your math test tomorrow

Staying zit free

Making the soccer team

Unlimited texting plans

Excellent list. No quibbles from us whatsoever. Though the specifics may change from person to person, there's no doubt that your priorities—relationships, performance, appearance—are the priorities of virtually everybody else your age. But if you'd allow us to make a small adjustment to whatever list you came up with, we'd like to squeeze in one more word:

You.

Chances are, you think that you—and all the things that make up you, like your health—are about as sexy a topic as the history of the pencil, but we're here to flip that notion upside its head, beat it with a stethoscope, and show you something you may never have thought of before: Your body is the vehicle you need to fulfill every wish that you have, and keeping it healthy will make it more likely that you'll succeed in fulfilling those wishes. What we're talking about here is more than just the bodily functions that you may normally associate with the word *health*. When we talk about health, we mean your brain, your relationships, your feelings, your identity, and your mood, as well as those bodily functions—all the things that make you feel the way you feel, think the way you think, and act the way you act.

Take a few minutes each day to focus on the health of your body and mind, and you'll be raring to go after what you want in life—whether it's having great relationships, getting into a college you want, or following your dreams to become the next Beyoncé, the next Peyton Manning, the next Chris Rock, the next J. K. Rowling, the next Steve Jobs, the next great teacher, software engineer, doctor, parent, or whatever it is you want to be.

This book is going to answer three big questions: Am I normal? Am I liked/loved? Who am I? What may surprise you is that each one of those questions (and the many answers that come with them) has *everything* to do with your health.

Your health is about becoming you.

Rest assured: We're not here to preach to you about the dangers of getting heart disease down the road or how to make sure that you don't need a hip replacement when you're a grandparent. We're here to talk to you about your body, your issues, and your questions—the stuff that concerns you today. The great side effect, of course, is that taking control of your body now will give you the foundation for leading a long and healthy life.

To help us understand your most burning questions, we got intel from Health-

Corps—a national organization modeled on the Peace Corps that sends recent college grads into high schools around the country to help teens realize how fascinating their bodies are. HealthCorps mentors teach adolescents not only how to improve their bodies through healthy eating habits and exercise but also how to develop the mental skills and strategies they need to navigate day-to-day challenges as well as prepare for the future. The aim of this book is to provide you with all the information you need to thrive, to grow, to splash around in the pool of life and have one heckuva great time.

So what are we going to talk about? You mean, besides guys, girls, and sex? We'll also cover the questions that you most want answered:

- How to get more sleep and have more energy

- How to improve your memory

- How to improve the appearance and health of your skin

- How to figure out whether you're in love—and how to maintain great relationships, romantic and otherwise

- How to achieve your ideal weight and size

- How to improve your memory (gotcha!)

- How to keep from getting sick

- How to make decisions about drugs, alcohol, and other teenage temptations

- Plus a whole lot more

Pretty quickly, you're going to realize that this isn't your average school textbook. We're not planning to preach to you, lecture you, or wag our pointer fingers at you.

We're here to talk. We're here to answer questions. We're here to make a few jokes. We're here to start conversations. And we're here to get you thinking about your health in a way that you just might not have thought about it before.

In each chapter, we're going to spend a little time explaining the science of your body, because in order for you to take ownership of your body, you need to know how it works. The human body is a magnificent symphony of organs, chemicals, and processes that control everything from your movements to your moods. When you understand how your body functions, it's much easier to keep it in good working order and to make any changes you might want.

After that brief biology lesson, we're going to spend the bulk of each chapter talking about what's important to you. We'll answer your most pressing, essential, and even embarrassing questions ("Exactly what happens during a pelvic exam?"), so that you can arm yourself with your most powerful decision-making weapon: information. At the end of each chapter, you'll find our "Fantastic Five"—tips and activities to improve your health and help you understand yourself a little bit better. In the back of the book, where we provide an exercise program, teen-friendly recipes, and our twenty-five top health tips for teens.

Before we get going, we do think it's important that you know a bit about how we view teen health. So keep these themes in mind as you're reading.

◎ **The teen body is unique.** There's a lot of health info out there about children, and a lot about adults, but not much about teens, who are in many ways different from both kids and grown-ups. So we're here to explain those differences and focus on the things most important to you, since your body is in this period of limbo between the two ends of the bodily spectrum.

◎ **Simplicity rules.** Some of you may need health overhauls, yes; you may just need tweaks and nudges in the right direction. (And even if you do need overhauls, tweaks and nudges are the way to start.) Healthy living doesn't have to be hard; in fact, it's pretty easy once you know the basics. We'll steer you in the right direction. The truth is that it takes only two weeks for a behavior to become a habit, so if you do want to make changes, you can. And it's simpler than you think.

◉ **Good health comes from good decisions.** Almost all positive health characteristics—from white teeth to a fit physique—stem from making smart decisions. Likewise, the reverse can also be true. As you'll learn, the teen brain isn't completely wired to make rational decisions. That's because at this age, the emotional centers of your brain are on full throttle, sometimes overriding logic and common sense. So we're not blaming you for taking risks or experimenting, but we will show you that much of your health is within your own hands if you make wise choices.

◉ **You have rights.** Now is the time when you're beginning to take over responsibility for your own health: the foods you eat, the sports you play, the people you hang with, the risks you choose to take or avoid, and the level of comfort or discomfort about those choices you're willing to tolerate. We're not going to be judgmental; while we are indeed parents, we're not *your* parents, and we're not you. All of the information we provide here comes from the perspective of thinking about your rights, your privacy, and your healthy transition into adulthood. While we hope that you feel comfortable discussing with your parents the important issues raised here, we understand that for some of you that is not going to be the case. We also believe that all teens deserve to know what's happening to their bodies and how they can promote and protect their own physical and emotional well-being.

◉ **You should challenge your beliefs.** 'Fraid to say it, but the truth is that there's a good chance you've been exposed to—and now believe—a lot of myths when it comes to your health and your body. Our job is to bust 'em up. So: Do diets really affect acne? Is cramming for tests really bad for you? Does eating fat make you fat? Should you really judge a book by its cover? We don't want myths governing your world; we want you governing your world. And we're going to arm you with the info you need in order to do just that.

◉ **Your self-identity and emotions influence virtually every aspect of your health.** Part of the whole trick of mastering your health is finding out who you are, and that's a real tough thing to do at any age, let alone in the teenage years. This theme is sprinkled throughout the book and addressed head-on in several chapters. But keep in mind that even when we're talking about what seems like a nitty-gritty health topic, there are emotional and psychological issues that are connected to it. Your mind and body are as linked together as Romeo and Juliet, PB and J, and Abercrombie and Fitch.

We believe that after you read this book, you'll have a deeper understanding of your brain and body—and will truly appreciate the biological majesty that takes place within the cozy confines of your skin. But don't let your learning stop with just this book. If you've got a question, ask us, via Facebook, Twitter, or youdocs@gmail.com. Or use our website, at www.doctoroz.com, to research tens of thousands of health issues.

Our hope, of course, is that you'll take all of this information, talk about the issues we raise, and make your own decisions about the life you want to lead in this challenging, yet exciting, time in your life. After all, this isn't about us. It's about us helping you get to a very good place, a place where . . .

You know you.

Activity: Get to Know You

Before thinking about your health and well-being, it's a good idea to take inventory of where you are right now.

Figure 1 **Circle of Life** Look at each section below and place a dot on the line marking how satisfied you are with that aspect of your life. For those areas of your life with which you are dissatisfied, please mark the dot closer to the inside of the circle. Marking a dot toward the outer part of the circle indicates happiness. After you have completed the circle, connect the dots. You will see the areas of your life that are satisfying and those where you may want to spend time finding more balance.

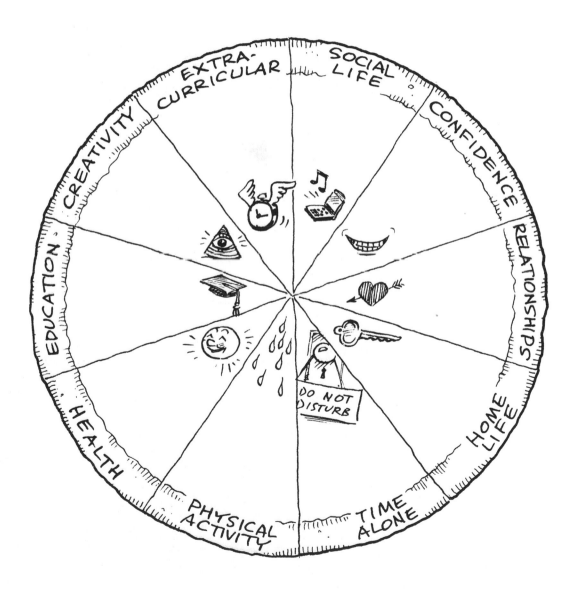

PART ONE

Your Body,
Your Looks,
Your Health

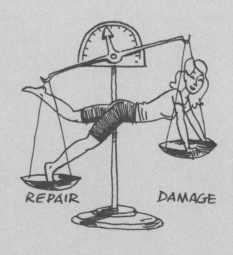

REPAIR   DAMAGE

What You Will Learn

- ◉ The purpose of skin

- ◉ Skin's three layers

- ◉ How skin gets damaged and stays healthy

- ◉ The best way to care for skin

- ◉ Prevention and treatment of acne

1

Show Some Skin

Keeping Your Flesh Healthy from the Inside Out

To understand the importance of skin to your body, just think about the kind of skin you may find in your backpack, purse, or pocket—namely, in the form of the skin that covers your cell phone, iPod, or laptop. Whether your skin is designed with zebra stripes, team colors, or glitter, it's obvious that your techno-focused skin serves two purposes: One, it provides a layer of protection for your precious cargo, and two, it tells the outside world something about your personality.

In a way, your natural skin does the exact same thing (minus the glitter, perhaps). Skin has many functions, such as protecting you against the sun, but it also serves as a visual interface with the outside world—which means that skin quality affects a lot of other issues, such as self-confidence. People tend to make snap judgments based on appearance—including skin—and although that might seem unfair, it's something we've been programmed to do evolutionarily. Clear skin communicates, "I'm healthy and a good choice for a mate!" It's no wonder, then, that we're surrounded by images in magazines, on billboards, and on TV of perfect skin. The truth is, perfect skin is unrealistic, and most of the images you see in magazines and on advertisements have been retouched to give models the appearance of supersmooth flesh. Real skin has pores, pimples, hairs, blemishes, and all kinds of, ahem, beauty marks.

Your bodily skin is your casing, so it's in your best interest to learn how to protect your protection—and put your best skin forward.

Whether you're dealing with *No, not now!* zits or just want to improve the overall quality of your skin, learning the basics about how and why your skin works will help you manage any issues that might, er, pop up.

The Biology of Skin

There's a good chance that, as a teen, you spend more time worrying about your skin than pretty much any other part of your body. And we don't blame you. No matter whether you're black, brown, white, tan, or yellow, your skin communicates quite a bit about who you are and how healthy you are.

And while some folks may criticize you for spending more time in the cosmetics aisle of the drugstore than you do on your homework, there's absolutely nothing wrong with trying to keep your skin healthy looking. Why? Not only does healthy skin make you feel better, but it also makes you healthier, too. That's because your skin really is a proxy for how well the rest of your body is working. Translation: If something's going haywire on the outside, chances are that something's doing the same thing on the inside. And we're all for improving both.

Before we get to the ins and outs of how to keep your skin healthy, smooth, soft, and blemish free, let's take a look at the structure of skin and the many purposes it serves.

Though it is certainly used as a selling point on everything from magazine covers to beauty ads, the main purpose of skin is a simple one: Serving as sort of a sausage casing (not that we think of you as a concoction of pig innards), skin keeps all of your organs, tissues, and fluid from oozing out onto the sidewalk, and it also acts as your literal body of armor, protecting those organs and tissues against outside invaders, from the sun, to mosquitoes, to the gross stuff in locker rooms, to pigeon poop.

One of the neatest things about how skin works is that it not only keeps things out, but at the same time it also soaks things in (like lotions and tattoo ink). This can sometimes lead to a biological dilemma, as in the case of sun rays. Your body needs sunlight to produce vitamin D,★ which is essential for helping your bones absorb calcium, among other things. But the downside is that too much exposure to sunlight damages skin, leading to wrinkles and possibly cancer down the line. It's a tricky balance, no doubt.

Covering an average of eighteen square feet, your skin is your body's largest organ and has many more purposes than just physical protection.

Skin also:

◎ **Protects against infections.** Germs from the outside world travel to your inside world via three main systems—your lungs (through your nose and mouth), your intestines (through your mouth), and your skin (all over).[†] Since your skin stops the outside world from getting in far more than the other two areas, it is your protective key.

◎ **Sends important signals to your brain via touch.** For example, if you burn yourself, and it hurts, your brain receives the message to get your fingers away from the lighter you're holding up at the end of the rock concert. And that message comes courtesy of your skin. If your fingers are touching fire

---

★ Don't be confused by all the different kinds of vitamin D. Vitamin D in milk is good, but it needs to be converted to a more active form—vitamin D3—before we can use it. When we refer to vitamin D in the book, we mean the active form, D3. The best ways to get it are through the sun (just ten minutes in the sun without sunscreen) or in a supplement.

† Four, if you count sexually transmitted infections, which travel through the vagina, anus, penis, and mouth, which we cover in chapter 8.

and you feel no pain, the flames may have already killed the part of the skin containing pain-sensing fibers. So what's the big deal? If those nerve endings are dead, your brain won't get the message, and you won't remove your fingers from the flame, leading to more severe injury. Drugs that alter your brain function can prevent you from recognizing pain, potentially leading you to hold the lighter until your fingers are permanently damaged. Not good either.

◉ **Helps you heal.** That's what scabs do. They provide a layer of protection and moisture to allow skin to fuse together over a wound. (By the way, picking a scab interrupts and slows down the healing process, because the healing cells are pulled off when you peel off the scab.)

Now let's look at the way skin is structured.

Your skin comes in three layers (see figure 1.1):

Epidermis: This is the outside layer made up of proteins called keratin. It has no sensory fibers, so it literally feels no pain. Dead cells continually slough off and are replaced every six to eight weeks. The dust you see in your house? If you keep your windows closed, the majority of it is caused by your dead epidermis, plus that of your house guests.

Dermis: The next layer, the dermis, is the thickest of all, and it's where those sensory fibers live. Those nerves make you react when someone scratches your back just right. Elastin fibers within the dermis work like rubber bands to help keep your skin tight and young looking. Sun and smoking destroy elastin and can eventually cause wrinkles. We'll tell you later how you can help keep your skin tight by nourishing it with a key compound for growing elastin.

Subcutaneous tissue: In this layer, sebaceous glands secrete lubricants (oil) to protect your skin, while apocrine glands send chemical messages called pheromones to the world around you. (More on them in chapter 15.) Sweat glands found here

Figure 1.1 **Skin Deep** Skin is made up of three layers—including those internal layers that work like rubber bands to help keep skin elastic and glowing. Damage can come in the form of sun and smoking, which weakens those internal layers, making skin more prone to wrinkling and other problems.

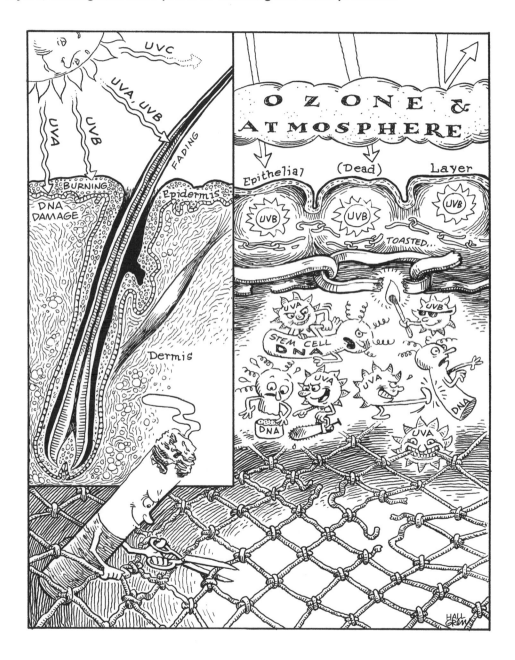

release fluid that evaporates to cool you down during exertion, while hair follicles produce—you guessed it!

Now let's get to what you really care about: what causes your skin to not glow the way it once did or to glow too much—in other words, to shine like an oil slick. As you now know, your skin is covered with hair follicles, and at the base of each is a sebaceous gland. This is a good thing, because that oil (called sebum) gives skin its natural moisture, which helps keep it soft. But as is the case with ice cream and music volume, you can have too much of a good thing.

Every day, hair follicles shed dead cells that line them, and those cells can get mixed in with the oil. These dead cells and sebum can plug the pores (tiny holes) in your skin, forming blackheads. (Doctors call them "open" comedones, pronounced *comb-a-dones.*) Now, when a pore stays blocked for too long, the body tries to protect itself from bacteria on the surface by sealing the pore off with a thin layer of skin. Unfortunately, bacteria can sometimes become trapped under this thin layer of skin. The body recognizes those bacteria as foreign invaders, and sends in the troops to fight off the little buggers. Our body's defense system includes white blood cells, which race into battle, turning the now covered blocked pore into a whitehead. As white cells invade the site, they recruit more blood flow to deliver even more white cells to the area. (See figure 1.2.) The result: a big, juicy pimple. (See Q&As for our recommendation on how to prevent and treat them.) Doctors also call whiteheads by a technical name—specifically, "closed" comedones, because the skin has now made a layer closing off the blocked pore. In contrast, blackheads have not yet sealed off the pore from the open air.

Add to this mix androgens: hormones that include testosterone, dehydroepiandrosterone (DHEA), and their cousins. The androgens work at the skin level to create more pore-clogging oil. For both guys and girls, use of a medicine called spironolactone (brand name, Aldactone) can help block androgen formation in the skin. For girls, taking birth control pills can help to minimize outbreaks by increasing your production of the sex hormone binding globulin, which not only mops up extra androgen, but also makes it harder for skin cells to recognize androgens. And of course there are risks to this medicine.

Figure 1.2 **Zit Happens** Hair follicles trapped under the skin can become infected, causing bacteria to build up, leading to inflammation. The result: pimples. Excellent hygiene and diet can minimize the damage. For more severe cases, medication may be a good option to treat the infections.

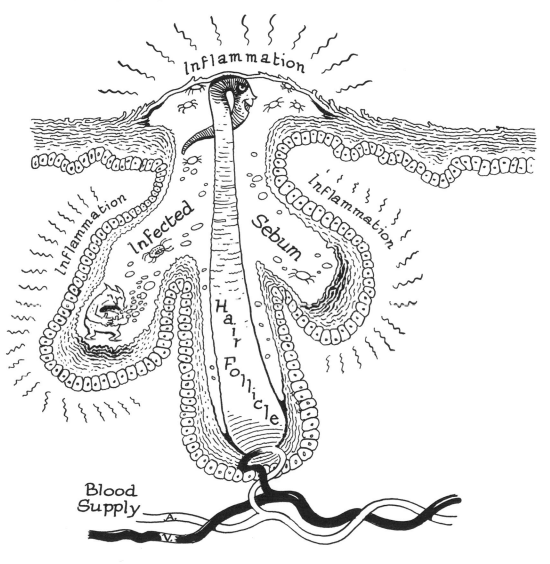

While pimples are unpleasant, the biggest threat to the health of your skin is the sun. Being exposed to sunlight gives you much needed vitamin D (important for strengthening your bones and protecting against cancer), but overdoing it will damage your skin—and leave you with wrinkles, or worse. How does this happen? Ultraviolet radiation from the sun weakens those elastic collagen fibers that give skin its tautness. And the sun's radiation, which penetrates below the surface, causes particles called free radicals to float around in your body and damage your genes, which is what can lead to cancer. Overexposure can certainly lead to a painful burn, but the effects last much longer than your burn will. Doing it over and over and over again (that goes for tanning as well as burning) is a surefire way to make your skin look old—no matter what your age.

Understanding the basic biology of skin will provide the foundation for you to learn all the things you can do to make your skin shine. But so far, we've just touched the surface of what can happen to your skin and what you can do to protect it. For more info, take a look at our YOU Qs to see how you can make your skin shine.

The YOU Qs
You Ask, We Answer, You Decide

So what's the best way to prevent blemishes from breaking out in the first place?

First, having *a healthy, well-balanced diet* is a good start. (See chapter 3.) Make sure that you eat mostly healthy fats, like omega-3 fatty acids from fish and walnuts and omega-9s found in olives. That's because it appears that inadequate consumption of healthy fats or consumption of saturated fats is linked to increased acne. And above all, it helps to have a master plan when it comes to washing your face. It's much better to eat well and practice good hygiene than to just rely on medication to fix your acne.

Explain good face hygiene. It's not just soap and water?

Soap and water are important, yes, but there's a little more to it than that. Following this plan, you can help keep your skin looking healthy and smooth, with minimal blemishes:

Step 1: Wash with pH-balanced soap. Every person has an acid mantle (like cellophane) that forms a protective layer over the skin to inhibit the growth of harmful bacteria and fungi. If it loses this acidity, skin becomes more prone to damage and infection. How do you lose the acidity? By washing your face with ordinary soaps, which are usually basic (the opposite of acidic), which ends up removing the mantle that seals in moisture. The benefit of using a pH-balanced soap: Your pores will look smaller if they're kept free of oils and dirt. Ideally, you should wash your face twice daily, and you don't need to spend more than a few seconds doing it. Excessive rubbing can aggravate acne. Skip the soaps with colors and fragrances, too. They just add residue and increase the chance of an allergic reaction.

Step 2: Moisturize. Typically, your skin soaks up moisture to keep itself looking fresh and smooth. Healthy moisturizers don't disturb the acid mantle of the skin or clog pores. We prefer natural moisturizers, such as squalene (made from olives), avocado oil, walnut butter, aloe, and cocoa butter, and ones that are proven to be hypoallergenic—meaning that they don't cause allergic reactions. Apply moisturizer while you're still damp from the shower to seal in the moisture after lightly patting yourself dry.

Step 3: Use sunblock. The sun is your skin's biggest enemy, and using sunblock will keep your skin looking healthy and young. (See page 14.)

Why can't I just pop a pimple?

Every teen (and most adults, too) has the same urge: Pop that date breaker! The problem is that when most pimples are popped, they ooze a little bit of pus (white cells that eat up bacteria), and more of it gets pushed below the skin. *Pus is pretty inflammatory, and if it gets into the oil gland that lives at the base of the hair follicle, oil gets released below the skin, causing further inflammation.* If enough oil gets released, you can wind up with a tract, or highway, connecting one hair-follicle-and-oil-gland structure to the next one, causing your skin to cave in a bit, making a pizza face and eventually causing scarring.

Now, there is an alternative to squeezing that won't cause your pimples to spread. If you take a sterilized needle (stick it in boiling water or hold it over a flame), you can poke it through the very tiptop of the pimple (where it's white) and let the pus out. Never penetrate deeply; you don't want a gusher. If it hurts, then the skin isn't dead, and it's not ready to lance. No squeezing; that defeats the purpose and will slow down healing. Be careful not to jab, rip, or poke. Then wash with soap and water.

Big warning: We'd rather that you have a dermatologist pierce the zit with a needle, because you do risk scarring if you do it the wrong way. While the chance of causing major damage by lancing a garden-variety pimple is small, you do have to be careful to keep the area sterilized and to not damage neighboring tissue. You're just taking the very tip off to ease the inflammation. Wash your hands thoroughly before and after touching pimples, to avoid spreading the infection to other pores.

I've tried the diet and hygiene approach and it hasn't worked. What's next?

You can *start good skin care* now. Washing with an antibacterial soap twice a day is the first line of defense, and a relatively simple one.

Those of you with simple blackheads and whiteheads will want to use a topical keratolytic medicine, which unblocks the pores (examples include adapalene, or Differin; and topical tretinoin, or Retin-A), plus something that kills bacteria on the surface of the skin (topical clindamycin, benzoyl peroxide, or erythromycin)—a double whammy in the fight against acne. (*Topical* means that you apply the ointment, cream, or gel directly to the skin. Erythromycin may not work as well, as the bacteria get resistant or outsmart the drug.) For those who have blackheads and whiteheads and want to keep it simple, azeleic acid (brand name Azelex) unblocks the pores and kills bacteria on the surface of the skin. It also helps even out the pigment of the skin so you don't end up with lighter and darker areas from acne scarring.

More than a few pimples, but not quite a pizza face? You might want to use benzoyl peroxide topically in addition to a different topical antibiotic. The two work better applied together than they would if used individually. You can use over-the-counter or prescription formulations of the former, while your pediatrician or a dermatologist will need to write you a prescription for the latter. For a higher price, there are many combo meds, such as the topical antibiotic clindamycin containing benzoyl peroxide; the best of these call for only one application a day, rather than the standard twice a day. That's a bonus for those who don't like much fuss when it comes to face or skin care.

If your acne is bad enough—with blemishes on the face, and perhaps pimples on your back or chest as well—then you might want to use an oral antibiotic (taken by mouth) in addition to the topicals, to kill the bacteria already trapped under the skin. You can be on an antibiotic for years without a problem, although sometimes you have to change to another one if the bacteria that love your skin become smart enough to eventually resist the drug. Girls can use either birth control pill alone (see chapters 6 and 8), or in conjunction with the antibiotic.

If these strategies don't work, then you need to talk with your dermatologist about your possibly going on Accutane, which is the pill form of isotretinoin. If you're a girl and think you might need Accutane, it's worth trying the birth control pill route first, since Accutane makes periods irregular and also causes birth defects if you get pregnant while taking it (or shortly thereafter). Guys, you're not off the hook, as the medication can also cause liver damage, making annual blood tests necessary. Before trying Accutane, both girls and guys should have maxed out on whatever topicals and oral antibiotics they have used (meaning using all medications faithfully and washing your face twice a day). If that has not cleared up your face in six to eight weeks, then it may be worth pursuing Accutane.

Note: When you make a change in your skin care, especially for acne treatment, it takes about six to eight weeks to see a difference. If your acne regimen isn't working after that, it's time to go back to the doctor. There's a silver lining to all this: Those of you with really oily, pimple-laden faces may actually have fewer wrinkles later in life as compared to your dry-skinned, pimple-free classmates now. Your naturally elevated production of skin oil protects you better against aging and wrinkles—assuming that you don't smoke, keep your arteries young (see chapter 3), and avoid too much sun.

What's your recommendation for sunscreens?

We know the last thing you want to hear is our "We remember when" stories, so we'll keep them to a minimum. But the truth is that we know plenty of adults who didn't protect their skin from the sun when they were young, and now they're upset because their faces look like subway maps, with all the crisscrossing wrinkles. The fact is, not protecting your skin against the sun is absolutely one of the most damaging things you can do to your body. Skin cancer, particularly melanoma (the most lethal and invasive skin cancer) is being found more often and in younger and younger folks, partly from changes to the ozone layer and partly from increased sun exposure, with repeated sunburns adding to the risk for cancer.

So here are our recommendations: Nanoparticled zinc oxide (and titanium dioxide if you do not sweat—titanium dioxide turns gray when mixed with sweat) sunscreens protect immediately, and newer versions of these sunscreens form a thin film rather than making you look as if you'd smeared crayon or cream cheese all over your face, like the older versions (of your mom's and dad's teenage years) did. All the rest of the sunscreens—called chemical or organic sunscreens—take twenty minutes to absorb into your skin before protecting. *You need to slather all sunscreens on thickly (1 millimeter is how they are tested for SPF effects) and apply them evenly,* making sure not to miss any spots such as the back of the neck, the top of the ears, and any exposed scalp. Most of us don't put on enough sunscreen, and if that's the case with you, then you're getting only a fraction of the effectiveness (if you're putting on SPF 30, it's could be more like SPF 15 or SPF 10). Ever wonder what the heck the SPF (sun protection factor) numbers truly mean? SPF 15 means that you'll get the same damage in fifteen hours of sun exposure with the lotion as you would in one hour without. The problem is that you need to reapply, as you sweat it off, swim it off, and so on. When you get to the higher numbers—SPF 30, 45, 50—they start acting more like a mechanical barrier, more similar to zinc oxide than the lower SPFs.

You really need 1 to 2 ounces of sunscreen (about the size of an egg or a Ping-Pong ball) to cover your whole body. Because you'll use a lot of it, cheaper is often better. Tip: A bottle of sunscreen ought not to last longer than a week on your next beach vacation.

Look for products that are hypoallergenic and noncomedogenic (don't block pores); while not a guarantee against pimples and rashes, they're less likely to cause skin problems than other formulations. "Water resistant" means that the sunscreen will stay on your body past the first droplet of sweat when you are hot. But even if it says "water resistant," reapply it after swimming. By the way, hats and T-shirts don't provide enough SPF protection. Hats provide an SPF of 10 at the most and T-shirts only about SPF 5, but sun-protective clothing with higher SPFs are available.

How bad can tanning beds really be? Everyone uses them.

Tanning beds use fluorescent lights to produce UV radiation, 95 percent of which is UVA, the worst kind for inducing skin cancer. *UVA is linked directly to melanoma and nonmelanoma skin cancer. Melanoma is the one that can kill you and likes to invade, going far beyond "skin deep."* Your generation has a higher risk for melanoma than all prior generations, due to the changes in the ozone layer; you can magnify that risk exponentially by tanning with a tanning device and tanning outside without protection. Sunless alternatives are safer, such as products that contain dihydroxyacetone (not the healthy fat DHA)★, which reacts with the layer of your skin called the stratum corneum to produce darkening that begins within an hour of application, peaks in eight to twenty-four hours, and fades over five to seven days. These products can be self-applied or sprayed on at a tanning salon; the latter allows for more even distribution. You want to make sure to test a product somewhere inconspicuous, like the back of your wrist or your inner arm, to make sure it doesn't make your skin look orangey. Don't use on your lips or in your eyes. (See chapter 3.)

What can I do about stretch marks?

Striae, or stretch marks, appear commonly during adolescence—around breasts, hips, thighs, or anywhere else the skin is growing and stretching. They can also occur when individuals inject anabolic steroids or use strong topical steroids for a prolonged period in a specific area. Many scars will fade on their own, especially if you avoid sun exposure to the scarred area, as it makes the scar worse. *If you feel the need to do something more, you can try putting vitamin E lotion or cream on them to get them to fade.* If this is not working after three to six months, you can ask your doc or a dermatologist about topical tretinoin (brand name, Retin-A), or about pulsed dye laser therapy. Insurance does not tend to cover that procedure in the United States.

★ The other DHA is the healthy fat that makes you want to be known as a fat head. (See chapter 3).

What can I do to make scars look better?

As explained above, *vitamin E lotion can help them heal.* Also, keep them out of the sun, as sun worsens scars. If you are going to be out, keep them either covered with clothing and/or with total sun block. (Zinc oxide works great.)

I'm really thinking about getting a tattoo. What do I need to know?

Let us guess: An eagle? A flower? A tribute to Usher? Tattoos can have great stories behind them, for sure, but singer Jimmy Buffett perhaps described tattoos most accurately: "a permanent reminder of a temporary feeling."

If you're going to get one, you need to think carefully about where you have it put, and who you want to see it at what ages and stages in life. Remember, you may have bare arms, thighs, back, shoulders, whatever, at some time. Ideal sites for tattoos to be shared with only a privileged few include around your waist, hips, or upper cheeks—those on your backside, not on your face. That means you can hide them for that college interview, as opposed to tattoos emblazoned on your arms, chest, or ankle. Careful if it's in a foreign language: Does it really say what you want it to say? Are the letters backward, the way they would be if you looked at yourself in a mirror versus reading them on a page?

If you do get a tattoo, you need to make sure that the artist uses a new needle (watch him remove it from the sterile package), and pay more for new unopened ink, so that you don't get any blood-borne infections such as the human immunodeficiency virus (HIV) and hepatitis C. Also, getting rid of a tattoo is a lot harder than getting one in the first place. It requires several expensive laser treatments, and sometimes even then you're left with a shadow. Laser bubble tattoo paints, which can be totally busted and removed with one laser treatment, are just coming on the market, so ask for them if you're not sure that you'll want to live with that *Glee* tattoo forever.

How about piercing?

Piercings are reversible; you can always take them out. But you may be stuck with a scar, or keloid (pronounced *kee-loyd*); that's when you get thick scar tissue around the site. Darker skin may be more at risk for developing keloids, which can be difficult to remove. So be careful where you pierce. A scar near your belly button may end up just looking like a smile or a frown, but keloids can be a bummer, especially if they're on your nostril or along your eyebrow line. *Make sure that the person doing the piercing uses a new needle* for the safety reasons we mentioned above. Warning: The not-so-visible piercing sites may hurt, because those nerve endings are designed to be fairly sensitive, as opposed to earlobes, which have fewer sensory fibers.

I've always had bad BO. I can't find a deodorant that helps. Any advice?

If you smell funkier than a Black Eyed Peas track, there's probably a good explanation. But the actual composition of your sweat is based on your genes and the food you eat. For instance, garlic will pass quickly into your skin and share itself with others. Also, our major sweat glands, or eccrine glands, release a sterile solution that attracts smelly bacteria in some people. These secretions are stored in coiled circular glands that cover our entire skin surface. *Washing frequently helps, but sometimes a quick course of topical antibiotics, from your doctor, followed by a probiotic is the best anti-odor solution.*

I sweat so much that I soak my shirt, and it's really embarrassing. What can I do?

Hyperhidrosis, or excess sweating, is a common plight among teens and adults. It can happen in the armpits, feet, palms, face, or elsewhere, and can be embarrassing if it occurs at an inopportune time. While it's not the most embarrassing thing that will ever happen, we understand that it's a real problem that people like to have fixed. For whatever reason, supersweaters have more active sweat glands than most people. You can get prescription antiperspirants that contain higher concentrations of aluminum hydroxide or aluminum chloride than ordinary deodorant, such as Drysol (20 percent) or Certain Dri (12 percent). These can be applied three nights a week at bedtime and washed off in the morning. After it is working well, it can be applied once or twice a week (and still washed off in the morning) for three to six months until sweat production has subsided. Most people can then back off and not use any of the medicine for another three to six months, then repeat the cycle. Some folks will get a red itchy rash with these—it's less likely if you don't shave immediately before applying. If no response is seen despite using three times a week, you can actually apply the antiperspirant, wrap the area in plastic wrap, then unwrap it in the morning and wash off with soap and water. Keep this up several times a week until those sweat glands calm down. If these strategies are not working, a dermatologist or plastic surgeon can inject the area with botulinum toxin type A, better known as Botox, which will paralyze the nerves that stimulate the sweat glands. Injections need to be repeated one to three times a year. You can also have the sweat glands destroyed surgically, but very rarely is that kind of drastic procedure needed.

What kind of cosmetics should I get?

Going to the beauty counter is like going to the supermarket: There are millions of products, and many times you have no idea which ones are healthy and which ones aren't. Some offer double robbery: They both weigh down your skin and lighten your pocketbook. Look for products that list an active ingredient and a particular concentration. Vitamins and supplements in skin lotions, creams, and potions usually have to be in the 1 to 10 percent range to really be effective. The formulations also need to be pH balanced, and the active ingredient must be able to penetrate the skin; for example, vitamin A works at a much lower concentration. Your best bet is to try reputable brands, but even some of those use ingredients such as collagen that could enter the skin only in a science-fiction movie. You can find out more about this at youbeauty.com.

Remember that cosmetic products are just that: cosmetic. Products that make therapeutic claims must be scientifically proven to be safe and effective and are regulated as drugs by the FDA. Most ingredients in cosmetics have not been proven effective for skin health. The ingredients that have been shown to have scientific backing are vitamin A, vitamin B_3, vitamin B_5, vitamin C, vitamin E, alpha hydroxy acids, ferulic acid, and coenzyme Q10, (ubiquinone), while niacinamide appears to be best for promoting elastin production and preventing wrinkles.

★ FANTASTIC FIVE: STEPS FOR SUCCESS ★

1. **Don't treat your skin like a second-class citizen.** Spend some time with it every day. It will be with you for a long time. Wash twice a day to prevent acne, moisturize with inexpensive moisturizers, use the right medicines (over-the-counter and/or prescription) if necessary, and slather on sunscreen when you're out and about.

2. **Diet plays a big role in the health of your skin.** Make sure to get two or three servings of protein a day, such as nuts or fish. Aim for a minimum of 30 to 50 grams of healthy fat a day and limit your intake of the five food felons. (More in chapter 3.)

3. **One of the biggest detriments to healthy skin: stress.** As your immune responses get weakened by stress, that increases the likelihood of developing blemishes and bad skin. We can't promise you a stress-free life, but for healthy skin, we recommend you take steps to manage your stress. (See chapter 10.)

4. **Ask yourself:** What do I do to take care of my skin on a day-to-day basis? What can I do differently? Do I judge others by the surface of their skin? Can I "get past the skin" to understand the other valuable parts of that person, even if I don't like the look of their skin? What might I be missing?

5. **Test your skin.** Take our YOU Test below, answering yes or no, to determine what kind of skin you have:

    1. Does your skin look dull or flake like a snow globe?

    2. Does your skin look like a bathroom floor, with a shiny, slippery texture?

3. Does your skin feel itchy and taut like sausage casing?

4. Do you have pores that are enlarged like craters, or clogged pores, or acne?

5. Does your skin react to cosmetics containing alcohol, synthetics, fragrances, and artificial colors?

6. Does your skin appear consistently moist, vibrant, and plumper than a squishy cantaloupe?

7. Does your forehead, nose, or chin appear oilier than a fast-food kitchen, while the skin around your cheeks, eyes, and mouth is normal or dry?

ANSWER KEY

If you answered yes to questions 1 or 3, you have *dry* skin.

If you answered yes to questions 2 or 4, you have *oily* skin.

If you answered yes to question 5, you have *sensitive* skin.

If you answered yes to question 6, you have *normal* skin.

If you answered yes to question 7, you have *combination* skin.

What You Will Learn

- How hair grows

- The best way to maintain healthy hair and minimize damage

- Why teeth are important indicators of overall health

- How to fix problems with teeth and nails

- The root of bad breath

2

More in the Mirror

How Your Hair, Teeth, and Nails Hold Clues to Your Overall Health

If you're a typical teen, then you've probably been told that your life pretty much goes like this: A quarter of your time is spent at school, and a quarter is spent in bed. The other half? Divided equally between being on your smart phone and in front of the mirror, or doing both at once.

No judgment from us; it's how your and every other teen brain works: You work, you rest, you socialize, and you do everything in your power to make sure you're looking your best when you work, rest, and socialize.

There's absolutely nothing wrong with taking pride in your appearance, but keep in mind that being overly self-critical can have unhealthy effects. You already know that your skin is proxy for your entire health. The same is true for everything to do with your appearance, including your hair and teeth.

But for our era, the truth is that many of us may feel as if the eyes of the world are on us at all times, and appearance means so much. With the feeling that you're the star of your own movie, you may also become obsessed with flaws that nobody else would notice. That vulnerability makes you even more vulnerable to clever marketers who want to sell you products that you may or may not need.

As we did in the last chapter about skin, we want to take the discussion one step further and explain how seemingly superficial concerns—about hair, teeth, and nails—can also have health implications. They not only provide clues as to what's going on inside your body but also play a role in attracting others, developing relationships, and defining your identity. (Chimps, for example, spend a lot of time grooming each other, and that behavior is an important part of forming bonds and the mating ritual.)

How healthy we are, in many ways, defines how beautiful we are. But we all have different ideas about what beauty is, right? There are those who try to conform (wearing conventional makeup, plucking their eyebrows, waxing their chests) and those who manipulate their appearance to make a statement or stand out from the crowd (hello, purple fingernails and hot-pink highlights!). And that's certainly what makes everyone unique. We'll be giving you some of the nuts and bolts about what's healthy for your appearance, but we also urge you to pause for a moment while you look in the mirror and think about the big picture and what it all means.

So if you'll allow us to interrupt your chatting/texting/Skyping for a moment, let's take a look at your looks.

The Biology of Hair, Teeth, and Nails

Hair

We tend to think of our hair as simply an accessory to our looks—mere ornamentation. So whether you wear it up, down, messy, clean, dirty, or in a purple-tinted Mohawk, your hair says a little something about your persona.

In addition to the image it helps project, hair also serves a biological function, no matter what part of the body we're talking about. The hair on your scalp protects you against the sun, and your eyelashes act as your first defense against bugs, dust, and other irritating objects, like errant spitballs, while hair in your armpits and groin acts as a lubricant to help you move without chafing. Back in the days of cavemen, when every person wore about as much clothing as an up-and-coming pop star, the hair in your nether regions camouflaged your reproductive parts from generation-threatening spears and acted as wicks for chemicals of attraction called pheromones, which we'll talk about in a few chapters.

Here's a cool fact: The average person's head has up to 150,000 hair follicles; the body, 5 million. That number is constant over a lifetime and is hereditary, so only thickness, condition, and whether you lose the strands that sprout from those follicles can change. Each one of those strands grows about six inches a year, slightly faster in the summer than in the winter. Women between the ages of sixteen and twenty-four pump it out the fastest.

While it may seem that your hair is as far removed from your internal organs as your clothes or jewelry, each hair follicle has its own blood supply. Because of that, hair is greatly influenced by your health choices and diet. Hair is also under the delicate control of hormones, which is why many older men have beards and hair on their chests and male-pattern baldness on their heads, and women don't. (At least not typically and why both gray with age.)

As you can see in figure 2.1, your hair is made up of two distinct structures: the follicle and the shaft. The follicle, a tubelike segment in the epidermis, sits under the surface of the skin and extends down into the dermis. Remember? That's the

Figure 2.1 The Mane Issues

Hair is a living entity that's made up of several layers and lubricated by our natural oils. Some of the things that we do to primp our hair (like drying or bleaching it) can damage it.

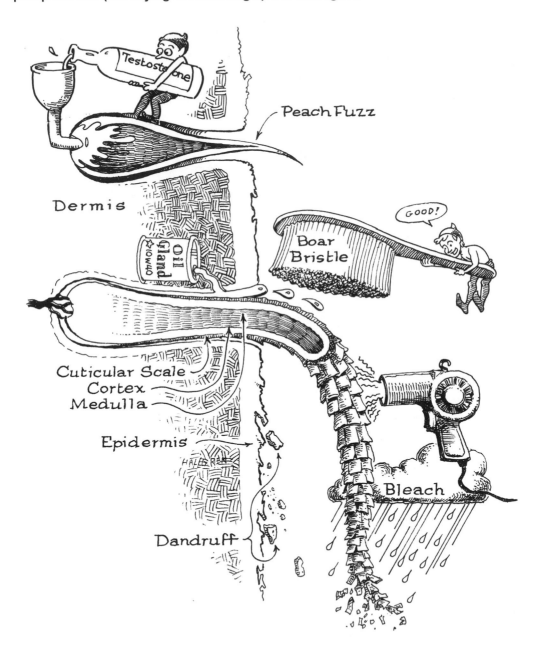

thick layer of skin that we discussed in chapter 1. The base of the follicle contains tiny blood vessels that nourish the cells. The living part is the bulb at the base, or root, while the shaft—the part of the hair that we see above the skin—is actually dead. Pretty crazy, huh? Now, that hair shaft is made up of a protein called keratin. The inner layer of the hair shaft and the middle layer make up the majority of the shaft.

To keep your hair shiny, it needs some oil—not the kind found in the pantry or at Jiffy Lube, but the kind that's secreted from the sebaceous glands in your skin. Surrounding your hairs are tiny muscles that give you goose bumps, standing your hairs on end when you're cold or watching a scary movie. These muscles also squeeze the glands that lube up your hair, which produce sebum: your own natural hair and skin conditioner, rich in vitamin E.

In terms of growth, hair goes through its own life cycle; a biological process dictated largely by your genetic disposition. There are two main phases:

Anagen (active): Cells in the root are dividing quickly and pushing the hair out. This stage typically lasts two to three years per hair follicle.

Telogen (resting): This phase lasts for about a hundred days on the scalp. Consider it hair hibernation; the follicle is completely at rest. And these are the hairs that fall out and you find in your brush or clogging your drain.

For your hair to have the shine and shape that you want, it needs protein and healthy fat—not directly, mind you, but through your diet. Therefore, eating healthy sources of protein and fat provides a better foundation for good hair health than any store-bought product you may use. And that also means that a big enemy of healthy hair is disordered eating, as you won't have full hair or great shine if you have an inadequate or unhealthy diet.

The best nutrients for hair health are biotins—B vitamins found in nuts, egg yolk, and avocados—and healthy fats, like those found in salmon, canola and olive oils, walnuts, and flaxseed. Taking half a daily multivitamin twice a day will help, too.

Teeth

Your teeth, in addition to helping with a wide range of tasks besides chewing, are also a very clear marker of your health. Of course you'll need a dentist and dental hygienist to thoroughly assess the health of your teeth and gums, but there are some things that you can inspect yourself. It helps to know a few basics about oral health before you begin.

Your teeth are bonelike structures made up of different minerals such as calcium. Like the bones elsewhere in your body, your teeth are constantly in a state of balancing two opposing processes: (1) remineralization, in which minerals crystallize to form the structure of the tooth, and (2) demineralization, in which bacteria from your saliva breaks down those minerals (the process in your skeleton works similarly, but not exactly the same—take the saliva out of the equation, add a few other factors). This tug-of-war between remineralization and demineralization is ongoing, and as you might guess, you can do things that tip the balance in either direction. For example, brushing with a fluoride toothpaste helps the remineralization process, while eating lots of sugar feeds the bacteria that produce tooth-eroding acids. Drinking carbonated colas, which are highly acidic, also eats away at tooth enamel. When the "de-" process outweighs the "re-" process, little pits called cavities begin to form, and your teeth decay. (If you do have cavities, insist that your dentist not use fillings made of mercury, which can be toxic.)

When we talk about the health of your teeth and gums, we're really concerned about bacteria that can set up shop in between your teeth. Plaque—that sticky gunk made up of bacteria, saliva, and yesterday's dinner—can build up between your teeth and under your gums. If that happens, it triggers inflammation in the gums that leads to periodontal disease, otherwise known as gingivitis (and that stimulates inflammation in your arteries and throughout your body, and inflammation in arteries causes wrinkles and impotence as well as heart attacks). So, just two minutes of dental hygiene in the morning and evening can make a huge difference in whether or not you grow up to look like a prune. It can even partly determine how much you'll enjoy sex. That's right: Inflammation from your gums travels through your circulatory system, leading to inflammation of blood vessels that reduce the delivery of oxygen to your

Figure 2.2 **Chomp Chomp** While lots of stuff can go on in your mouth, like bad breath and dry mouth, clenching your jaw can create lots of tension and pain.

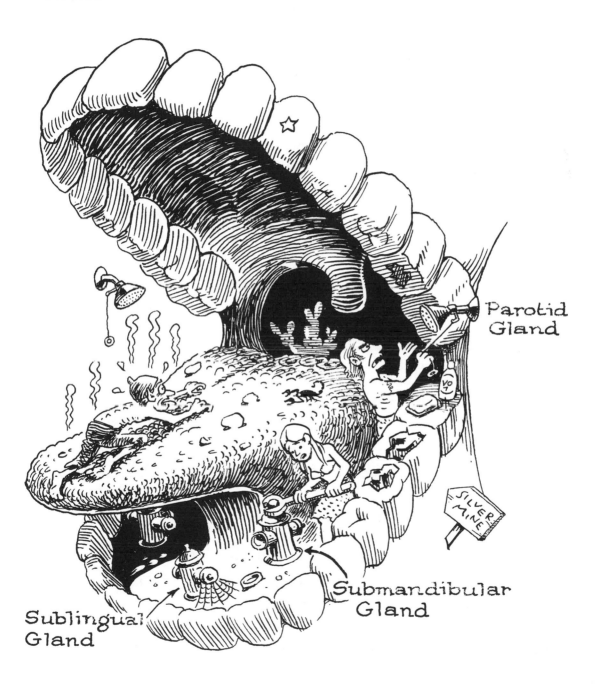

skin, causing premature wrinkles, as well as to other parts of your body, including the sex organs.

Oral health also includes the way your jaw works. A quick jaw primer: Wiggle your jaw around. Go ahead; nobody's looking! Your top teeth are fixed to your skull, while your lower jaw has the flexibility to move front to back and side to side. If the top and bottom are misaligned, your upper teeth can't adjust, so you end up wearing down your teeth. That inhibits the ability of the jaw to work efficiently, causing the back teeth to wear down as well. (See figure 2.2.) Grinding and clenching, which is common among teens, can injure your jawbone joint, called the TMJ (temporomandibular joint). If you're a grinder (which can be caused by misalignment) or a clencher (which can be caused by stress), you'll want to have your bite analyzed so that you can be fitted for a night-guard mouthpiece that prevents you from grinding or clenching while you sleep. It's one of the reasons why orthodontics (braces) can be so important; they help straighten out a misalignment in your teeth and jaw. (More on braces below.)

Nails

There's not a heck of a lot you need to know about your nails, but lots of teens do spend a heck of a lot of time either manicuring them, decorating them, or gnawing them. So it's good to learn a little about them. Your nails are composed of laminated layers of keratin, the same protein found in your hair and skin. Each nail has several parts, including:

◎ **Nail plate:** the visible hard part of the nail.

◎ **Nail folds:** the skin that frames the nail plate on three sides.

◎ **Nail bed:** the skin beneath the nail plate. The cells at the base of your nail bed are the ones that actually produce the fingernail or toenail plate.

◎ **Cuticle:** the tissue that overlaps your nail plate at the base of your nail. It protects the new keratin cells that slowly emerge from the nail bed.

🌀 **Lunula:** the whitish, half-moon shape at the base of your nail underneath the plate.

Your nails grow from the area under your cuticle (called the matrix) the same way that hairs grow from follicles. As new cells grow, older cells die, become hard and compacted, and are eventually pushed out toward your fingertips.

Fingernails—which, incidentally, grow faster than toenails and grow faster over the summer than over the winter—lengthen about one-tenth of a millimeter a day, which means that it takes a fingernail about four to six months to fully grow out. But what we're really concerned about isn't the growth rate but the health of our nails; to make sure they're smooth, without ridges or grooves, although these are often normal variants. Ideally, they're uniform in color and consistency and free of spots or discoloration.

We hope you can see how appearance isn't just a vanity issue, but it's one that does have many different health implications as well. That said, we know you've certainly got a lot of questions about your appearance—and what you can do to make your hair, teeth, and nails shine and sparkle. So fire away.

Cuticle

Nail Fold

Lunula

Nail Fold

Nail Bed

Nail Plate

All my friends have different opinions about shampoo, conditioner, and all that. What's your take?

Here's our three-step process for maintaining healthy hair:

Step 1: Shampoo. Before getting into the shower, gently brush or finger-comb your hair to loosen up tangles and residue. When washing your hair, treat it delicately. Leave hair hanging down and gently massage in shampoo starting at the roots and working down. You don't need a lot to clean your hair. Most shampoo just washes away the protective oils.

Step 2: Condition. Conditioner creates shine and preserves hair's health by giving it smoothness and protecting it against damage. For volume, condition only the middle and ends of your hair, where it's most susceptible to damage. For shine, condition the entire strand. Do it every time you use shampoo. If your hair is dry, try skipping the shampoo part some days and just apply conditioner and rinse thoroughly. Or just use water.

Step 3: Dry. Don't rub your hair with a towel or twist it tightly into a turban. Wet hair is delicate and breaks easily. Pat it gently and squeeze it with your towel or use a superabsorbent towel sold at salons. A wide-toothed comb is the best way to detangle and distribute styling products when hair is wet. And keep any dryers at low-heat settings. High hair-dryer heat (and that from curling irons) causes the water under the cuticles (the outermost layer of the hair) to form bubbles that stress and break the hair, leaving those dreaded split ends.

Any shampoo recommendations?

Your physical activities, your use of styling products, and your hair type will usually determine how often you need to shampoo. If washing every day makes your hair too dry, try every other day or every third day. Or you may have very oily hair that needs washing more than once a day. If you condition when you shampoo, it could be that you need to shampoo daily but need to adjust the level of conditioning. Ideally, *use a pH-balanced shampoo that's gentle.* We love shampoos from these makers: Aubrey Organics, Quinessence, So Organic, Avalon Organics, and Organic Excellence. But you know your hair best. If it looks shiniest and healthiest using 99-cent generic shampoo and conditioner, with no split ends and a nice fragrance, then by all means, have at it! More expensive does not necessarily mean a better product. If you swim frequently in a pool, use shampoo that removes chlorine because the chemical dries out hair, leading to split ends, and can turn blond hair slightly green.

What about coloring hair? Is that bad for me?

Artificial coloring on your hair is the equivalent of artificial coloring in food: It may make it look as pretty as can be, but *it's not always the healthiest thing* you can do to your head. There is some suspicion that permanent black hair dye can cause leukemia and lymphomas. Temporary hair dyes are safer than permanent ones and won't cause lasting damage to your hair.

Bleaching, on the other hand, will really run up your hair bill as you try to stop permanent damage. Here's why: The pigment of your hair comes from the inner two layers. When

you bleach your hair before you color it, you damage the shingles that create the covering of the hair shaft (see the illustration on the previous page). The dye then slips through the gaps in the outer layers, and the hair cells swell to give your hair a different color. But the damage the bleach caused allows the dye to slowly slip out of the hair, so you end up losing the full body and color of the hair faster than if you just left it alone.

If you decide to color your hair yourself, follow these steps:

◎ Don't leave the dye on your head any longer than necessary. Rinse your scalp thoroughly with water after use.

◎ Wear gloves when applying hair dye (nitrile gloves are the best when dealing with chemicals), and carefully follow the directions.

◎ Never be a home chemist and mix different hair dye products: You never know what you might create.

◎ Make sure to have adequate ventilation in whatever room you're using. (Windows open, folks!)

What about dandruff? How do I get rid of the flakes?

Dandruff results from inflammation of the scalp as well as from a fungus that loves the dark, warm jungle you call your hair. The way to treat it: frequent washing with a medicated shampoo that helps control the scaling. The medicine calms your immune system so that your scalp doesn't itch and you don't scratch off the epidermis. *Look for antimicrobial and antifungal shampoos* that contain ingredients such as tar, selenium sulfide, zinc pyrithione, ketoconazole, or ciclopirox. One other solution: green tea applied to your scalp. Green tea contains a chemical that's been shown to help. Unfortunately, green tea doesn't work when it's mixed with other chemicals. Just make a strong cup of green tea and apply it directly to your scalp. But cool it first! You do not want to burn the fungus if your scalp is attached.

My hair is thinning. Why?

There's an old myth that guys inherit baldness from their mother's father—if he's bald, you're doomed (domed?). But the truth is that baldness comes from both parents. While it's typically something that happens as you get older, sometimes hair can start thinning as early as high school. *Male-pattern baldness occurs when testosterone is converted to another chemical*, dihydrotestosterone (DHT), that causes hair to fall out. But hair can also start thinning because of poor nutrition or eating disorders, so you'll want to try straightening out your diet first. If your thinning hair does appear to be hereditary, we recommend thinking about topical treatments that inhibit conversion to DHT—Rogaine (minoxidil) and Propecia (finasteride). Minoxidil works by increasing the anagen growth phase and enlarging the hair follicle, while finasteride inhibits the conversion of testosterone to DHT (by blocking that enzyme we mentioned earlier), which causes hair loss. Research shows that two-thirds of men who use finasteride slow down hair loss. And the earlier this drug is used after noticing hair loss, the more effective it will be. But this drug has that pesky little side effect of occasionally (rarely, actually) leading to decreased sexual desire and difficulty achieving an erection. Interestingly, minoxidil was originally used to treat high blood pressure, but researchers noted that it had a strange side effect: It grew hair on the backs of hands, cheeks, and fingers, and that's how it developed as a hair-loss treatment. When it comes to other products or procedures that claim to grow hair—everything from the Hair-Max LaserComb to Scalp Med—you should be wary of a wallet transplant. Yours to theirs. No potions or lotions other than minoxidil and finasteride have been shown to predictably increase hair growth or prevent its destruction.

Alopecia areata, an autoimmune disorder, can also cause hair loss. In autoimmune disease, the body's immune system, which normally protects us against germs, goes haywire and starts attacking the body itself—in this case, the hair follicles—as if it were an infectious intruder. The hair can fall out in small areas, which is the most common form, or you can lose the hair on your entire head and body, including eyelashes, underarm hair, and pubic hair. There are many treatments for it, so if you are losing patches of hair, it is definitely worth asking your doctor what you can do. Ignoring it does not tend to make it go away.

I have a friend who's pulling her hair out; I just know it. What's the story?

Some kids compulsively wrap, twist, twirl, or pull their hair out: scalp hair, eyelashes, eyebrows, or hair elsewhere. *It is called trichotillomania, and it can be an unhealthy form of coping with stress or an unconscious habit.* These folks have irregularly shaped patches of hair loss, with hairs at different lengths, as they do not break evenly when tugged. The scalp sometimes can bleed if someone is chronically pulling his or her hair out. This is a habit that deserves some help and support to break.

It helps to keep your hands occupied. Try wearing a hair scrunchie or bracelet around your wrist to play with when you feel the urge to pull your hair. Or take up origami, doodling, or other activities that keep your hands busy. You can also try specific relaxation techniques such as deep breathing or yoga, but it's most important to try to manage the stress that's usually the source of the problem.

If your friend has patchy hair loss and you are trying to figure out if she is pulling it out or having some other problem, the following chart can help you.

Process	Appearance
Trichotillomania	Hairs with uneven lengths in a patch, with some hair broken off just at the base.
Alopecia areata	Smooth scalp with no hair at all in affected area(s).
Ringworm (tinea capitis)	Broken-off hairs that look like little exclamation points at the scalp, in a patchy area. This one calls for a special antifungal, griseofulvin, which you take for a month or more, and often an antifungal shampoo such as Selsun Blue or selenium sulfide shampoo used two or three times a week

What's the best way to get rid of unwanted body hair?

There are lots of options for dealing with significant amounts of unwanted body hair. *Some teens prefer shaving or using an at-home depilatory cream that will re-*

move the hair as a first-line treatment. Some prefer waxing. If you choose the latter route, ask for a cooler-temperature wax, which doesn't hurt as much when the follicle is ripped from the skin (after being stuck to the wax). Other people are turning to laser therapy, which works on dark-pigmented hair; the laser travels down the hair follicle and zaps it so that it never grows again. Some prefer electrolysis, where the hair is fried off with an electrical current. If you're going this route, make sure a trained pro does it.

I have really curly hair that I want to straighten. What's your recommendation?

We recommend *blow-drying your hair and flattening your curly locks with a flat-iron*. Brazilian Blowout and similar smoothing solutions contain toxins like formaldehyde—the stuff they use to preserve the remains of dead animals, such as embalming fluid. Ew. Formaldehyde is toxic and should only be used in well-ventilated areas and never on your hair.

What do I need to know about shaving?

Here's how we recommend a good shave, whether you're taking care of your face, legs, or other areas:

- ⊚ Rinse the area with warm water, then press a warm washcloth against it for a minute or two (to help soften up hairs to be shaved).

- ⊚ Shave with short strokes in the direction of hair growth (not against the grain); don't pull the skin and make sure to use a sharp razor every time.

- ⊚ Aftershaves are okay to use (unless they cause a burning or tingling sensation that's too uncomfortable); you can also try a moisturizer instead.

- ⊚ If you experience razor burns (tiny bumps of inflammation), you may want a lotion like bacitracin (or another antibiotic lotion clindamyacin) to ease inflammation.

Why doesn't pubic hair grow like the hair on our heads?

Short, coarse, and curly, public hair never gets a chance to grow long because it has a short growth period. Within six months, the follicle dies and the hair falls out. Pubic hair, which acts as a buffer to reduce chafing, *provides a large surface area to disperse pheromones (the chemicals of attraction).* When it grows in—one of the first signs of puberty—it starts as downy, straight hair, and then progresses to coarse, curly hair that starts to form a triangle above and around the genitals. Fully developed, pubic hair may extend out to the thighs, and for guys, up to the belly button (creating more of a diamond of hair than a triangle).

Lemme guess. You also have the ideal way to brush teeth?

You're catching on quickly. When waiting for class to end, two minutes seem like an eternity. Chatting with friends, two minutes go by in a flash. At the bathroom sink, *two minutes* is the time you need to spend brushing your teeth to clean them adequately and reduce plaque. Use a soft brush and rub the bristles up toward the gums. Change your toothbrush every two months. Those newfangled ultrasonic brushes amaze many dentists with their plaque-fighting abilities (and some come with built-in two-minute timers). We actually prefer sonic brushes, since they produce more than thirty thousand brushstrokes a minute, compared to about five thousand for the typical electrical ones. In addition, the sonic brushes spray into the crevices of teeth to clean beyond where the tips of the bristles actually touch. In other words, they're more effective at dislodging plaque. To use one, follow these instructions:

◎ Wet the bristles and use a small bit of toothpaste.

◎ Place the toothbrush bristles against the teeth at a slight angle toward the gum line. Power up.

◎ Apply light pressure to let the brush do the brushing for you. Don't push too hard!

◎ Gently and slowly brush across the teeth in small back-and-forth motions so the longer bristles reach between your teeth.

◎ Do the outside top teeth, inside top teeth, outside bottom teeth, and inside bottom teeth for thirty seconds apiece. Then clean the chewing surfaces and anywhere else that may have stains. Feel free to brush your tongue, too, to help prevent bad breath.

No matter how you brush, make sure you floss—something that four in five of us still don't do. When you don't floss, you're not cleaning 40 percent of the tooth. Dentists consider flossing even more crucial for preventing tooth decay and periodontal disease than brushing. The floss should barely pass between each tooth and should gently touch the gums. If your floss breaks, try the thicker or waxed stuff, or Oral-B's Glide brand, which is made with Gore-Tex material. Your dentist can also file down the "contact points" between your teeth. Whatever you do, don't just jam the floss in between your teeth, or you'll cut your gums and your bathroom sink will look like a war zone.

My teeth aren't white at all. Which products or procedures do you recommend?

Teeth whiteners contain a chemical called hydrogen peroxide. The oxygen hits the stains and breaks them up; then you wipe them off into oral oblivion. The upside is that teeth whiteners are inexpensive and can be purchased at your local pharmacy. The downside is that hydrogen peroxide can cause temporary tooth sensitivity and/or gum irritation. If this occurs, try a desensitizing toothpaste and a soft toothbrush.

For bigger bucks, you can have your teeth whitened in the dentist's office, where a high-intensity light is used to activate the oxygen. While over-the-counter methods rely on longer periods of contact time (a half hour for ten days to two weeks) to deliver the oxygen, office treatments are quick and painless. Here's a rundown on your options:

In-office whitening: Fastest and strongest effects, up to ten shades lighter, but costs $500 to $1,200.

Brush-ons: Best over-the-counter method. You can see results four shades lighter. Great options are Rembrandt Whitening Wand, BriteSmile to Go pen, and GoSmile Daily, but the first two are reusable, so bacteria can build up; GoSmile is single use, so there are no hygiene issues, but it is more expensive. These brighten the back teeth better than the strips do.

Strips: You can get four to six shades lighter, but only on the front six teeth.

Tray and gels (in-office or OTC): It's an older technology and has potential for gum irritation, so it's best to do with a doc. At home, the temptation is to abuse it, which can lead to tooth sensitivity.

Whitening toothpastes: An everyday experience, these toothpastes remove stains from teeth by polishing or chemical removal.

The ideal combo: If you can afford it, use an in-office whitening, then follow up with brush-ons and toothpastes at home.

Studies have shown that repetitive whitening (using safe, low concentrations of the active ingredients) gives longer-lasting results. Just be sure not to repeat more than once every two weeks, or you'll thin the enamel. Home whitening strips don't appear to harm enamel.

Do I really need braces?

The main reason to have your teeth straightened is that it's harder to keep crooked teeth clean, which leads to gum disease and tooth decay. But you may also be interested to know that crooked teeth harbor germs that cause bad breath. Also, from a cosmetic point of view, it's important to have a nice smile not only to improve your self-image but also to improve the way that others perceive you. Studies have shown that people with straight teeth are seen as smarter and actually earn more money than people with bad teeth. This is especially true for women. People with overbites are generally considered lower in intelligence. People with good teeth are perceived to have better hygiene and overall are considered more attractive. For those who don't need drastic realignment, Invisalign is a great option—it's a series of transparent molded plastic forms that fit over your teeth and gradually move them into place (they need to be removed when you eat). It's virtually invisible and no more expensive than traditional braces, and there are also teen versions available. It also takes about the same amount of time, and is covered by Medicaid in many states and most other health insurance that covers orthodontics.

My mom says a tongue piercing is bad for my health, but I think she's just saying that because she doesn't want me to get one. Is she right?

She's right. They're horrible for your teeth: *The clicking of metal against your teeth can chip away at the protective enamel,* plus they change the way foods taste—who wants that? But while we're on the subject, here are some cool things you can tell from your tongue: Inflammation may be a sign of nutrient deficiencies; if your sense of taste diminishes, it could mean that you have a zinc deficiency, something easily rectified by taking a daily zinc tablet.

Will brushing take care of bad breath?

Bad breath, or halitosis, develops for a lot of reasons: from food getting trapped in pockets in the tonsils, from the stomach, and from the tongue—where the stench from bacteria buildup can clear a room, as well as get stuck in braces. One good way to handle bad breath: *a tongue scraper, which removes bacteria and takes some of the stink away.* You need only about ten seconds. Just take the scraper and run it over your tongue. If your breath is just relentlessly offensive, talk to your dentist, who might even prescribe a few days of antibiotics. Your friends (and dates) will thank you.

Is it normal to have excretions come out of your tonsils? Does this cause bad breath?

Tonsils can have "crypts" or little pockets that food can get caught in, getting broken down by mouth bacteria and generally causing smelly breath. If you have a problem with bad breath, mouthwash really can help by dislodging the trapped food bits when you gargle with it, and it can help kill off unwanted overgrowth of mouth bacteria. You need some mouth bacteria, but not so much there that your breath stinks.

What do you do about white spots on teeth?

White spots can come about for any number of reasons, including a decalcification in the tooth's enamel or even decay. Above all, keep brushing and flossing as normal and talk to your dentist, who may be able to suggest some procedures that will help with the discoloration, such as *bleaching* and *microabrasion,* which can remove the spots. And don't use whitening strips, which may make the spots even brighter.

What are wisdom teeth?

Back in woolly mammoth days, *wisdom teeth were nature's version of a backup system—giving you one last set of teeth that would come out by the age you would have destroyed your molars.* Why are they called wisdom teeth? Hopefully, you would get them by your midteens (sometimes later), when you were wise enough to take care of them properly. But unlike for your relatives ten thousand years ago, hopefully your molars haven't fallen out yet. Because of this, crowding often occurs when wisdom teeth erupt, causing them to come in sideways. Cockeyed teeth can't be cleaned and will destroy adjacent teeth—which is why they're often removed in a minor surgical procedure.

I have a friend who has a nasty fingernail. What's the best way to treat problem nails?

Depends on the injury or problem. Most minor nail injuries heal on their own, but they might be unsightly for a while because nails take a heck of a long time to grow. Here, some common nail-related issues:

White spots: These small, semicircular spots result from injury to the base (matrix) of the nail, where nail cells are produced. They'll eventually grow out.

Splinter hemorrhages: A disruption of blood vessels in the nail bed can cause fine, splinter-like vertical lines to appear under the nail plate. Caused by injury and some drugs, splinter hemorrhages resolve spontaneously.

Ingrown toenails: Improper nail trimming, tight shoes, or poor posture can cause a corner of the nail to curve downward into the skin. Ingrown nails can be painful and sometimes lead to infection. To avoid infection, see a podiatrist (a foot doctor) rather than attempting to saw away the nail yourself. Your doc will numb the toe and trim the ingrown nail.

Finger cracks: Second only to a stubbed toe, a pesky hangnail (or a finger crack, technically) wins the award for the smallest, most annoying pain in our lives. How do we get them? When humidity is low, your fingertips and cuticles can crack. Best prevention: Use a moisturizer routinely to keep your skin from drying up. And if you do crack up, try Johnson & Johnson's Liquid Bandage (like Krazy Glue for your skin) to seal the cracks and eliminate the pain within seconds.

I hear a lot of people saying how bad nail polish is for you. Is that true?

In fact, nail polish is likely the most toxic cosmetic there is. *Polish includes poisonous substances such as formaldehyde, phthalates, acetone, toluene, and benzophenones.* Phthalates, solvents for colors, are toxic to the nervous system; acetone and toluene, which keep the color in liquid form, evaporate quickly and fill the air with noxious fumes, putting your respiratory system at risk. The other substance we fingered, benzophenones, may cause cancer.

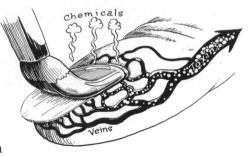

If you apply polish in adequately ventilated rooms, it's probably okay, but surely you shouldn't be changing your polish several times a week, as some teens are known to do. Also, don't use nail polish remover more than twice a month. Instead touch up the polish. When you do need a remover, avoid those containing acetone, which dries nails and is seriously bad for you. We know you'll roll your eyes, but acetone is so toxic to your eyes, nerves, and lungs that it's a good idea to go to the Home Depot and find one of those air filters that will protect your lungs and brain if you use it. Repair splits or tears with nail glue or clear polish.

My parents get after me to stop biting my nails. Any tricks?

To stop your nail-biting habit, *try carrying a squishy ball to squeeze or a rubber band to snap or applying bad-tasting nail polish to keep you from gnawing away.* You can also play with a scrunchie around your wrist or try origami or anything else to keep hands busy and away from your mouth. Need something to crunch on to help you get through a stressful time? Try celery sticks.

SOLVING THE MANE PROBLEMS

Issue: Damage

Many people damage their hair while primping and styling, often without even knowing it. Here are the major offenders:

Excessive combing: Over time, excessive combing and brushing, especially of wet hair, can cause the delicate cuticle scales to lift and, in extreme cases, peel away. Forget those one hundred strokes a night. The idea was to move oil from the scalp into the hair to give it shine. But if you comb aggressively when hair is wet, it will be damaged.

The wrong tools: Using the wrong combs and brushes, especially on fragile, chemically treated hair, can remove the cuticle layer in large portions, creating porous and dull hair strands. A wide-toothed comb is best.

Back-combing and teasing: Back-combing and teasing are extremely harmful, since they tug in the opposite direction of the cuticle scales, which can eventually rip them off, leaving the inner area exposed.

Heated appliances: When too hot or used on wet hair, heated appliances can actually cause water under the hair to boil, creating permanent welts that weaken and dull the hair shaft and set the stage for breakage. Never use ceramic appliances on wet hair. If possible, do not blow-dry your hair.

Issue: Split Ends

A split end develops when the hair's cuticle layer is severely weathered or missing, causing the exposed shaft to fray like a piece of yarn. Wind can cause hair to tangle and make it hard to comb, which can eventually lead to split ends.

Solution: Give your hair a dose of protection and intense moisture by using conditioner daily. Regular trims help, too.

Issue: Lackluster Locks

Daily environmental wear and tear and a buildup of styling products both contribute to dry and dull hair.

Solution: A mild shampoo will remove residue. But be careful you don't overdo it and strip the hair of all its natural oils. A deep conditioning (leave the conditioner on for ten minutes) will give you softness as well as shine.

Issue: Oily Hair

When hair follicles release an excessive amount of the natural protein sebum, hair can look flat, oily, and greasy.

Solution: An oily scalp needs consistent care. When you shampoo, massage into the roots and all along the length of the hair. Another habit that may increase the appearance of oily hair is frequent grooming. Combing, brushing, and running your fingers through your hair aid in the movement of sebum from the scalp down the hair shaft, so try to handle your hair as little as possible.

Issue: Lackluster Hair Color

No matter how permanent your chemical hair color claims to be, all dyes will fade with time. The sun, air, and harsh shampoos all contribute to a lackluster shade.

Solution: When coloring, use a semipermanent rather than a permanent hair color system. Semipermanents are far gentler than permanent dyes and are designed to fade over time, allowing you to replenish your color sooner without causing as much damage. Use shampoos and conditioners designed for maintaining dyed hair.

★ FANTASTIC FIVE: STEPS FOR SUCCESS ★

1. **Think maintenance.** Creating daily healthy habits for care of your hair and teeth will make the process automatic, so that you don't even have to think about what you need to do to maintain good looks and optimum health.

2. **Floss!** It's perhaps the most underappreciated step that you can take for your health. Take two minutes to brush several times a day, and then floss to prevent and dislodge pesky plaque from your teeth.

3. **The most common cause of hair loss in teens is inadequate nutrition; specifically, not getting enough protein and healthy fat.** Best foods include olive and canola oil, salmon, avocado, egg yolk, tree nuts, and legumes (like peas and beans).

4. **Solo work:** Experiment with different shampoos and conditioners every few weeks and see what changes you notice. Does one make your hair feel softer? Is another more drying? Can you find the least expensive one that works best?

5. **Discussion:** We tend to "type" people according to their appearance (grungy, geeky, goth, crunchy, preppy, and so on). Is this unfair stereotyping? Or do people cultivate certain appearances because they want to be associated with certain groups?

What You Will Learn

◎ The hormonal power struggle that controls hunger

◎ How metabolism works

◎ Guidelines for healthy and unhealthy eating

◎ The ins and outs of eating disorders

◎ How to read a food label

3

Weighty Issues

The Ins and Outs of Nutrition, Hunger, and Diet

Yes, you could say that this entire book is all about your body—your brain and your skin, your hair and your muscles, and so on. But, this chapter may be one of the most important bodily chapters of them all, because we're dealing with a subject that can be very much at the core of not only your health status but also your identity.

If you think we're going to leave the discussion of shapes and sizes to geometry class, you've got another thing coming, because here we're going to talk about all of the issues surrounding your body shape, your weight, and the health issues associated with the two extremes: being too heavy or too thin.

In teens, we're often concerned about those at either end of the spectrum because attaining and maintaining a healthy body weight right now sets you up for a healthier future. Being overweight or underweight can also affect your life right now—physically, socially, and emotionally. In this chapter, we're going to explain how you can determine what a healthy weight is for you, take you through the biology of hunger, and give you the nuts and bolts of healthy eating.

We know it can be tough to be a perfect eater when you live in a world that bombards you with fast-food choices and advertisements, but we believe that if you can establish smart eating habits right now, you'll be laying the groundwork for a healthy, adventurous life—because you'll be fueling your body properly to handle all of the amazing things that you want it to do.

The Biology of Hunger

At the center of any weight issue, there's one key element: food. Eat too much and you're going to be sporting extra pounds; eat too little and you're going to screw up your metabolism. Either way, you alter your body's biological processes and set yourself up for some serious health problems.

We'll take you through the entire digestion process in chapter 17 (from going in one end to going out the other), but here we'd like to give you an overview of the basics of good nutrition.

You may know that foods are essentially broken into three subcategories: protein (found in meat, fish, eggs, nuts, and beans), carbohydrates (found in grains, fruits, and vegetables), and fats (found in butter, eggs, meat, fish, oils, and nuts). Each one serves different purposes in the body. Protein, for example, is an essential building block for muscle. But they all serve one main purpose: providing energy to your bodily systems and organs.

All food is eventually broken down into units the body can use. Protein is broken down into amino acids, the foundation of every cell in your body. Fats are utilized to protect nerve cells (see chapter 9) and are an excellent source of energy that can be stored for long-term use. The sugars in carbohydrates are all converted to glucose, the body's principal source of energy. Many people think that the way you get fat is by eating fat. That can be true, but it's misleading. Any of the three types of nutrients can make you fat if you ingest too much of it. As your body processes food, it will shuttle that food's nutrients throughout your body—to feed your brain or fuel your biceps. Any extras that can't be used are essentially put into a doggie bag and saved for later, in the form of fat stored in your body.

Healthy eating entails paying attention to both the quality and quantity of food you consume. You want enough calories to keep your body energized, while at the same time making sure that your meals are balanced with foods from each of the three groups. Furthermore, you want to make sure you're choosing healthy options from within each food group. Think of the sugar rush you get when you drink a Coke and eat a sugary cereal for breakfast. (Actually, we wish you wouldn't.) Now compare that to the feeling you get when you eat a bowl of oatmeal with a glass of low-fat milk. They may contain the same calories, but one meal is packed with nutrients, while the other is made up mostly of sugar. The healthy choice—the oatmeal, in case you hadn't figured it out—contains fiber and a little bit of fat, which takes longer to digest, so you stay fuller longer. It also contains nutrients that improve function and fight disease. The unhealthy choice might give you an initial burst of energy, but those calories are nutritionally "empty" and will only lead you to crash and crave another fix. The quality and quantity of food you eat have a major influence on your appetite regulation—how your body and brain know they want or need more food. Let's take a look at how it all works.

In the center of your brain sits the hypothalamus, a key command center for your body. (See figure 3.1.) Among the biological functions it controls are temperature, metabolism, and sex drive. The tiny structure also controls your appetite—not just for food but also for thirst, sleep, and even for that special someone. Hidden in your hypothalamus is a satiety center that regulates your appetite for food via two hormones that regulate whether you feel hungry or full: ghrelin and leptin. Let's take a look at how they work.

Your stomach and intestines do more than hold food and produce belches that register on the Richter scale. When your stomach is empty, its inner lining releases this feisty little chemical called ghrelin. When your stomach is growling, it's this

Figure 3.1 **Satisfaction Guaranteed** In your brain, you have satiety centers for food, thirst, sleep, and sex. Your actions help influence hormonal levels that make you feel satisfied. Sometimes they can be confusing—for instance, a hungry feeling may actually mean your body is thirsty. A glass of water can sometimes curb that hungry feeling.

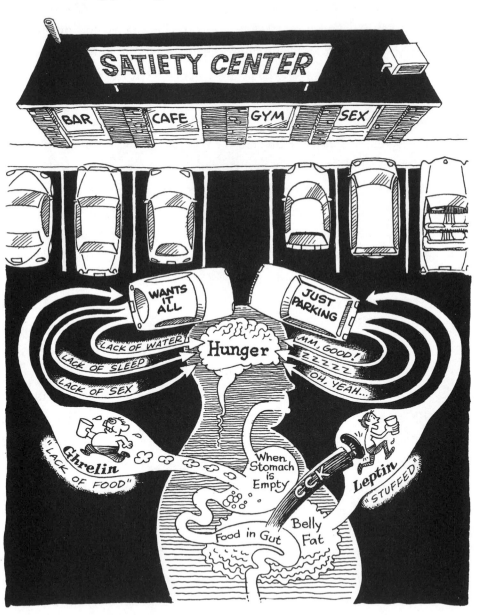

gremlin of a hormone that's sending desperate messages that you need more food. Ghrelin makes you want to eat. When you diet through deprivation (not eating enough food), the increased ghrelin secretion sends even more signals to eat, overriding your willpower and causing chemical reactions that give you little choice but to go crazy in the pantry. Your stomach secretes ghrelin in pulses every half hour, sending subtle chemical impulses to your brain—almost like subliminal biological messages: Cheese fries! Milkshake! Triple burgers! When you're *really* hungry, those messages come fast—every twenty minutes or so—and they're also amplified. So you get more signals and stronger signals that your body wants food. After long periods, your body often can't ignore those messages. The chemical cattle prod stops when you eat; when your stomach fills, your ghrelin levels go down, thus reducing your appetite. (See figure 3.2.)

On the other hand, there's leptin, produced by fat tissue and by stomach cells, that tells your brain that your body is full. Here's how the two work together: Ghrelin works in the short term, sending out those hunger signals two or three times an hour. Leptin works in the long term, so if you can get your leptin signals up, you'll have a greater ability to keep your appetite in check. Leptin can outrank ghrelin.

But all foods are not created equal when it comes to stimulating leptin. In particular, highly processed foods, especially those that contain high-fructose corn syrup (HFCS—recently rebranded as corn sugar), are less likely to stimulate leptin production or leptin-like response from your brain than foods containing a healthy balance of protein, fat, and carbohydrates.

The fructose in HFCS, which sweetens soft drinks and salad dressings, isn't seen by your brain as a regular food—in contrast to the type of fructose found in fruit—so it tells your body to keep eating. Even low-fat foods that contain HFCS can wind up high in calories, partly because you overeat without the brain signaling, "Hey! You're full! Put down that fork!"

The power struggle between ghrelin and leptin also involves other chemicals, specifically those that influence mood such as serotonin (see chapter 12). Ever notice how easy it is to drown your sorrows in a pint of Häagen-Dazs? That's because simple sugars in foods such as ice cream increase your levels of this neurotransmitter, which makes you feel good. But that feeling quickly fades, and your brain, craving

Figure 3.2 **Hormones and Hunger** Two hormones—leptin and ghrelin—battle to control your hunger. Increased levels of leptin help you stay satisfied, while increased levels of ghrelin make you want to gorge. Eating good-for-you foods can help influence those hormone levels to keep you satisfied throughout the day—and avoid the highs and lows that can come from chowing down on sugary foods.

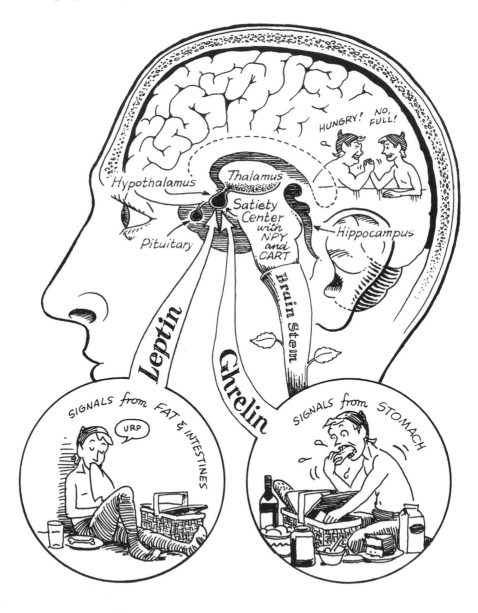

to feel good again, commands you to seek more of those simple sugars to recapture that feeling. And when you don't get enough sleep, ghrelin goes up and leptin goes down; it's why we crave sweet and starchy foods when we're tired, to give us that pick-me-up feeling.

The highs and lows we get from emotional eating can set the stage for weight gain. Your goal, then, is to keep yourself well rested and emotionally balanced so that you're in a steady state of satisfaction and don't experience huge hormonal highs and lows that make you binge on empty calories. Starvation—which can also be a response to stress or depression—can cause similar highs and lows. For more on eating disorders, see the discussion below.

Now, extra calories aren't the only thing that affects whether you're fat, thin, or just right. Another factor is your metabolism, or the rate at which you burn the calories you consume. Only 15 percent to 30 percent of your daily intake of calories is burned through intentional physical activity such as exercise, walking, or dancing. You burn most of your calories by keeping your heart pumping, your brain remembering your math equations—your body just performing everyday functions. However, that doesn't mean that outside influences don't slow down and speed up your burn rate. Any movement speeds metabolism, including fidgeting (called "nonexercise activity thermogenesis" in scientific lingo, or NEAT for short). Every increase in body temperature of 1 degree increases your metabolic rate by 14 percent. Eating protein appears to do the same thing naturally, by the way. When you sleep, your metabolic rate decreases by 10 percent. Perhaps most shockingly, when you starve yourself for more than twelve hours, your metabolic rate actually goes down by 40 percent! This is because when you skip meals, your body senses a dietary disaster and quickly goes into storage mode rather than burning mode. That's how our ancestors survived famines: by storing fat when they were deprived of food. And there you have the primary reason why deprivation diets don't work for losing weight.

Some of your metabolism is indeed genetic; you're born with a certain burn rate. That's why some rail-thin people can eat a lot and not get fat (which doesn't necessarily mean they're healthy, by the way). But you can control your metabolism to some extent by exercising, eating steadily throughout the day rather than bingeing, and consuming good-for-you foods—which we'll discuss in greater detail below.

So what are healthy foods versus unhealthy foods?

Generally, they can be classified into these two groupings:

Healthy ingredients: lean protein (like skinless turkey and chicken, fish), healthy fats (like omega-3 fatty acids, unsaturated fats), healthy carbohydrates (100 percent whole grain), fiber (oatmeal, vegetables, psyllium husks).

Unhealthy ingredients: the five food felons: (1) added simple sugars, (2) enriched (or bleached or refined) flour, (3) added syrups like HFCS (corn sugar), (4) saturated fats (four-legged animal fats, two-legged animal skin, coconut and palm oils), and (5) trans fats.

First, avoid simple sugars and syrups. Saturated fats and trans fats are other ones to avoid. Finally, stay clear of enriched, bleached, or refined flour. All three words mean that the flour has been stripped of its nutrients. All of these in excess can contribute to obesity and lead to other long-term health risks. Use flour made with 100 percent whole grains instead.

And the ideal is to eat those healthy foods in balance: a little protein, healthy fats, and healthy carbs at each of your meals. Lean proteins include chicken, turkey, fish (great for those omega-3 fatty acids). Healthy fats (you need at least 30 to 50 grams worth a day) include olives, natural peanut butter, olive oil, hummus, and many other Mediterranean-style foods. Healthy carbs that can also get you needed fiber include things cooked with chia seeds and whole grain flour, anything whole grain, whole wheat pasta, brown rice, and don't forget your fruits and veggies. We'll show you some well-balanced recipes in our YOU Tools, starting on page 375.

How do you read a food label?

What are proper portion sizes?

A serving of protein usually means 3 ounces of meat/chicken/fish/tofu, as in three slices of lunch meat or a piece of chicken the size of your palm. Two tablespoons of peanut butter would make one serving of protein. You need two or three servings of protein a day. With respect to fat intake, portion sizes are trickier. The goal is to get a minimum of 30 to 50 grams of fat a day (the good kind), and it helps your body if you spread those out over at least three meals. For fruits and veggies, you need five or more palm-sized servings a day, minimum.

HAND SYMBOL	EQUIVALENT	FOODS	CALORIES
Fist	1 cup	Rice, pasta Fruit Veggies	200 75 40
Palm	3 ounces	Meat Fish Poultry	160 160 160
Handful	1 ounce*	Nuts Raisins	170 85
Two Handfuls	1 ounce	Chips Popcorn Pretzels	150 120 100
Thumb	1 ounce	Peanut butter Hard cheese	170 100
Thumb/Tip	1 teaspoon	Cooking oil Mayo, butter Sugar	40 35 15

* 1-ounce sizes vary based on density of foods.

I see calorie labels everywhere. How many calories do I really need?

There's such a wide range depending on individual needs. Most of you will need a minimum of 2,000 calories a day just to keep your body functioning. But athletes—and those of you growing (most of you are!)—may need significantly more than that. If you're actively trying to lose weght, don't go below 1,500 to 1,800 calories a day.

Eating fat makes you fat, right?

No, not quite. *Eating too many calories—whether they're protein, carbohydrates, or fat—is what contributes to weight gain.* But as we discussed, the key to controlling weight gain is to eat the right foods that will help keep your appetite hormones level so you don't get those intense hunger pangs that make you feel like gorging (see figure 3.3). And when it comes to fat, your brain actually needs healthy fat in your diet. Fat in your brain is not excess-calorie fat; it's used to myelinate (or hard-wire) your neural pathways. The fat helps you learn or get more coordinated. Without adequate fat, your brain capacity shrinks (see page 175). DHA omega-3 fat makes up about 60 percent of the fat in your brain. It is your "smart fat." Here's a little more about fat.

Many teens and adults aim for a low-fat diet in an attempt to be healthy. But what many don't realize is that a low-fat diet does not mean a *no*-fat diet. Your brain and body need a minimum of 30 to 50 grams of healthy fat a day for a reasonable fat diet, and a standard diet can easily include 70 to 90 grams of fat a day. Many dieters think that it's okay to eat only 5 to 15 grams a day, or to eat no items over 5 to 8 grams a day, or to obey other extreme dieting dictates. Unfortunately, this is not the best strategy; lack of fat in a diet can lead to loss of myelin, the fatty sheaths that surround nerves and allow messages to be transmitted from brain to body and back. Moreover, the cerebral cortex—the part of the brain that does all of your key thinking—actually shrinks if you don't get enough dietary fat over a long enough period of time. Besides keeping your brain fit and functioning, fat is also responsible for the shine and texture of your hair and the firmness of breasts in girls; if you lose enough weight and body fat, they get saggy. Healthy fats include fish oils, and omega-3s from algae, salmon, walnuts, olive oil, and avocados.

How about diet pills, or even laxatives—can they help you lose weight?

This one is a no-brainer: *Diet pills do help you lose weight, but they can stop your heart.* Acting as amphetamines, or speed, diet pills may suppress appetite for hours after you take them, but the way the hunger center works, most people will set themselves up for a binge when the pills wear off, leading to a vicious cycle of starving, bingeing, starving, bingeing. Inadequate calories cause the body to eventually break down heart muscle for food; with a weakened heart muscle, adding a stimulant such as diet pills can cause the heart to develop an abnormal, life-threatening irregular rhythm that can cause sudden death. And some pills come with the great side effect of anal leakage. (We'll give you two guesses as to what that means.)

Speaking of which, laxatives often are used to "cleanse" or empty the body of food and stool. They tend to cause cramps and diarrhea, with more and more required to achieve the same effect over time. With repeated use, the bowel gets distended, causing further bloating, gas, and cramping. Chronic loss of bowel tone can be frustrating, with a feeling of being "big" persisting or worsening over time. And both diet pills and laxatives are often associated with missed meals—snapping your body back into its famine response, resulting in slowed metabolism and a shift to store calories to survive the deprivation.

I really am watching my calories. Why do I look bigger?

When you starve your body, certain predictable changes occur. If you aren't eating enough food, and in the right balance, your body will try other ways to get what it needs. One big change occurs in your gut, where digestion happens. *If you are eating too little fat or protein, or not enough calories overall, or not enough fluids, your body will slow down the semidigested food's movement through your digestive system to try to "catch" any of the missing nutrients before the food reaches the colon.* At the same time, more time is used to draw off every drop of water from the bowel contents, making you more constipated. All that extra time means more opportunity for food in the intestines to break down and produce gas, making you more bloated. This bloating can be so extreme that certain teens who restrict their calories will look and feel seven months pregnant between meals—like those starving kids you see

Figure 3.3 **Department of Energy** The three major types of energy are contained in carbohydrates, proteins, and fats, which can come in healthy or waist-busting forms. Complex carbs enter the blood slowly, so we do not tax our hormones. Amino acids are converted inefficiently to sugars, and fats cannot be converted at all. Fats come in forms our bodies recognize (like nuts) and naturally less common forms that poison us (like trans fats). Most foods, like meat, are a combination of energy sources; as the food digests (or sometimes rots) in your intestines, nutrients are absorbed in different places. By the way, even though the liver is the symbolic center of the metabolic universe, the intestines, as evidenced by your bathroom time, aren't really a closed loop.

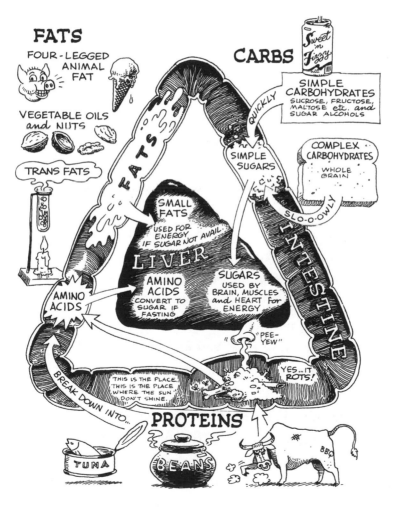

in photos from famine-stricken countries. Gas-X and other over-the-counter or prescription remedies won't change this bloating or feeling of being full early in a meal; the only cure, or relief, is to start eating, day after day and every day, with better amounts of the right food groups. If you improve the calories but still get too little protein or too little healthy fat or too little fiber or magnesium, you'll still be stuck with slow-moving bowels. The good news is that this whole bowel mess is reversible: If you start eating better every day, and for weeks at a time, you can speed up movement through the bowels and experience less bloating. It takes time and patience, but you'll know you're getting better when you start having normal bowel movements (that's the poop) each day, with less of an overly full feeling with each meal, and less bloating in between.

What's an eating disorder?

Living in the world today, many teens (and children and adults) are pretty conscious of their appearance in general, and their weight and body shape in particular. It's nearly impossible to avoid the perfect-body-focused impact of society and the media. (See more below.) In addition, some people have individual and family factors that make them more susceptible to critical self-judgment and more demanding of personal "perfection." What's more, certain times and situations in life contribute huge amounts of stress and challenges. When all these factors combine in certain ways, it can create a setting for developing an eating disorder.

Eating disorders in their extreme form seem to burrow into the brains of their victims, take over their thoughts and grow stronger every day. People with eating disorders build a "fat box," where every comment, every situation, is filtered through the box and distorted, so that it comes out as a criticism or demand. "You look great today" becomes "You usually look fat." "You look so healthy" becomes "You're eating too much." "I love your hair" becomes "I can't find anything nice to say about the rest of you."

EDs also take over their victims' self-perceptions. People become unable to see the "real" image of themselves in the mirror, seeing someone much larger or with a distorted body shape. People with severe eating disorders often go to sleep thinking about food and wake up thinking about food. Every bite is an internal struggle. The "eating disorder voice" grows to be much louder than the individual's true voice, and constantly berates and threatens. "You are a fat pig with no control!" "If you eat that cookie, you're going to be totally disgusting!"

A major part of fighting back against an eating disorder is for the sufferer to learn to hear and strengthen his or her own voice, so that he or she can make active decisions instead of giving the power to the disorder. Though to the outside observer, eating disorders seem to be all about the affected person's *behavior* related to food, they really are brain diseases, controlled by distortions in *thoughts* and *perceptions*. (Note: in milder forms, some bites or meals are challenges, but the thought process does not go on all the time. If any part of this rings true, speak to your doctor about it, as eating disorders are better prevented early, before the unhealthy behaviors get hard-wired into your brain as a default coping strategy.)

Eating disorders probably developed as a survival mechanism; in times of famine, the group would need to migrate (think run on the treadmill for a prolonged period of time) with little to eat (induced starvation) until they found a better living situation. It was in each person's best interest to survive the famine. When food was plentiful, it made sense physiologically to store some nuts up for the winter, or develop extra padding to survive the next famine. That's why fertility goddesses are all roly-poly, as fertility would not occur in the starved state, but only in times of plenty. And now that we have no sabertooth tigers to outrun, and most developed countries have plenty of food so no induced famine, nature seems to be activating that gene at the most inopportune times, with kids or adults creating similar starvation and overexercising patterns in an unhealthy way. Adaptive now? Not so much. Detrimental to health and well-being? Definitely.

◎ People with anorexia nervosa (AN) have an intense fear of becoming fat or gaining any weight, even though they are often underweight. They seriously restrict their caloric intake and are generally acutely aware of every calorie that goes into their bodies. Besides restricting, people with anorexia may also binge and purge, but the resulting calories consumed are less than the average person, and much less than is needed for healthy functioning.

◉ People with bulimia nervosa (BN) have episodes of eating much more than the average person would eat in a particular time period, and they feel out of control of their eating during this time. Then, they do something to "get rid of" the calories. This may include vomiting, using laxatives or other medications, fasting, or excessive exercise.

◉ There is also a group of eating disorders that do not quite fit into either of the other categories; we call them eating disorders not otherwise specified (EDNOS). People with EDNOS may not meet the rigid medical requirements of an AN or BN diagnosis but feature similar food-related behaviors. Or they may have unusual routines or rituals related to food—for example, only eating foods of certain colors, or chewing food and spitting it out.

So what are the signs of an eating disorder?

These are some of the classic signs. Any of them sound familiar?

◉ Preoccupation with appearance, body shape, or weight, with the preoccupation getting in the way of daily life.

◉ Consistent sadness, frustration, or anger about body image.

◉ Frequent self-deprecating comments.

◉ Frequent comparison to others regarding appearance, body shape, or weight.

◉ Excessive concern about a body part that seems average or okay to others.

◉ Increasing self-consciousness.

◉ Secrecy related to eating or exercise habits.

◉ Dramatic or steady weight loss and/or extreme weight fluctuations (big ups and downs).

- Severely restricting food intake.

- Bingeing.

- Refusal to eat certain foods.

- Obsessing over body weight, calories, food, or dieting.

- Unusual eating rituals, such as rearranging food on the plate, excessive chewing, eating food in a certain order, or having to measure all food consumed.

- Making excuses to avoid mealtimes and eating, including claiming food intolerances or allergies when none actually exist.

- Complaining often about feeling fat.

- Excessive exercise, even during bad weather or sickness; needing to get rid of calories consumed.

- Vomiting, diet pills, laxative use, or other forms of purging.

- Frequent weighing.

- Refusal to eat in front of others.

- Consistent denial of hunger.

- Attempts to hide appearance with clothing or posture.

- Moodiness, depression, withdrawn personality.

Everyone says it's good to lose weight. Really, what are the risks of losing too much weight?

The main risks include:

⊙ When your body does not receive enough calories or nutrition, it starts breaking down muscles in all sorts of places. One of its last resorts is to metabolize heart muscle for energy. Losing heart muscle can cause your heart rate to slow to fewer than 50 beats a minute; the average for a teen is around 60 to 80 beats per minute. When that happens, you are at risk for sudden cardiac death if you add exercise, caffeine, or other stimulants. In addition, the heart can develop abnormal cardiac rhythms. The more life-threatening ones include prolonged QTC syndrome, in which it takes too long for your heart to repolarize after depolarizing, a process it needs to perform automatically with every beat.

Fortunately, these serious effects are reversible if you start eating more and more nutritious food; think veggies and whole grains, with healthy fats like chia seeds. When you start eating better, the added calories and nutrients go to the heart first, then the brain, the other major organs, and the bones and muscles, with "padding," or love handles, a relative luxury that could only come much, much later.

⊙ Loss of brain tissue (cerebral atrophy). You may find yourself reading the same paragraph over and over in order to comprehend it, or having a hard time with short-term or long-term memory.

⊙ Loss of bone tissue (called osteopenia). This can give you little-old-lady bones at a very young age, with significant risk for stress fractures (breaks in the bones caused by overuse and weak bones).

⊙ Euthyroid sick syndrome. In this condition, your thyroid gland, located in the front of your lower neck, starts to slow down your metabolism if it does not see enough energy intake.

- Delayed puberty (with loss of your ultimate adult height if you start young enough) and loss of periods (amenorrhea), which can lead to loss of bone tissue.

- Kidney failure, liver failure, other organ failure if you lose enough weight.

- Tons of cosmetic issues can occur also, including problems with teeth, nails, hair (dry, thin, and brittle), and skin (drying out and bruising easily).

- People with eating disorders can have various other mental health challenges simultaneously, and sorting this out can be a bit of a "chicken and the egg" situation. For instance, depression can be a reaction to the chains that the eating disorder wraps around your life, or it can be the underlying cause of the eating disorder. Another person may have extreme perfectionism that gets his life out of balance, like obsessive-compulsive disorder. (More in chapter 12.)

What can I do about eating disorders if a friend has one?

Treatment usually involves a team approach, including doctors, parents, nutritional counseling, and psychological counseling. The therapist ends up serving as a "life coach" or skills builder, helping your friend develop better coping strategies so that they don't just use the eating disorder as a default coping mechanism ("I'm stressed, I don't eat; I'm stressed, I overexercise"). This ends up being the opposite with binge eating disorder, which can lead to obesity: "I'm stressed, I eat. I'm stressed, I don't want to exercise." Either way, the person needs new and better skills to handle stress.

Part of the way to overcome eating disorders is *establishing a healthy environment*. If your friend used to enjoy doing an activity with you, try to engage her in the activity, as long as it is a healthy one. Also, avoid the "weighty speak"; don't comment on food, body, dieting, or anything weight related, because the person with the eating disorder is likely to misinterpret whatever you say or find it "triggering," which means it gets her own eating disorder thoughts spiraling out of control.

I try to watch what I eat, but I feel like I'm hungry all the time. Help!

The reason some people eat is because their satiety centers (the place in the brain that lets you know whether you're hungry or not) are begging for attention. But sometimes, those appetite centers want things to quench thirst, not to fill the stomach. Thirst could be caused by hormones in the gut, or it could be a chemical response to eating; eating food increases the thickness of your blood, and your body senses the need to dilute it. A great way to counteract hunger is by drinking—but not the stuff that contains unnecessary, empty calories, like sugared soft drinks. Your thirst center doesn't care whether it's getting zero-calorie water or a mega-calorie frappuccino. *When you feel hungry, drink a glass or two of water or milk first, to see if that's really what your body wants.*

Do you have tips for losing weight in a healthy way?

Sure, here are a couple of our favorites:

Pick, stick, and automate. Yeah, sure, variety may be the spice of life, but it can also be the death of healthy eating. When you have a lot of choices for a meal, it's a lot easier to slip out of good eating habits and into fried-ham-induced bad ones. One way to avoid excess fat intake is to eliminate choices for at least one meal a day. For teens, that's most often breakfast. So find two or three healthy breakfasts that you like—say, oatmeal, cereal with low-fat milk, yogurt with fruit, all-natural peanut butter on 100 percent whole wheat bread—and stick to them every day. Every day. Yes, every day. When you make it an automatic choice, you won't make errors in choosing something unhealthy.

Don't surround yourself with eaters. Here's a concept we're betting you've never heard quite this way: Obesity is an infectious disease. No, no, no, it's not as if anyone's going to sneeze cheeseburger bits into your arteries. Nevertheless, there is a major infectious component to obesity: It spreads through social networks. Just consider one study that shows that if one of two friends is obese, the other's chance of becoming obese increases by 171 percent. That's why it's crucial to consider what and *whom* you surround yourself with. If you socialize with the every-day-is-a-reason-to-eat-lasagna crowd, chances are you're going to be knee deep in ricotta without much chance of digging yourself out (except via fork). But if you surround yourself with a healthy set of friends, you'll adopt healthier habits. Does that mean we suggest you ditch any overweight friends? Of course not. But it means be aware of your surroundings and try to make changes that can get you on track or support your own good health. The flip side is also true: If you surround yourself with peers dieting inappropriately, you are more likely to make bad choices.

Plan for hunger. Keep on hand emergency foods and items that can help you kill cravings, like V8 juice, carrot sticks, an apple, or a handful of nuts.

School lunches are horrible. Your advice?

Almost one-third of US youngsters eat fast food every day—and that means they consume more calories and eat fewer good foods than on days when they don't eat fast food. Almost all schools offer healthy alternatives for lunch. *Instead, why not pack yourself a peanut butter sandwich on 100 percent whole wheat bread, and a cut-up apple sprinkled with lemon juice?* Or a PB and J sandwich (on 100 percent whole wheat bread), a piece of fruit, a small bag of carrots for the crunch, and a water bottle. If you do choose the school lunch option, try to make nutritious choices. In addition to eating the fruit, vegetables, and low-fat or no-fat milk that is offered and avoiding anything fried or blanketed in brown sauce, get a group together to advocate for healthier options within your school. Create a committee to work with the school lunch coordinator to develop healthier recipes (baked not fried), substitute low-fat cheese for full-fat cheese, 100 percent whole wheat bread for white bread, and so forth. Here *you* can be the teachers.

People blame the media for how bodies should look. What's your take?

The media has been called the "Superpeer," both shaping and reflecting society. But the playing field is not even: websites such as the Dove Campaign for Real Beauty (www.dove.us/#/cfrb) can show the roles of airbrushing and other techniques to change reality into fantasy. Celebs have the advantage of stylists, makeup artists, and Photoshoppers who digitally manipulate their images. *Even so, they have been known to suffer from eating disorders and various addictions to try to change a* look when not being airbrushed, at the expense of their health and happiness. This aspect of their lives is not glamorous and can ruin their careers.

It helps keep things in perspective to realize the standards of beauty have changed over time. In 1980 researchers studied *Playboy* magazine centerfolds for several decades, showing a shift from a voluptuous Marilyn Monroe figure; to Twiggy, who was the first to glamorize what is now known as the starved Kate Moss look; and then to Twiggy plus breasts, or the standard Victoria's Secret model. Marilyn Monroe actually weighed around one hundred fifty pounds and was a size 12 to 14; size 00 is a relatively modern phenomenon. If you are blessed with the current shape consistent with the current media's standard of beauty, that may be great, but don't see your looks as your only or most important asset— identify all sorts of strengths that you have, as looks can be fleeting (think aging), but your identity needs to last you a lifetime.

Same goes for those of you who see all the imperfections in yourself; the most valuable diamonds have flaws, and you can learn to appreciate many aspects of yourself. Don't just dwell on the superficial, but on what is inside, and have your actions be a window into your character. Are you kind? Compassionate? Artistic? Inspiring? What are the adjectives that best describe you? How would you like to be described? Act in a way that will generate those adjectives.

★ FANTASTIC FIVE: STEPS FOR SUCCESS ★

1. **Aim for balance** at every meal: lean protein (beans, nuts, chicken or fish), healthy fats (a few walnuts/peanuts or avocado slices), and healthy carbohydrates (100 percent whole grain bread, oats, chia, quinoa), and fruits and vegetables.

2. **Never skip breakfast**. Breakfast revs your metabolism and sets you on a good path for the day. Ideally, you'll want to eat three modest-sized meals evenly spaced over the course of each day, with two small, healthy snacks in between.

The steady eating will help you avoid the highs and lows that are associated with bingeing.

3. **It's okay to go off the farm every once in a while,** and your teen-age metabolism can handle the occasional splurge, but we want you to get in the habit of recognizing healthy foods and eating them the majority of the time. You can treat yourself, but it's when those treats become a habit that you'll get into trouble—now and in the future.

4. **YOU Activity:**

Food Diary

Ever thought about what you eat, when, how, and why? This is designed to be fun and informative. Stay free of negative judgments. Keep track of your meals over the course of a day and see what you learn about yourself.

	WHAT DID YOU EAT AND HOW MUCH?	HOW HUNGRY WERE YOU, ON A SCALE FROM 1 TO 5?	WHERE WERE YOU?	HOW DID YOU FEEL?	WHAT DID YOU NOTICE?
Breakfast					
Morning Snack					

	WHAT DID YOU EAT AND HOW MUCH?	HOW HUNGRY WERE YOU, ON A SCALE FROM 1 TO 5?	WHERE WERE YOU?	HOW DID YOU FEEL?	WHAT DID YOU NOTICE?
Lunch					
Afternoon Snack					
Dinner					
Other					

5. **Solo work:** If you have trouble with your weight and find yourself hungry all the time, we recommend that you start recording your hunger levels, so you can really get in tune with how your body is feeling. Throughout the day, record your level of hunger as measured by this scale. Stay tuned to what your stomach is telling you. This process will help you really feel your hunger, so that you can let your stomach, not your emotions, dictate your habits.

Empty tank = hungry. It feels as if you haven't eaten since kindergarten.

Half tank = edge is off. You're okay, not desperate, like maybe when you're getting home from school.

Three-quarters tank = satisfied and not hungry. You can go much longer without food. You just ate nuts before dinner.

Full tank = full and comfortable. It's the way you feel after finishing an average-portion, healthful meal.

Overflow Level S = stuffed. You could've stopped two scoops of pudding ago.

Overflow Level OS = overstuffed. Audible groaning detected.

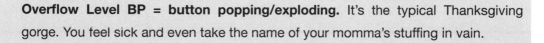

Overflow Level BP = button popping/exploding. It's the typical Thanksgiving gorge. You feel sick and even take the name of your momma's stuffing in vain.

The way to apply this is, every time you find yourself reaching for the cheese sauce or cookie box, rate your hunger. Then think about whether you're reaching for the leftover lasagna because you're truly hungry or for a reason that has absolutely nothing to do with hunger. Ideally, you'll want to stay in the three-quarters to full-tank range—satisfied at all times. And you'll get there by eating regularly throughout the day.

What You Will Learn

- The benefits of exercise

- How your muscles, bones, and heart develop

- How to overcome exercise obstacles

- How to get started on an exercise plan

4

Move It

There are some times when you want absolutely no part of sweat: during your oral report, when you're on a date, if you've found yourself on the wrong end of a principal's scowl. But other times, we hope that you love the idea of sweat—of moving, of exercising, of biking, hiking, dancing, or doing anything that gets your body shaking.

When you're physically fit, you have more energy, a more positive mood, more self-esteem, and overall better health. Being fit should be a goal for everyone, and the great thing is that you don't have to be a size 2 or have rock-solid abs to be fit.

The side effect, of course, is that being fit also helps prevent (or combat) obesity—

and it goes a long way toward helping you achieve your ideal body shape. One of the reasons why we have an obesity epidemic is because we simply don't move enough. We plop down on the couch or bed or futon or floor, dart our eyes toward our preferred screen (TV, video game, mobile phone, iPad), and don't move until someone tells us that the pizza is here.

Eventually, that causes a health crisis.

In this chapter, we're going to explore the basic biology of movement, specifically as it relates to your muscles, bones, and heart—and why being fit is important for both your health and your waist size. (In the next chapter, we'll deal with more advanced topics, like sports injuries.) We should also say that we're not in the business of telling you what kinds of exercises you have to do. Our goal is to help you understand why the body needs movement, so you then can find the fun activities that work for you—so you'll keep wanting to do them over and over again.

The Biology of Exercise

Why in the world do we even need to exercise? I mean, those darn school gym shorts are so bleepin' ugly. Lots of reasons, actually, but here are just a few of the benefits:

- Exercise increases your metabolism so that you burn energy at a faster rate than if you didn't exercise.

- Exercise reduces your appetite.

- Exercise helps you sleep better.

- Exercise stimulates the release of endorphins, chemicals that stimulate the pleasure centers in the brain.

- Exercise helps decrease depression and increase positive attitude.

◎ Exercise decreases the risk of lots of health problems, like heart trouble and even memory problems.

◎ Down the road, exercise helps prevent wrinkles and fosters more years of sexual functioning and pleasure. (We know: bad visual, but you'll care when you're there.)

They're all very good reasons not only for your long-term health but, as you can see, for your short-term health, attitude, mood, and overall well-being.

When we think about the basics of fitness, we tend to think about the entire skeletal system, which means not just your skeleton but also how your muscles, bones, and joints are put together. The skeletal system gives you the ability to stand up straight and protects your internal organs from severe damage during skateboarding falls, car accidents, and extreme sports. Giving your bones their get-up-and-go are your muscles, with your joints acting as the connectors and motion directors. (More on joints in the next chapter.) In addition, we think of the heart—especially because of its role in endurance sports such as running and swimming. So let's take a look at how they all work.

Muscles: We have 650 of them in our bodies, and they all play a part in helping to give us the strength not only to perform well in sports but also to get our bodies through the day.

Muscles are made up of tissues that contract and relax. They're kind of like an extendable ladder that snaps together and shortens when you pull or apply tension at one end. When you release that tension on the muscle or ladder, it relaxes and extends. (See figure 4.1.) Your energy intake (healthy food, not flaming nacho cheesy fries) provides the power for your muscles to contract and relax. Work them and feed them right, and they grow. Starve yourself long enough, and you start breaking down those muscles to fuel the rest of your body and little by little get weaker. Eventually you start noticing it, unless all your attention is elsewhere, as happens with eating disorders.

Muscles grow after they're used. Lifting weights, doing push-ups, or performing

Figure 4.1 **Muscle Up** Proteins serve as the building blocks of muscle. When you work your muscle, you damage it—but then the muscle grows and rebuilds itself in preparation for the next time you work it. Muscle isn't just important for appearance. It uses ATP to contract, so it helps burn fat, too.

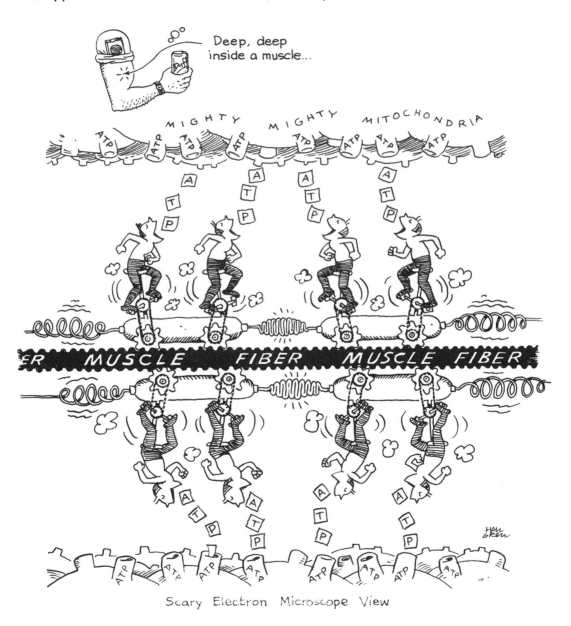

Scary Electron Microscope View

any kind of exercise that requires you to push or pull damages the muscle fibers; the soreness you may feel afterward comes from toxins released by muscle tissue when it is damaged. When you're done, the muscles say, "Forget this, we're not going to be damaged again. We're going to build up to be even stronger than before," which is why they get larger. For those who are overweight or looking to maintain weight loss, the great thing is that muscle actually helps you burn fat much faster than fat or other tissue. So if you're looking to lose weight, in addition to watching your calorie intake, build some muscle to increase the fat-burning engines in your body.

Bones: They may be useful for Halloween parties and playing fetch with Fido, but your 206 bones serve many more purposes than that. They protect your inner organs, store calcium and other minerals, act like levers to help you move, and, in their marrow, produce red and white blood cells and stem cells. Chances are, you may not think about your bones unless you break one of them, but even in your body today, they're important for all of your daily functions and movements.

Unlike that skeleton in your closet, bones are living organs, constantly building and reshaping themselves from before you are born until the day you die. In fact, bone is the only organ that regenerates itself. (Skin comes close, but when you cut your skin, you don't actually grow new skin; you heal with a scar, which isn't really skin, since it doesn't have hair follicles and can't stretch, or sweat.) Broken bone regrows itself, with the ability to become just as strong as before a fracture. The only downside is that darn cast you're stuck with for four to six weeks and the four to six months it takes the bone to resculpt itself to full strength. During the healing process, the muscles supporting that bone can weaken, requiring time and focused energy to regain their strength and endurance.

The second intriguing thing about bones is their physical structure. Most people think of bones as solid, hard all the way through. Actually, their physical structure is more like that of Swiss cheese: a solid mass dotted with tiny holes. (See figure 4.2.) Two kinds of cells work day and night to shape bone. Osteoblasts build up the structure, while osteoclasts, like little Pac-Men, break it down. The osteoblasts fill in the empty spaces with calcium and other minerals to make your bones hard and dense,

Figure 4.2 **Construction Zone** Bone is continually breaking down and building up. Osteoblasts help form the foundation of bone (which is more like Swiss cheese in structure). Calcium and resistance exercises push osteoblasts to help build strong bones.

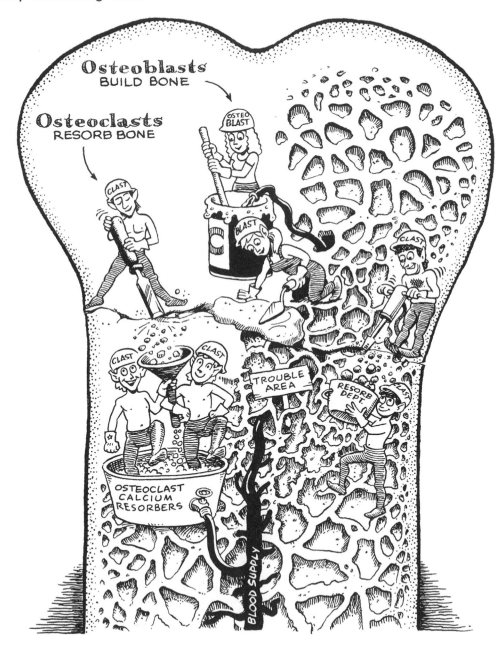

while the Pac-Man osteoclasts chew up that bone and spit the calcium back into your bloodstream to circulate throughout the rest of your body.

Just as exercise improves your muscle, it also builds your bone strength. In particular, weight-bearing exercise, which is just about everything except swimming and cycling, really helps kick up the bone-building process. Bone's biggest enemy—besides, perhaps, a patch of black ice—is soda (or pop, if you're from the Midwest). Chemicals found in soda, such as phosphorous, may lead to bone loss, and the caffeine may interfere with the body's ability to absorb calcium. We suggest drinking low-fat milk or calcium-fortified OJ instead of soda pop! Your bones' best friends are vitamin D, calcium, and magnesium. A solid 40 percent to 60 percent of your bone mass is deposited during early puberty (ages ten to twelve for girls, fourteen to eighteen for boys), with an extra 10 percent added during your twenties. Bone density peaks by the time you're thirty, with bone loss happening after that. So, now is the time when you want to max out your bone density by doing resistance exercise and getting plenty of calcium and vitamin D.

Heart: You probably think about your heart when it comes to other things in life—your relationships, for instance—but that blood pumper plays the starring role when it comes to exercise. You know it, too. Just run a lap in PE class, and you can feel the thump-thump-thump through your shirt and in your throat. As your body moves and burns fuel, in the form of the sugar called glucose to produce energy, it requires oxygen, and your heart has to beat faster to circulate more oxygen-rich blood to the tissues that need it. (The motion is less like the beating drum that we typically think of; it's more like the wringing out of a wet towel. The heart squeezes blood to pump it in and out of the circulatory system.) At the same time, your blood picks up waste in the form of carbon dioxide and carries it back to your lungs, where it is breathed out and fresh oxygen is breathed in.

Some people think the heart is the most important part of the body, as reflected in phrases such as "He's all heart." The most common heart finding in young people is a murmur. Heart murmurs can occur from birth through your geriatric years. The most common type that occurs in adolescence is a simple flow murmur, which is "benign," meaning not a problem. Think of a flow murmur as hearing water flow-

Figure 4.3 **Beating the System** The SA node rules your heart rhythm with quick conduction of the AV node; that electrical system can be shorted out by rogue cells from the other parts of the atrium and cardiovascular system, especially the pulmonary veins. The effect: irregular beats.

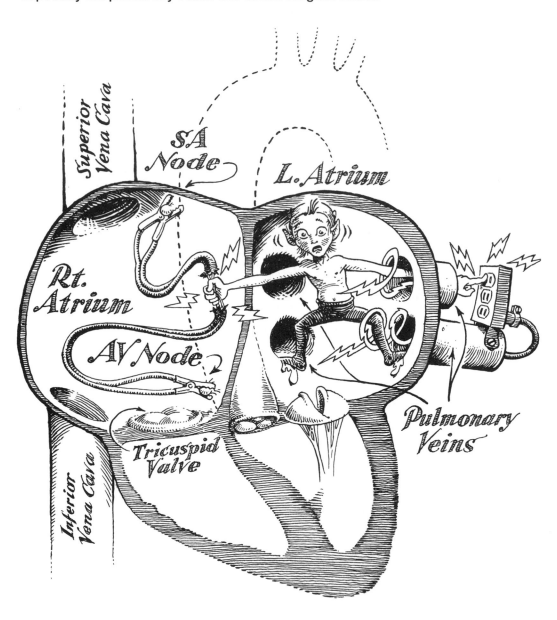

ing through the pipes in your home's boiler room; you can hear a *shush-shush* sound as the pump in your basement pumps water to all parts of your building or house (a regular heartbeat sounds like a drum). In your body, a flow murmur is what your doctor hears with a stethoscope as your heart contracts and sends blood through your arteries to the rest of your body. More rare heart murmurs often come with other symptoms, such as fainting, shortness of breath, or funny feeling heartbeats. If you experience these symptoms, see your doctor as you may have been born with heart disease that has gone previously undiagnosed. If he hears a normal heart and you have a normal ECG (electrocardiogram; you know, like you see on *Grey's Anatomy,* with the little line that goes up and down on the graph, measuring each heartbeat?), then you can rest easy that you have a normal heart.

A rare heart disease that you could have since you were born, undetected until teen years or later, is called congenital cardiomyopathy, where your heart doesn't pump right or respond well to stress—meaning it might just stop permanently if faced with exercise, caffeine, cocaine, speed, or any other stimulant, such as your best friend's ADHD medication. A pediatrician should be able to pick this form of heart disease up with a good history and a physical, especially if you get tired or dizzy with exertion or have fainted—scenarios in which your smart doctor would have gotten an ECG (those little rhythm strips that you see on every medical television show—and don't worry, they don't involve needles). Other serious conditions include ones that weaken your heart muscle. A starved heart acts very different from an athlete's heart, which is a big, juicy, high-performing, run-the-fifty-yard dash-in-six-seconds-flat kind of a heart. The athlete's heartbeat may be as slow as that of someone with an eating disorder, but we doctors can tell the difference on an ECG: The eating disordered heart has a little, bitty ECG spike reflecting depolarizing then repolarizing, which means there is not much heart muscle transmitting the charge. In an athlete's heart, there is a nice, thick heart muscle, so the time to depolarize and repolarize is longer, making a nice, tall spike on each beat of the ECG.

Another heart problem that may get diagnosed in the teen years occurs as part of Marfan syndrome, which affects one out of four hundred kids. Marfan syndrome and certain connective tissue diseases can damage the heart, as they can cause blood vessels such as the aorta—the main blood vessel taking blood from the heart to the rest of the body—to "dissect," or balloon out, and potentially burst. The key point here is that if you have an illness that affects your heart, work with your doctor closely—there are lots of things that you *can't* do, but there are tons of things that you *can* do, with your doctor's and cardiologist's advice. But the heart disease that affects most people in their lives is hardening of their arteries. We're seeing this already starting in some youngsters at age nine and docs are even operating on people in their twenties. (See figure 4.4.)

The biological bottom line: The way your muscles, bones, and heart get stronger is by working them and challenging them. When you do that, your body responds and develops to make you a healthier and stronger person.

Figure 4.4 **A Work of Artery** Your body tries to repair nicks in your arteries (caused by such things as cigarettes) by using cholesterol as plaster. That buildup can start as a teenager and cause a blockage and heart problems even in people in their twenties.

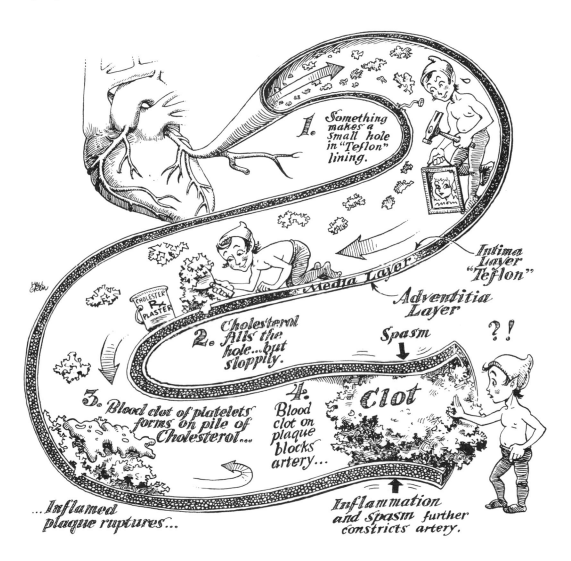

I haven't exercised at all. What's the best way to get started?

We recommend that you *start by simply walking thirty minutes a day at a brisk pace.* (Wear running or walking shoes, to provide the best support.) That will help you prepare a base level of fitness for your muscles and heart. We also recommend that you do our YOU Teen Workout—a workout that will challenge your muscles and make you stronger—three times a week. See page 367 for the workout, which you can complete in fifteen minutes and which doesn't require any equipment.

Why does it matter if I have strong bones? Don't I just need to worry about that when I get older?

Strong bones help reduce the risk of a break during a fall. And they also give you a strong pillar of strength for sports. Thinning bones don't just happen to little ol' ladies these days. Osteopenia and osteoporosis (diseases of thinning bones) have their roots in childhood, which is why your mom was so persnickety about you drinking all your milk with calcium and vitamin D as a kid. During early puberty for girls (ages eleven to fourteen years on average), and late puberty for boys (fourteen to eighteen years), bone is getting deposited at a high speed, with your osteoblasts working harder and faster than those Pac-Man osteoclasts. During your teen years, your bones need 1,200 milligrams to 1,500 milligrams of calcium a day, or the equivalent of four to six dairy servings a day. (One serving equals a cup of milk or calcium-fortified orange juice, three slices of cheese, or one yogurt.) If you don't like dairy or are lactose intolerant, you can try Lactaid pills/chews before eating or drinking dairy products or soy milk, rice milk, or calcium supplements in pill or soft chew form. Viactiv soft chews contain 500 milligrams of calcium, plus vitamins D and K, and come in great flavors such as milk chocolate and caramel. Two a day provide 100 percent of your calcium needs. We like the Adora brand chocolate calcium supplements, too (500 milligrams calcium plus 400 IUs vitamin D in each). If you get in four to five dairy or soy milk servings, you can skip a calcium supplement. If you consume three servings, take one 500-milligram calcium supplement that contains at least 400 IUs of vitamin D. Under three servings, take two supplements, ideally at least an hour apart.

It's important to stockpile bone during adolescence because up to 90 percent of bone mass is acquired by age eighteen in girls and age twenty in boys. After age thirty, the osteoclasts start to gain on the osteoblasts, leading to gradual bone loss if you don't maintain your calcium intake and do weight-bearing exercise.

The biggest pain about osteopenia and osteoporosis is that you can have it and not even know it. If you fall while doing that triple-jump turn on a bike or skateboard, you can at least rationalize why you broke your arm. But if you step off a curb funny and break your ankle, something is seriously wrong. There are certain things that weaken your bones. Chronic use of steroids (the kinds you swallow, not the kind you inhale for asthma), kidney disease and other conditions can weaken your bones. But in teens, the main offender is a diet deficient in calcium, especially in those with eating disorders. Preventing osteoporosis in the first place is a lot better than a future filled with fractured bones.

I hate exercising because my back always hurts.

You might not think it, but back pain is actually common in adolescents. There are different causes of back pain, but a muscle spasm—which can leave you gasping for breath or be a dull ache that won't let up—is the most common kind. In a spasm, the paraspinal muscles around your backbone can tense up for no good reason. Poor posture can be one of the culprits. To remedy this, *whenever possible, suck in your stomach and butt muscles at the same time.* You need abdominal muscle strength to protect your back. This tends to straighten your spine—and, as a bonus, can help you build that washboard stomach. Yes, you need abdominal strength to protect your back. Other causes of back pain include switching from high-heeled to low-heeled shoes or vice versa, wearing shoes that don't fit, doing lots of heavy lifting, sleeping on a bad mattress or bed, and being overweight, for the simple reason that it's harder on your spine to carry around more weight.

Another simple back-strengthening exercise is to get down on all fours and arch your back like a cat, hold it for three seconds, then curl your back and hold it for three seconds. Do three reps of these. Next, extend an arm and the opposite leg, and hold it for three seconds. Do three on that side and three on the other side.

I hurt, too. But it's my neck. What's that all about?

Neck spasm, or when your neck muscles tense up, has a fancy medical term: torticollis, or wryneck. Here your sternocleidomastoid, trapezius, or scalenus muscles (the neck ones) are in spasm, leaving your head more tilted to the side than one of Harry Potter's owls. It can happen on one side or both sides of your neck and can last for varying amounts of times. The most common cause is trauma. If you develop torticollis, nonsteroidal anti-inflammatory analgesics such as ibuprofen (Advil, Motrin) and naproxen (Aleve) can help, but not acetaminophen (Tylenol), which treats pain but does not get rid of inflammation. A 400-milligram dose of ibuprofen (two regular-strength pills) every six hours usually does the trick for the typical person weighing between 140 and 200 pounds. Use less if you are smaller, but no matter what size you are, be sure to take them with two glasses of water. *Massage, hot showers or baths, and use of a foam neck brace, also called a cervical collar, can also help.* The pain may last up to a week or a week and a half. If it lasts longer, see a doc.

What if I just hate exercise altogether?

You don't have to do formal exercise to get the benefits. Find something that makes your workout feel more like playing, and you'll still build your heart, muscles, and bones. *It could be hiking or dancing or anything that gets your heart rate really going.* Tennis is a game that you can learn now and play for life. If you play a sport like soccer that doesn't require extra strength training, learn a few strength exercises and do them for just ten minutes three times a week to help build up your muscles to prevent injuries. Going for a walk in the woods once a month is lovely, but doesn't count as regular exercise; you need to find something vigorous you can do at least three times a week.

What's the most important body part to work on?

While working out your biceps and calves may be nice for showing off at the pool, the biggest bang for your buck comes when you work *the foundation muscles in your body's core*. These muscles—especially the ones in your abdominals, which oppose your back muscles—help provide the support, muscular strength, and stamina. Do core exercises religiously three days a week to work your abdominals and lower-back muscles. See some moves on page 367.

I've heard many weight lifters have protein shakes before and after workouts. What's the story?

Until recently the research wasn't clear whether adding protein after a workout increased muscle size by causing water to gather in muscles. More gold-standard studies have shown that it does more. Adding 30 grams or so of protein after resistance workouts (whey shakes, nuts, or salmon burgers are good choices) increases muscle size by about 10 percent, but increases strength and power in the muscles worked by a whopping 15 to 50 percent compared to carbohydrates and electrolytes only. This isn't before a workout, which can cause you to gain extra fat, not muscle.

A lot of my friends are into hot yoga. Are there benefits to heating up? What about risks?

Hot yoga, or Bikram yoga, involves doing twenty yoga poses in a room that can be up to 105 degrees, with 40 percent humidity. Why the heat? *It's supposed to help you get a deeper stretch.* Many people love it, though the research is mixed when it comes to whether it's a beneficial exercise. Some side effects include nausea and dizziness, especially from dehydration. So hot yoga is not a good idea if you are suffering or recovering from an eating disorder, Crohn's disease, as well as anything that puts your body at risk for nutritional depletion or dehydration. But if you're already fit and healthy, with no eating disorder on the horizon, it should be safe to give it a shot, assuming that you stay well hydrated and get appropriate energy intake. (That means a balanced diet, silly!) Don't wait until you are thirsty to rehydrate; by then, you are already about 25 percent dehydrated.

Okay, I'm ready and excited to start an exercise plan. What else should I keep in mind?

Great! We don't want you to overdo it right from the start (best intentions can backfire if you start out too quickly), so follow our guidelines in the first question, and also keep these things in mind:

- Stay hydrated during exercise. That means guzzle water. You don't need energy drinks, which tend to contain lots of calories, unless you're exercising for over an hour at full tilt or unless your doctor specifically tells you that you need the extra energy intake or need to gain weight.

- Remember that *technique and good form are more important than how much weight you lift*. You'll get stronger and reduce your risk of injury by doing exercise the right way. Before starting a weight-training regime, ask an instructor or trainer to show you the proper form.

- In addition to doing exercises that work your heart (cardiovascular exercises) and muscles (resistance training), we also want you to think about balance and flexibility,★ which will make you strong and keep you injury free. Our workout includes moves that will help you in that area. But it is nice to stretch your muscles (after they're warmed up).

- Don't think that exercise has to be boring or has to be done in gym class. Take a bike ride. Go for a hike. Use the stairs instead of the elevator. Find a workout buddy. You can always make smart choices about how to be more active in your everyday life.

★ Interesting note: During growth spurts, it's not uncommon to become klutzy because, among many reasons, your body is changing faster than the vestibular system in your brain can rewire to create a new sense of yourself in space. The vestibular system is what helps provide balance and a sense of space and place.

I've been told I have scoliosis. What does that mean, and is it a deal breaker for exercise?

Scoliosis means a curve to the spine, making it look like an S. The doctors don't define it as scoliosis unless the curve measures 10 degrees on X-ray, so really minor, subtle curves don't cause problems.* *Scoliosis can start when you're just a kid, but usually it develops in adolescence, affecting 3 percent to 5 percent of all teenage girls, but only 15 percent of those cases are serious enough to require any treatment.* Guys, you have it easy: Scoliosis affects only one boy to every seven or eight girls. If it starts before you hit a growth spurt, it can progress faster and be more of a problem if you don't receive the right interventions. (More on that in a minute.)

To check your spine, your doctor should bend you forward, as if you were trying to have your hands touch the floor, with your legs straight. The doc will look at your spine from behind you. Any curve is visible then, and if it looks like it may be 10 degrees or more, the doc will order an X-ray to measure it.

Scoliosis doesn't hurt, unless the curve is really curvy: 30 degrees or more. People with severe curves (40 degrees to 50 degrees) who do not undergo appropriate treatment may suffer slightly compressed lungs in adulthood, making it harder to breathe.

If your curve is greater than 25 degrees, you usually are referred to an orthopedic surgeon (think bone doctor) for bracing, with the brace worn for roughly twenty-two hours a day until the spine matures and the curve has stopped progressing. Once the curve has remained stable for a year, the orthopedic surgeon will gradually reduce the time you need to wear the brace, until eventually you won't need it at all. The braces fit easily under clothes and actually make you look taller and straighter. You can usually participate in all sports; in fact, any physical activity is strongly encouraged. You may have some restrictions, but you can work out a specific plan with your doctor. Even swimming is okay: You just put

---

* Some really subtle curves may be because one leg is slightly longer than the other, throwing the hips out of alignment, so it looks like a curve. Normal people may have $\frac{1}{16}$ of an inch difference between legs, but if that difference is $\frac{1}{4}$ of an inch or more, sometimes it takes a foot insert (think a Dr. Scholl's pad) on the side of the shorter leg to straighten out that spine.

the brace back on as soon as you are out of the pool and dried off. Only those with severe curves need surgery, so don't let the term "orthopedic surgeon" throw you off. If you get prescribed a brace, use it as instructed, to minimize the chance you'll need surgery.

★ FANTASTIC FIVE: STEPS FOR SUCCESS ★

1. **If you're not already exercising, find an activity (or activities) that you love;** that gives you a sense of play or fun. You'll be more likely to stick to regular exercise the more engaged you are.

2. **Start slowly.** It's not only best for your body, so you don't shock your system, but you also don't want to make your new routine so hard (and your muscles so sore) that you don't want to ever do it again.

3. **Grab a buddy.** Exercise is more fun when you do it in pairs or groups. So find a friend who's in similar shape to you and wants to get in better shape, or someone who's in just a little better shape than you and wants to get better with you.

4. **Solo work:** Try our YOU Teen Workout on page 367. We also recommend the workout program in the book *The Dorm Room Diet*, written by Dr. Oz's daughter Daphne.

5. **Discussion:** With your friends or family, discuss what barriers to exercise exist in your school, home, community, state? What are some concrete things you could do to overcome them?

What You Will Learn

◎ The parts of a joint

◎ The makeup of knees, shoulders, and ankles

◎ How to treat muscle strains and pulls

◎ The lowdown on energy drinks and other sports supplements

5

The Sporting Life

Beyond the Basics to Advanced Fitness

If you've embraced the fit life, or want to, then you may be the kind of person who loves playing, competing, and using your body to experience a lot of natural highs in life, whether on the field, on the court, in the pool, at the track, or at the Ping-Pong table. If that's the case, then you may very well be pushing your body to the limits—and perhaps experiencing some of the risks and side effects of doing so.

In the last chapter, we learned about muscles, bones, and the basics of the cardio-vascular system. In this chapter, we're going to take things one step further—giving you a heads-up on some of the injuries that can result from more demanding physical activity, so you can learn how to avoid problems and excel at your chosen sport or activity.

The Biology of Joints

You've already learned about the importance of keeping your body strong via your muscles, bones, and heart—all of that holds true for everyone from the beginners to the advanced. Those of you twisting, turning, cutting, stopping, sprinting, tackling, bashing, and doing all of the other things that come with most athletic endeavors (or with your daily life, from lifting groceries, to hoisting backpacks, to taking out the trash) should also know a little bit about the parts most vulnerable to injury: your joints, which serve as the intersections where bone meets bone. As with traffic accidents, the intersection is where a lot of the action happens, because that's where a lot of forces come together. Same holds true for your body.

Let's look at your joints. Joints—particularly hinge joints such as elbows and knees—are made up of various parts. (See figure 5.1.) They're designed to bear weight and move the body. Here are the parts that make up your joints:

Collagen: a type of tissue that serves as the scaffolding upon which everything else is built.

Tendons: collagen fibers that attach muscles to bones.

Ligaments: soft tissues that connect bone to bone. Joints with few or weak ligaments, such as the shoulder, allow more motion, while joints with strong support structures, such as the hip joint, are more stable but have a smaller range of motion. We like to call these biological trade-offs. For more mobility, you get less stability—and vice versa.

Cartilage: gives our bodies form before our bones are mineralized after birth, and continues to give structure to our ears and noses. In the rest of the body, it serves as the plate of soft tissue at the ends of bones that prevents bone-on-bone clanking. The cartilage between bones acts as the internal shock absorber for your joints, while muscles are the external shock absorbers. As an example, the meniscus—car-

Figure 5.1 **Nice Joint** All joints—including the knee—serve as intersections between bones and soft tissues. They act as shock absorbers in the body. The knee joint is frequently at risk of being damaged because of such things as stop-start sports and even hormonal changes in girls. In case you didn't notice, these names aren't quite medically correct. Heh.

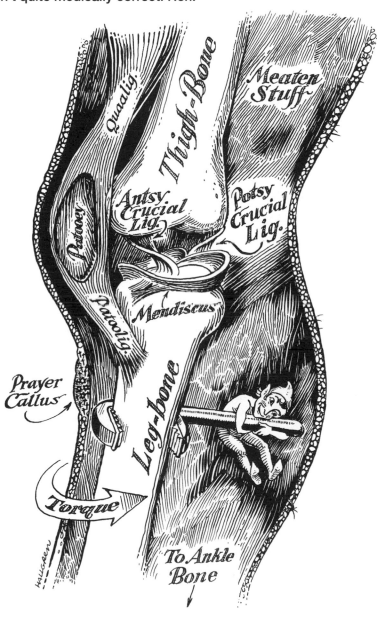

tilage that's especially vulnerable to injury—works as a key shock absorber in the knee. Since it does not have a blood supply of its own, cartilage needs to get nutrients from the surrounding synovial fluid. (See below.)

Synovial fluid: joint oil, if you will. In a normal, healthy joint, the cartilage is smooth, and the synovial fluid is as pure as spring water. If a joint becomes injured, infected, or inflamed, you can produce too much synovial fluid, which leads to painful swelling.

Now let's look at the joints most at risk of injury for teen athletes.

Knees: Sandwiched between your two longest bones, which are the femur (thigh bone) and the tibia (shin bone), your knee works like a door hinge. It bends in only one direction, backward, never sideways or forward. Check it out, but not too hard. Because of its limited range of motion, along with the heavy load it carries, plus the potential of torque (twisting motions), your knee is at risk for strain and injury.

The most common injury? A torn meniscus. The meniscus adds stability to the knee joint. Shaped like a suction cup, it keeps the round bottom of the thigh bone sitting nicely on the flat top of the shin bone. It also produces synovial fluid to feed and lubricate the cartilage. Your meniscus can tear if you're heading one way and then change direction quickly (think fast rally in tennis) or through force (think linebacker hit). Your knee is still going zig while your body has started to zag. It can also tear from overuse; for instance, from doing too many squats or other knee exercises. When the meniscus tears, it changes from shock absorber to inflamed sore area.

Tears in the meniscus or in your anterior cruciate ligament, or ACL—one of the four ligaments in your knee, and the most common female athlete injury—can be seen on MRI (magnetic resonance imaging—like an X-ray without radiation that also shows soft tissue). Treatment involves the use of anti-inflammatory medicines and RICE: rest, ice, compression (wrapping it), and elevation (keeping it propped up). Aggressive rehabilitation, supervised by a good orthopedic surgeon (don't worry, that doesn't always mean surgery) and physical therapist, can get you back in gear after a lot of hard work. Some tears may require surgery, however. (See more below.)

Shoulder: Each shoulder has two joints that connect three bones, the collarbone (clavicle), the shoulder blade (scapula), and the humerus, which is the long bone in the upper arm. These two joints allow you to rotate your arms in multiple directions. The top of the humerus lies on a shallow shelf of shoulder bone like a golf ball on a tee. Some shoulders dislocate easily because the humerus falls off the shelf like a golf ball off a crooked tee. (See figure 5.2.)

This ball-on-a-tee joint allows you to swing a golf club or a tennis racket, do the butterfly stroke or the backstroke, or wave wildly to your best friend bopping down the street. With all that potential motion comes the risk of injury, with the most common being a rotator cuff injury. Your rotator cuff is made of tendons and ligaments that keep the shoulder joints in place and allow you to move them in so many ways. Overuse 'em, as baseball pitchers often do, and you're at risk of tearing muscles or tendons around the shoulder. A doctor can diagnose a torn rotator cuff with a

Figure 5.2 **Shoulder the Load** The shoulder joint works as a ball-and-socket joint (as opposed to a hinge joint, such as in the knee). Overuse can result in strains in the rotator cuff, which is made up of soft tissue around the shoulder. (Your teacher may not like these names either.)

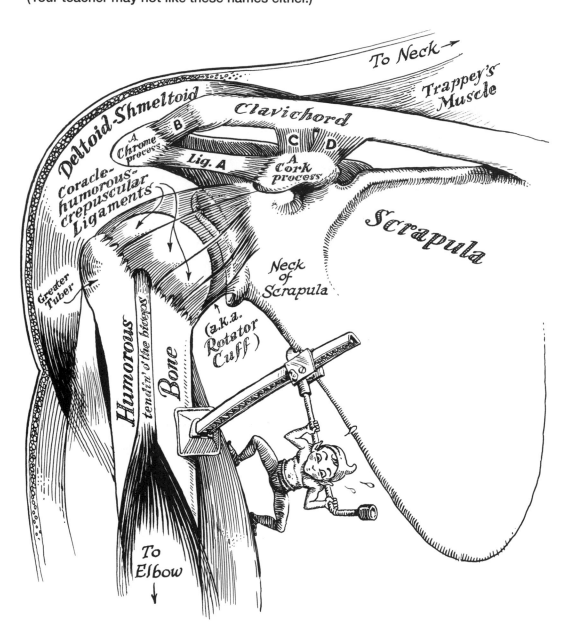

good physical examination, then confirm it with an MRI. Treatment is similar to any other tear: rest, ice, and anti-inflammatory medications. As with any issues of the joint, sports medicine doctors and certain trainers and coaches can help you avoid overuse injury and strengthen opposing muscles to keep your rotator cuff strong and in line.

Ankles: Sprains of any kind—injuries to the ligaments when they're stretched beyond their natural limits—constitute 20 percent of all sports injuries. They're particularly common in the ankle joint because the ligaments in the outer ankle aren't very stable, and because they can be vulnerable in sports where you do a lot of cutting and twisting. You land on your feet, your leg twists a different direction—voila, the ligaments are stretched and the ankle is twisted.

The treatment is RICE (see below), and to recover, you must include strengthening exercises. The aim is to regain full range of motion by bending your ankle in all four directions. As part of your recovery, you can wrap your foot with an exercise band and do these motions; that will provide a little resistance and make those muscles even stronger. Proprioception—knowing where you and your limbs are as you move around—is also important to help you regain strength in those muscles and ligaments. That's because teaching your body to stabilize itself when it's off balance is what strengthens them. You can work on it by rolling back and forth on a balance board or a board on a log, strengthening all of your ankle muscles. Doing this for five minutes a day can do wonders to keep that ankle from rolling or twisting as painfully.

Without question, athletics—whether they're through school, a club, a neighborhood group, or on your own—can provide some of the most rewarding experiences in your life, not just from a physical standpoint but also from an emotional perspective. Think of the relationships you develop and the life lessons you learn. We want you to take full advantage of all of those rewards—and to keep your body healthy while doing so.

The YOU Qs
You Ask, We Answer, You Decide

I seem to get a lot of muscle pulls. What's going on there?

They can happen for a number of reasons: quick cutting, not warming up before vigorous exercise, or starting an exercise plan without giving your body proper conditioning. Doing weight training to strengthen your muscles rather than just cardio exercise is the key to prevention. Two very common pulls we see in young athletes:

Hamstring pull: The hamstring—a group of muscles that run down the back of the thigh, supporting the hip joint and attaching to the lower leg—can be injured by overuse, especially if you're overstriding during a run. *Reinjury rates are 80 percent because scarring of injured areas creates more tension,* so stretching after a warm-up is especially important. Stretch after you use this muscle by putting your foot on a chair and leaning forward while bending at the hip until you feel tension in the hamstring. Hold for a minute and switch legs. Don't bounce, just gently stretch.

Groin pull. This partial tear of the adductor muscle group between the pubic bone and the femur (your inner thigh bone) is especially common when the muscle is cold and you've overexerted yourself. The best prevention is to stretch and strengthen the area. Lie on your back and spread your legs in the butterfly position, extending your knees outward so that you feel the stretch. Put a ball between your legs and squeeze to strengthen.

Heat, ice, which should I use?

Ice is nice for the first forty-eight hours after an injury to get the swelling down. Swelling comes from an increase in fluid or blood flow to an area, which slows down recovery from an injury and causes discomfort. The extra fluid makes the joint stiffer, weaker, and more painful. *Ice reduces the swelling*—and the pain. After the initial forty-eight hours of ice, some docs recommend ice, and others recommend heat to loosen up the joint or muscle, giving you more flexibility and allowing you to move freely during rehabilitation. That's why a hot shower or bath is so soothing by the third day after an injury. However, we don't recommend heat until the swelling has gone down.

Explain that RICE thing, would you?

If you do experience joint pain or related strains and sprains in the surrounding soft tissue, it's best to follow the RICE protocol:

Rest: Stay off the injured area.

Ice: Ice the area of injury, using an ice pack or a bag of frozen peas on the injured area for twenty minutes four times a day to keep down the inflammation and swelling. Protect your skin with a thin washcloth or towel.

Compression: Wrap the joint in an elastic bandage to help support the weakened tissues. Fit it snugly, but not so tightly that it causes pain or cuts off the blood supply.

Elevation: When you're at home, keep the injured part elevated—higher than the level of the heart—to decrease blood flow to the area and prevent swelling.

Do football players get the most ACL tears?

High school football players may get more prime-time play and louder fans than the girls' soccer team, but in terms of injury, *girls are eight times more likely than guys to tear their ACLs.* Girls' knees are less stable for several reasons: Their hips widen during puberty, which puts strain on the knee, plus the joint itself loosens due to hormonal changes. Yet another hormonal factor may come into play: Increased levels of estrogen around the time of a girl's period may weaken joints and ligaments. To help avoid ACL tears, you want to support the joint by developing your quadriceps muscles in the front of the thigh, so that they are balanced in strength with the hamstring muscles on the back of the thigh.

Do you recommend sports or energy drinks for working out?

Sports drinks may have some of the coolest commercials, but they're necessary *only if you exercise vigorously for more than sixty minutes in a row.* They rehydrate your body faster than plain water after long periods of exercise because they contain minerals and electrolytes that hasten the absorption of water. But if you drink nondiet sports drinks regularly or after short or not particularly strenuous workouts or as pick-me-ups in the morning or afternoon, you'll end up consuming more calories than you've burned. Also avoid the ones with caffeine, as they can make you pee more, leaving you dehydrated.

Some of my friends are taking creatine and other things to get stronger. What's your take?

Some athletes laud the supplement creatine as a wonderful muscle builder—making the difference between a homer and a long out, or between a world record and third place. Some studies show that creatine can increase power and speed as well as cellular energy, but the fact is that most of the gain in muscle size is due to increased water accumulation. Studies also suggest that a simple sugar and some protein—think an apple with a handful of nuts plus a bottle of water—can help muscles recover faster after exercise. Creatine, a naturally occurring substance produced mainly in the kidneys and liver, builds strength, but not aim, so you may be able to throw the football to the next field over, but not into the running back's hands. Or your serve could knock someone over every time, but you can't ever get it to stay in the court.

Some athletes try growth hormone or anabolic steroids in a misguided attempt to enhance performance. Use of these can wreak havoc on the body's metabolism, suppressing your own hormones from working well and giving you many other unwanted side effects like shrunken testicles and breast enlargement in boys. Shared needles used to inject the drug can lead to HIV, hepatitis, or other infections. *Use of such drugs tends to backfire, negatively affecting sports performance and long-term health by destroying joints and possibly causing tumors, among other problems.*

Are growing pains real?

Yes, growing pains are real. And they can be very uncomfortable. *Hot showers, hot baths, and occasional use of ibuprofen can help.* Save the latter for times when you can't get comfortable due to the pain, but the normal twinges of growing pains usually do not need meds. If pain is waking you from your sleep, it is worth asking your doctor about it. He or she can help assess whether these are simple growing pains, or whether something else may be going on.

★ FANTASTIC FIVE: STEPS FOR SUCCESS ★

1. **The central part of all movement comes from, well, your central part;** that is, your core. In addition to the abs, the core includes your hips, butt, and trunk. But we also recommend performing exercises that challenge your balance—to strengthen not only your core but also the little stabilizer muscles in your foot and ankle that will help prevent some sprains. Try doing some of your regular exercises using just one leg.

2. **Warm up.** Injuries often happen because people just jump right into exercise. Muscles need time to prepare for what's to come. So before you start a high-intensity workout, warm up with a light jog, some backward running, even some side-to-side shuffles and bodyweight squats. Those movements tell your body what's in store, whereas stretching does not; save that for after your workout.

3. **Practice the RICE method** for any muscle- or joint-related injury. It will help bring down the swelling and help you recover faster.

4. **Solo work:** Spend ten minutes before bed stretching your muscles, focusing on especially tight areas, like the hamstrings. Notice how you feel while stretching and afterward.

5. **Discussion:** Your best friend has offered you steroids to pump you up and improve your performance. What is the good, the bad, and the ugly on 'roids?

PART TWO

Boys, Girls, and Sex

What You Will Learn

◎ Why breasts change during puberty

◎ All about menstruation and hormonal changes

◎ How to treat PMS

◎ What are normal and abnormal gynecological changes

6

For Girls Only

The Female System Up Close and Personal

Right now your body is changing faster than your taste in music. The most obvious signs of these changes are physical: breasts, periods. But the same hormones that transform your body from that of a girl to that of a woman also affect your emotions. In fact, receptors for estrogen—the main female hormone, which you begin producing during puberty—are found not only in breast and reproductive tissue, as you might expect, but also all over the brain. So when you experience moments of high emotion, it's not just "girl drama"—it's likely your hormones talking. In this chapter, our goal is for you to understand the biology behind those hormones and appreciate the amazing things they do in spite of the ups and downs you may feel.

The Biology of Femininity

Here's the short of it: Puberty actually doesn't start in your reproductive organs but in your brain—and it can start early, as in ages eight to twelve for most girls. The hypothalamus, the command center of the brain, sends a chemical messenger called GnRH, or gonadotropin-releasing hormone, to the pituitary—another gland in your brain—which dispatches two messengers of its own, FSH (follicle-stimulating hormone) and LH (luteinizing hormone). These hormones travel to your ovaries and tell them, "Hey now, time to wake up and act pubertal!" When the ovaries get the message, they start producing estrogen, which tells your body to grow breasts and create that white discharge you may see in your underwear.

That's the big picture, but the story continues, and for girls, it plays out most prominently in two areas: the onset of menstruation and the development of reproductive organs, including breasts.

Breasts

As you get older, your breasts may serve the role for which they were intended: as the biological vehicle that carries milk from mom to newborn. But in the meantime and throughout your life, they may also serve other roles, such as contributing to feelings of femininity and attractiveness, both sexual and otherwise. (By the way, it may not seem like it, but according to studies of male views of female beauty, breast size ranks surprisingly far down the list of important physical attributes. See youbeauty .com for more on this.) Here's what you need to know:

Breasts are made of fatty tissue that lies on top of the chest muscle, or pectoralis muscle. Embedded within that fatty tissue are milk-producing apocrine glands. (See figure 6.1.) On the surface of each breast is a darker pigmented area called the areola, with a nipple at the center. (The nipple is just the part that sticks up when you're cold.) Under the skin, each breast is made up of fifteen to twenty wedge-shaped lobes with ducts running through them that connect the glands to tiny holes in the nipple.

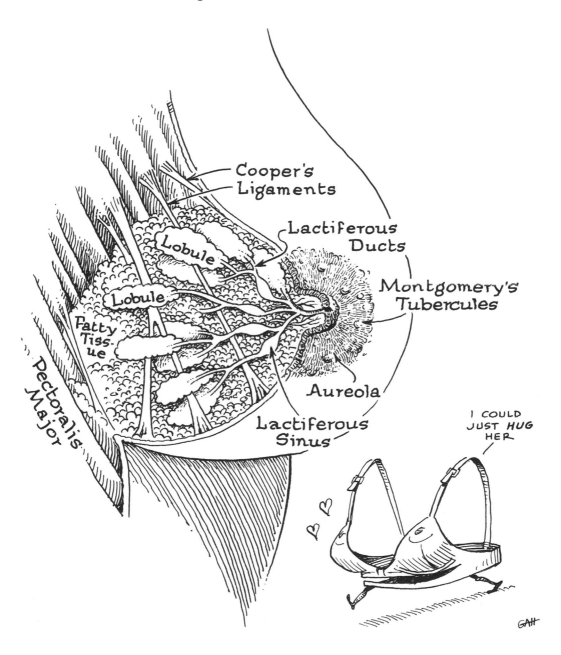

Figure 6.1 **Nothing but the Breast** Breasts are made up of fatty tissue over the pectoralis major (the chest muscle). Ducts carry milk that can be secreted for breastfeeding babies.

Cooper's Ligaments

Lactiferous Ducts

Lobule

Lobule

Fatty Tissue

Montgomery's Tubercules

Pectoralis Major

Aureola

Lactiferous Sinus

I COULD JUST *HUG* HER

GAH

When a baby breast-feeds, the milk comes out of these holes like water through a showerhead. Breast size, incidentally, has nothing to do with ability to produce milk.

Each lobe is made up of between ten and one hundred smaller lobules, and breast tissue extends all the way out to the armpit. The breast also has fibrous bands called Cooper's ligaments that extend from the skin to the pectoralis muscle below, providing power to "lift and separate." During puberty, breast size increases because of hormonal influences: Estrogen secretions cause an increase in fatty tissue and breast duct tissue, and the hormone progesterone instructs the lobules to grow. Breast development can begin as young as age seven, but usually things start happening between ages eight and twelve. If no change has occurred by the age of fourteen, it's worth asking your doctor about why your body is running late.

Breast development typically goes through a series of stages, starting with a little puffiness under the areola, or what we call a breast bud. About a quarter of women have breasts of different sizes and shapes; such asymmetry is typically not a problem and usually isn't even noticeable to anyone else. However, differences of at least two cup sizes from one side to the other can be corrected with bras or even with surgery if it really bothers you; see our Toolbox on page 400. It takes between three and eight years for breasts to be fully formed in shape and size. In the meantime, you can experiment with different bras to help give you the silhouette you want.

You probably have heard enough about breast health to know that women should perform self-exams to check for potentially dangerous lumps and bumps, but it's a little different for teens. A doctor should conduct a breast exam as part of your annual physical, but you do not have to examine your breasts until you reach age twenty as breast cancer doesn't tend to happen before then, and you can actually cause some problems by overexamining your own breasts. (See below.).

So what are some common breast issues? Well, there are a lot of normal changes that go on, especially during the menstrual cycle; your breasts can become hot, swollen, or sensitive. They also may undergo fibrocystic changes or develop potentially painful lumps and bumps that grow over the course of the menstrual cycle, then deflate when you get your period. You can deal with fibrocystic changes with good support bras or sports bras—especially right before your period. If you notice a lump or a bump, don't inspect it every day. Instead examine your breast at the same point in your next period cycle (usually a month or month and a half later), to see if it is the same size, shrinking, or growing. If it is the same size or smaller, that means you're experiencing fibrocystic changes of the breast and don't need to worry about it. If it is in exactly the same place, and growing, it may be a benign growth called a fibroadenoma, and you should consult your doctor and/or your pediatric gynecologist. The downside of fibroadenomas is that you eventually need to have them removed if they get bigger than a large grape, as they will eventually distort your breast anatomy. Think removing a grapefruit from the space versus a grape—the grapefruit has mushed the rest of the breast tissue out of the way, whereas something the size of a grape or marble has not moved much tissue yet.

Menstruation

Here's a fascinating fact: While you were still inside your mom, you had more than seven million eggs in your ovaries—more than you'll ever have in the rest of your life. By the time you were born, your ovaries contained one million to two million eggs, and at the beginning of puberty, about three hundred thousand. Over the course of your lifetime, you will release three hundred to four hundred total. (See figure 6.2.)

Unlike boys, who have a virtually unlimited supply of sperm, women have a finite number of eggs. That's why you need to wear a lead apron when you undergo X-rays: You don't want anything to happen to those eggs, or you may not be able to have babies. Beginning around the time you get your first period—a reproductive milestone known as menarche—and continuing until about age fifty, when you reach menopause and stop menstruating, your ovaries will generally release one egg a month, alternating sides.

The egg, or ovum, travels down something called a fallopian tube, hoping to become fertilized before it reaches your uterus. If it doesn't, the unfertilized egg will be released along with the lining of your uterus in what's known as your period. Sounds simple enough, but all of this actually involves some rather complicated choreography of hormones.

As mentioned above, it all begins when the hypothalamus signals the pituitary to

Figure 6.2 **Her Hormones** During puberty, your body begins to produce sex hormones, including estrogen, luteinizing hormone, and follicle-stimulating hormone. They all play various roles in your feelings, physical changes, and the menstrual cycle. The main purpose of sex hormones is to prepare the body to release an egg to be fertilized.

release follicle-stimulating hormone and luteinizing hormone, which in turn stimulate the ovaries to release estrogen. After a couple of years of puberty, that estrogen pulse is strong enough that an actual egg pops out. The casing of that egg, called the corpus luteum, produces progesterone, another hormone, which causes the lining of your uterus to get all plush and cushy and your breasts to get full. If the egg goes unfertilized, your estrogen and progesterone levels fall, triggering the shedding of the uterine lining, or endometrium; the lower hormone levels also cue your brain to start the cycle all over again.

You make a lot of estrogen in the normal menstrual cycle, and some of that female hormone can be converted into the male hormone testosterone, which can be a good thing in small amounts (think aggressive drive channeled into success in school, sports, or other activities) but can be a troublemaker in large amounts (think acne, thinning hair on top, and hair on chin or other unwelcome places).★

When an egg is released by an ovary, we call it ovulation. It can take a while for your body to get into the groove: Only 50 percent of girls ovulate regularly within the first two years of getting their periods, and 80 percent of girls don't ovulate regularly until five years after they began menstruating. Some women feel a cramp and may even spot a drop of blood at the time of ovulation. You can also tell when you're ovulating because your vaginal discharge will get slippery and stringy for a few days, as opposed to its normal cheesy or watery consistency. This increases the lubrication of your vagina and helps sperm swim up into your uterus at the time of the month when you're at maximum fertility. Your pheromones—the hormones that attract mates—are actually at their peak during ovulation; it's perhaps one of the reasons why you might feel more attractive or find others more attractive during ovulation.

The average age of menarche for American girls is twelve and a half years, usually two years after the appearance of breast buds and/or pubic hair. So girls who start

★ The male hormones, called androgens, are produced in both the ovaries and in your adrenal gland, and also from conversion of estrogen to androgen in the skin. These androgens get the body making pubic hair and underarm hair; in excess amounts, you can get hair in other, less welcome places, such as the chin, the upper lip, below the belly button, on the chest, or on your lower back. This excess hair is called hirsutism, and there are various things you can do about it (see page 36).

puberty at age eight will get their first periods around age ten. Girls who don't begin breast development until twelve won't start menstruating until fourteen. As doctors, we don't worry, as long as *something* is happening by age fourteen.

When you get your period, the blood may look clotty, or red, or brown, and smell a little meaty. While it may seem like there's a *lot*, girls and women only shed 5 to 8 teaspoons of blood per period, usually spread out over three to seven days. You may notice that your flow—that is, the amount of blood you release every cycle—is erratic, especially when you first start to menstruate. That's perfectly normal. If a period lasts more than seven days or is so heavy that you're changing your tampon or pad every hour, you should tell your doctor. She'll want to test the iron level in your blood to see if you have anemia. This deficiency in oxygen-bearing red blood cells can leave you feeling run down. If you are anemic, you'll need to take a daily iron supplement.

When you start having periods, it should actually be a time of celebration (privately or publicly—that's a personal decision). It means that all your girl pieces and parts are in place and working, with eggs to spare. In many cultures, it is considered a rite of passage into womanhood, when you are accepted into the tribe as a young adult, with added privileges and responsibilities. How does your family mark the occasion? Menstruation is often referred to sarcastically as "your friend," "your secret," and "being on the rag." (Substitute your favorite lingo.) It's a good idea to keep track of it on a calendar (*P* for period? *S* for spotting? *B* for bleeding?) so that you can learn your own menstrual pattern.

How do I tell my bra size?

Can you believe that an estimated four out of five women aren't wearing the proper bra? To measure yourself for a bra, you need *a measuring tape and a mirror*. You can do without the mirror, but it can be a bit awkward. Measure yourself around your chest, just underneath your breasts. Take that number and add five inches—that gives you your band size. If the total number is an odd number, round up to the next even number. For instance, if your under-breast measurement is thirty-two, you add five inches, making it thirty-seven, then round up to the next even number, which makes it a thirty-eight.

Next measure around the biggest part of your breasts, usually over the nipple line. Here's where the mirror comes in handy; you can use it to make sure that the tape measure stays level all the way around from front to back and around again to meet in front. To find your cup size, subtract your band measurement from your bust measurement. Then check the following chart to determine which cup size you are.

If all else fails, you can simply try on a bunch of bras and make sure that your breasts are not overflowing out the sides or top in a way that makes it them look funny; if that is the case, try a size up. Alternately, if your breasts aren't filling up the cups, go down one size. Cups and bras come in different shapes, so sometimes it is trial and error to make sure you get a brand and style that fits.

Difference Between Bust and Band Size	Cup Size
Less than 1 inch	AA
1 inch	A
2 inches	B
3 inches	C
4 inches	D
5 inches	DD (or E)
6 inches	DDD (or F)
7 inches	DDDD (or G)

Why do nipples get erect?

The original nipple erections stemmed from the need to feed babies. *Smooth muscles around the nipple plump up the nipple during stimulation from a child to facilitate breastfeeding.* But milk doesn't necessarily have to flow for your nipples to feel stiff. The conditioned response can also be triggered by other stimuli, like sexual arousal, cold, and fear. If you're self-conscious about your nipples, avoid sheer bras and go for ones with thicker fabric or even a little padding.

What if my breasts are uneven in size or if I don't like the way they look?

No one gets a perfectly matched set. However, most girls are not more than one cup size different. If you are a B cup on one side and a D on the other, it is worth asking your doctor about what is going on. *Many times, nature will fix the problem; your breasts keep growing all the way through your early twenties,* and most surgeons won't even consider breast surgery until they are fully developed. If the imbalance persists and bothers you significantly, breast surgery can either augment or reduce the size. Surgery is not a decision to be taken lightly, however, as it carries its own risks that may outweigh the cosmetic benefits.

Should you decide to let nature take its course, you can change your breasts' contour somewhat through resistance training, like light weight lifting or Pilates, to strengthen your pectoralis muscles. Exercising those pecs can keep your upper body toned and give your breasts extra lift. In the end, you should not judge yourself by your breasts. They do not define you or your sexuality any more than hair color does.

My breasts hurt sometimes, especially around my periods. What can I do about this?

Breast pain (also called mastodynia) is common before periods, and even before that, when the ovaries produce estrogen. This causes the breasts to swell, which can indeed hurt. Support bras or sports bras can make a big difference, as can regular exercise. You can try avoiding salt (that includes diet foods and diet pop, which usually contain high salt loads), caffeine, and chocolate, all of which can cause temporary breast sweling. Drinking a natural diuretic such as cranberry juice may help, but don't use diuretic pills, as they can affect your electrolyte levels and cause bigger problems. *Other remedies for breast pain with periods include hot showers or warm baths, relaxation and breathing exercises, 400 milligrams of ibuprofen up to four times a day, and even cabbage leaves placed over the area.* (They're said to draw out the pain.)

Extreme breast pain with periods may be caused by hormonal swings, and if the simple measures above do not help at all, you could consider starting a low-dose birth control pill to regulate the amount of hormone your body is exposed to. Other types of breast pain, not necessarily linked to periods, affect three to four out of every ten girls. Common causes include muscle pain (from too many pushups or activities that stress your pectoralis muscles), trauma to the chest (as in a softball to the breast; almost as bad as getting a ball to the nuts for guys), and nipple piercings. Regarding the latter: If it is red, inflamed, or has pus around it, get it checked by a doctor.

My breasts sometimes leak stuff. What is it?

Galactorrhea, or milky breast discharge, can occur if you examine your breasts too frequently—like, every day. It can also be caused by certain medicines, although rarely, or by a kind of benign tumor called a prolactinoma that can occur in the brain's pituitary gland. Prolactinoma can often be treated with medicines that stop the discharge and melt away the tumor. If it gets too big, however, it may need to be removed surgically. If you get a milky discharge from your breasts, your doctor will order a simple blood test to check your level of prolactin, the hormone responsible for inducing lactation. If it's normal, you don't have to worry about a prolactinoma (a tumor that secretes prolactin). If it's elevated, you'll need an MRI of the brain to see if growth is visible in your pituitary, where prolactinomas usually live.

Do I need to worry about breast cancer?

Breast cancer affects about one out of eight adult women, but it is generally not a disease of adolescents. However, breast concerns such as funny lumps, breast pain, and breast discharge bring a lot of teens to the doctor. As noted before, if you feel compelled to check your breasts, don't do so more than once a month, so you do not create a problem (breast discharge, for example) where there would otherwise be none. If you do notice a lump, here is what to think about: The majority of lumps are fibrocystic changes of the breast, a benign condition that causes lumpy areas that can be moved if you roll your fingers over them. They also pop up in different regions of the breast and do not stay just in one spot, varying with your shifting hormone levels. In contrast, fibroadenomas are benign growths that occur in breast tissue and stay in one place. They will keep growing—slowly—as long as they are left there. Fibroadenomas do not turn cancerous, but once big enough, they can be a real bother, so we tend to have them removed before they reach the size of a large grape. If you suspect that you have a fibroadenoma, you should get seen by an adolescent medicine specialist or a pediatric gynecologist well versed in the breast diseases of teenagers. Another way to tell the difference is to go on a birth control pill, which will help alleviate fibrocystic changes within three to six months but will do nothing for a fibroadenoma.

What Is PMS?

Premenstrual syndrome is a predictable set of symptoms that occur cyclically one to two weeks before your periods and end one to three days after you start bleeding. *Common symptoms include bloating, weight gain, breast tenderness, increased appetite and thirst, tiredness, worsening acne, constipation, chills and/or hot flashes, and mood changes, including irritability or depression.* Not all girls get all of those symptoms, nor do they always last the whole time. The exact cause isn't yet known, but it is thought that PMS sufferers have less serotonin running around (the feel-good neurotransmitter that we discussed in chapter 3; more on serotonin in chapter 12). About six out of every one hundred women get PMS so badly that it interferes with their daily lives.

How do you treat PMS? Swallowing 500 milligrams of calcium supplements with vitamin D (400 IUs) twice a day may help, especially for those not getting enough milk or dairy products. Some complementary therapies may work, although the jury is still out with respect to formal studies evaluating these. These strategies include using ginkgo biloba (gingko leaf extract) or *Vitex agnus-castus* (chasteberry) and eating carbohydrates. (Yes, that was in one study.) Nonsteroidal anti-inflammatory drugs, nicknamed NSAIDs (pronounced *en-seds*) for short, may help; examples include ibuprofen (Motrin, Advil) and naproxen (Aleve). Birth control pills, which regulate hormone levels, may also help, especially ones with every-three-month periods. Selective serotonin reuptake inhibitors such as fluoxetine (brand name Prozac) may also be recommended for severe PMS, as it allows your own serotonin to stay active in the space called the synapse before it is taken up and broken down. For those who don't want to take a pill every day, Prozac comes in once-a-week form.

Premenstrual dysphoric disorder (PMDD), the extreme of PMS, is often severe enough that a woman requires some sort of medical treatment to help her function. The treatments above may help, and it is definitely worth working with your doctor if this describes you.

What do I do about bad menstrual cramps?

You may know someone who gets such bad period cramps that she can't hang out or do anything on the worst day or two of her period. Some girls get cramps that are so bad they throw up and have to stay in bed. Period cramps, also called dysmenorrhea, occur when you make too many prostaglandins. These hormone-like substances are made in your egg sac, which releases an egg from your ovary, and they also get produced in the lining of your uterus. When the prostaglandins get secreted, they travel through the bloodstream, get to the uterus, and induce cramping. When it squeezes hard enough, the uterus contracts so hard that it can temporarily cut off its own blood supply. The body reads this lack of oxygen delivery to those tissues as pain. Some women's bodies overproduce prostaglandins, while other women seem to be hypersensitive to them. In other words, some girls are lucky enough to experience no cramps at all, and others regularly suffer for three to seven days.

If you suffer from severe cramps there are a few things you can try to relieve them. First add omega 3 fatty acids to your diet. Exercise and healthy diet choices can be effective; you can also try taking two of the 200-milligram doses or one 400-milligram dose of Advil or Motrin every six hours, or four times a day, which can keep your body from making so much prostaglandin. Acetaminophen (Tylenol) does not block the hormone that causes cramps, so if you feel better when taking Tylenol, the cramps are going away on their own anyway. Lucky you! If the ibuprofen does not work, ask your doctor for another NSAID called naproxen, which comes in 550-milligram tablets and needs to be taken in the morning and at night to work. The trick is not to miss any doses, as once your body makes the prostaglandins, you get the cramps. If these medicines in the right doses are not effective, the next step is another prescription medicine called mefenamic acid (brand name Ponstel). This drug comes in 250-milligram tablets; you take two initially and then one every six hours. Another option would be to start birth control pills, which suppress ovulation and thin out your utrerus lining; both the egg sac and the uterine lining are sources of those pain-inducing, cramp-causing prostaglandins.

What happens if my periods are really irregular?

It depends on what you mean by irregular. If the time between day one of your last period and day one of your next period is anywhere between twenty-one and forty-five days (three to almost seven weeks), it's perfectly normal. And it doesn't have to be the same every month. Some women are like clockwork from the minute they start menstruating; others may never be perfectly regular. If you're having periods shorter than three weeks or going more than three months between periods, it is worth mentioning it to your doctor. Stress, sexually transmitted infections (STIs), chronic illness, excessive exercise, weight loss, malnourishment, travel, and other factors can impact your periods.

So why do we even worry about missed periods? First, we want to make sure you are not skipping periods; it's important to steadily grow and shed your uterine lining, as letting it overgrow, can be a risk for uterine cancer down the line. *Too few periods can mean that you're not making enough estrogen, which poses risks to bone health.* In addition to calcium, vitamin D, and weight-bearing exercise, girls' bones need estrogen to build strength.

Now, if your hormones are "misbehaving," you may not be ovulating regularly, and you can get bleeding when it's not time for a period. This is fixable, so ask your doctor what you can do about this. If you're on the Pill or the patch, we call this breakthrough bleeding; your natural hormones are "breaking through" the amount of hormone delivered by the Pill or patch resulting in a small amount of bleeding. This blood can be more red, or more brown, or of a different consistency than normal period flow, or it can look exactly like a normal period. Breakthrough bleeding is a bother but not a problem, usually. (Girls who are sexually active should make sure that it is not a sign of a sexually transmitted infection; the STIs chlamydia and gonorrhea can be silent, or they can show up by throwing your cycle out of whack.) To manage the breakthrough bleeding, you have a choice: You can ignore it, knowing that this is your body's way of thinning out your lining. Or you can ask your doctor for a spare birth control pill pack to take a second pill a day (or a first pill, in addition to the patch) until the breakthrough bleeding stops. You are literally growing over unstable lining sites with the extra dose of hormones.

Is there a danger to using tampons?

Tampons, used properly, are safe and convenient. You can swim, horseback ride, walk, hike, and do any activity without fear of leakage, provided that you change them often enough. *The big danger comes from leaving them in too long.* If you leave a tampon in longer than six hours, you put yourself at risk for a life-threatening problem called toxic shock syndrome. With this, your body makes toxins from the vagina bacteria "super-growing" in the tampon, causing a massive release of toxins that attack your body and cause shock and potentially death. So make sure you take out a tampon before falling asleep, and don't keep them in for extended hours. Change them every three to four hours, ideally.

Is it normal to have discharge every day between periods?

Vaginal discharge can be absolutely normal or a symptom of infection. Pay attention to your vaginal discharge—you may notice that it changes in quantity and consistency along with your menstrual cycle. It's also good to know what your normal pattern is so that you can tell if something changes.

If you are having sex, it is always worth checking for sexually transmitted infections if your vaginal discharge changes; your doctor can order a simple urine test or use a Q-tip-sized swab to collect cells from the vagina or cervix to establish if you have an STI. The doctor may examine the sample under a microscope right there in her office or send it out to a lab. A vaginal swab can help determine whether or not you have overgrowth of normal vaginal bacteria (called bacterial vaginosis), yeast overgrowth (would give you a cottage cheesy, itchy discharge), or infection with the parasite trichomonas. Each of those is treatable with a pill or cream, depending on which one you have.

Normal vaginal discharge is usually whitish-yellowish but can vary in color depending on which bacteria are currently living in your vagina. Yes, you have bacteria there—and it's a good thing, too, as they protect you from overgrowth of more opportunistic bacteria that aren't supposed to be there. There can be lots of it or a little. It can be every day, 365 days a year; the good news there is that this usually means you are making a good amount of estrogen, a necessary requirement for developing strong bones. On the bad news side, normal vaginal discharge in some girls can drench underwear and require some girls to wear panty liners daily, changed a lot. Many girls are fortunate enough to have minimal discharge or not enough to even notice. For those with a profuse amount, you can try Vagisil, a cream that you insert like a tampon for three to seven nights in a row, to recolonize your vagina with a better balance of bacteria. Do not douche, as that can push vaginal bacteria up into your uterus, ovaries, or fallopian tubes, causing infection in those sites.

What about douching?

There's *actually no good reason (and no need) to stick a douche* (which rinses your vagina with water and other fluids) inside your body. Your vagina is a self-cleaning oven and will take care of all of your cleanliness needs by itself. Vaginal irritation and pelvic inflammatory disease are problems that occur in girls and women who douche regularly.

What happens at a pelvic exam? Why do you need it anyway?

Pelvic exams aren't necessary unless you have a specific problem; they're not even necessary for a physician to prescribe oral contraceptives. In fact, many sexually transmitted infections are diagnosed by a simple urine test and sometimes by a vaginal swab. You don't even need a pelvic exam to make sure that you got rid of an infection. However, if you have extreme lower abdominal pain, are pregnant and not sure of the dates of your last period, have been sexually assaulted, or have an unusual discharge with some abdominal pain, your doctor may decide to perform a pelvic exam.

In a pelvic exam, you get put in a really awkward position, with your tush hanging off the end of the examining table and your feet in these things called stirrups. The doctor uses a super-tampon-sized instrument called a speculum to gently open your vagina and take a look at your cervix. If you're over twenty-one years old and sexually

Bladder

Cervix

Vagina

Uterus

Anus

Rectum

active, she'll use two swabs to obtain samples for a Pap smear, which tests for cell changes that may indicate cervical cancer. (See chapter 8 for info on the HPV vaccine against the virus that causes cervical cancer.) Next the speculum is removed and the doctor inserts a gloved, lubricated finger in your vagina. With her other hand on your abdomen, she feels your uterus, cervix, ovaries, and fallopian tubes. *The whole pelvic exam takes only about two minutes, and with a sensitive doctor well versed in teenage health, it should not hurt, although you may feel slightly uncomfortable.* Some girls do not handle a vaginal exam well; for them, the doctor can perform a rectoabdominal exam instead, with the gloved finger inserted in the anus rather than the vagina.

What is PCOS?

Polycystic ovary syndrome (PCOS) is a common problem, affecting one in ten girls and women, and results in irregular periods, acne, and extra hair growth. *It occurs when hormone imbalances prevent eggs from maturing and being released from the ovaries each month; instead, the immature follicles form cysts in the ovaries.* With no egg released, there's no progesterone produced by the egg sac to balance the estrogen produced by the ovaries. This unopposed estrogen can lead to irregular periods, in which too few periods may be followed by prolonged heavy periods due to the excess lining made by all that estrogen. Some of this surplus estrogen gets converted to the so-called male hormone testosterone (women's bodies make it, too), causing acne and hair growth in unwelcome places. All that extra testosterone also increases the appetite, leading to weight gain in a majority of people with PCOS. Some patients also become resistant to the hormone insulin. This can bring about dark, velvety skin on the back of the neck, under the arms, or in the groin area, called acanthosis nigricans. While not dangerous, it is a sign of insulin resistance, which can lead to diabetes down the line. Parents often mistake it for dirt, but it is actually extra pigment in the skin.

How is PCOS treated? It depends on what symptoms you have. Birth control pills regulate the hormone level and the periods. What's more, they prevent acne, overgrowth of the uterine lining—a potential risk factor for uterine cancer later in life—and the continued overproduction of testosterone. Other hormonal methods, such as the patch or the NuvaRing, may also regulate periods. (For more on hormonal birth control methods, see page 159; for more on acne, see page 8.)

For girls with hirsutism (excessive unwanted hair), waxing, bleaching, depilatories, electrolysis, and laser treatment can help. Some girls choose to use spironolactone (Aldactone), a prescription medicine that works at the skin level to decrease hair growth and make the offending hair grow in slightly lighter and more fine. Girls with PCOS-derived insulin resistance should stick to complex carbohydrates rather than sugary items, get plenty of exercise, eat lots of fruits and vegetables, and drink plenty of water. A medicine called metformin (used to manage type 2 diabetes) can help the overweight person with PCOS drop five to ten pounds. It works best in conjunction with the birth control pill. Other ways to address the excess weight that often accompanies the increased appetite from the hormone imbalance are covered in chapter 12.

What is endometriosis?

Endometriosis describes endometrial tissue growing outside of the uterus, swelling and contracting on a monthly cycle. *It is a cause of major pelvic pain*—that is, pain in the pelvis or lower abdomen—and needs to be diagnosed by a doctor highly experienced in pediatric and adolescent gynecology, as it can look slightly different in younger teens than it does in women in their twenties or thirties. If someone has endometriosis, we usually treat her with a birth control pill, especially an extended-cycle brand such as Seasonale or Seasonique, to lessen the frequency of periods and reduce the pain to the level of normal period cramps. But if the pain continues to get worse, often a gynecologist will perform a laparoscopy, in which a thin fiberoptic tube with a tiny camera at the end is inserted through a small incision in your belly button. This way the physician can examine the ovaries and uterus without having to subject the patient to a major operation. If he sees wayward endometrial tissue, he can laser it during the procedure and put you on medicines afterward to help melt any other endometriosis away.

★ FANTASTIC FIVE: STEPS FOR SUCCESS ★

1. **Get to know your body.** Take a look. Use a hand mirror. Touch yourself and explore. The way to take ownership of your body from many different perspectives is to get to know all of the intimate details.

2. **To provide the best support for breasts (and reduce risk of discomfort and pain), get a bra that fits properly.** Know your correct size and try various styles. For athletic endeavors, wear a sports bra that you have carefully fitted.

3. **Your menstrual cycle doesn't have to be exact, but see your doc if you go less than three weeks or more than three months between periods.** If your doc does not handle adolescent gynecology questions, then see if you can find an adolescent medicine doc or pediatric gynecologist in your area.

4. **Solo work:** Chart your menstrual cycles and make notes of how you feel during those times. Learn your cycle patterns and feelings associated with those days to be more in tune with your body.

5. **Discussion:** Your best friend becomes a bear before and sometimes during periods. Do you bring it up gracefully or just lie low?

What You Will Learn

◉ The average penis size

◉ The role of testosterone

◉ The basic anatomy of testicles

◉ How male hormones can affect various bodily systems

7
For Boys Only

Fact: A teenage guy is gonna think about, laugh about, and obsess about (not to mention scratch at) the one part of his body that's different from a girl's. Heck, penis jokes have made millions for moviemakers—and probably sent the same number of students to detention. And while it's easy to make cracks about the male machinery, that doesn't mean you can't use your brain for something other than your best dirty-comic impression when talking about the male body.

Yes, there's a reason why we call them private parts: because, let's face it, it's not appropriate to expose them during, say, the weekend football game, or anywhere else in public, for that matter. But let's not mistake the word *private* for *taboo*. Though the male reproductive system is a little less complicated than the female's, it's still important to understand how the working parts—and the hormones that power them—fit into your overall health.

At virtually no other time in your life are such profound changes going to occur in your body that affect both your physical and mental sense of your own masculinity. Puberty is an amazing change, for sure—one that essentially elevates your status from boy to man. To explain it to you, we're going to go beyond a mere below-the-belt inspection of your fleshy parts to examine the chemical and hormonal changes that are happening in your body as well.

The Biology of Boys

Let's get one thing clear from the start: Penis size doesn't matter in terms of sexual function. A normal-sized penis is three inches or longer when flaccid, or not erect. That measurement is made from the base of the penis to the tip. For those of you with what docs call a "fatty pad" around your lower abdomen where the pubic hair is, don't panic: You need to push down and find where the penis starts; don't just measure the part above that fatty pad. (See more on size in this chapter's Q&As.) It's also quite normal for penises to come in lots of different shapes (a little bendy is okay) and styles (circumcised versus uncircumcised). All can do the job they were designed to do absolutely perfectly.

The penis is essentially a vascular organ; that is, it's supported in large part by the quality of your blood flow. So the most important thing in terms of penis health is keeping all of your circulatory pipes clear through healthy eating, avoiding smoke exposure, and maintaining good exercise habits.

The other fuel that powers your sexual organs and greatly shapes your masculinity is the hormone testosterone.

The first sign of puberty for boys, which usually occurs between ages ten and fourteen, is an increase in the size of the testicles, also referred to as your gonads. These sex glands, housed in a sac called the scrotum (see figure 7.1), wake up during early adolescence and start to pump out testosterone in response to chemical

Figure 7.1 **The Male Tale** The testes store testosterone—the male hormone that's responsible for the deepening voice, increased sex drive, and the growth of body hair. The testicles should feel soft and squishy with a soft lump in each. If you feel any hard lumps, see a doctor.

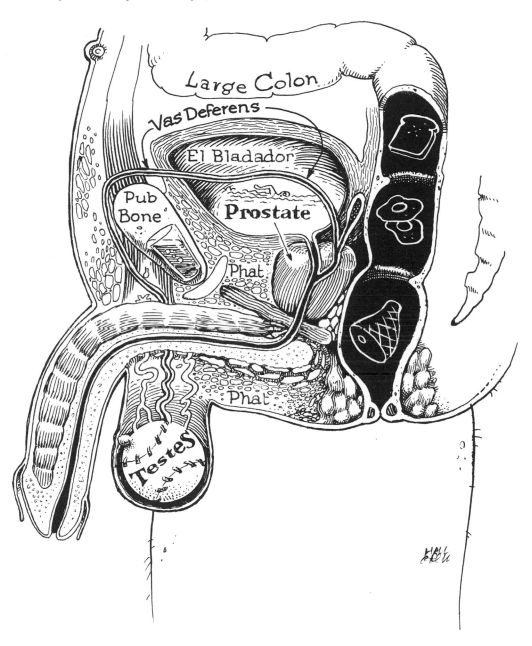

Large Colon

Vas Deferens

El Bladador

Pub Bone

Prostate

Phat

Phat

Testes

messages from your brain's hypothalamus and pituitary glands. Without any warning, you may find yourself shifting from thinking about trucks to thinking about sex. Testosterone is also responsible for your developing a beard and other body hair, your deepening voice, and your penis widening and lengthening. On the negative side, this hormone is the culprit behind a teen's breaking out with zits at the most inopportune times. (For tips on dealing with acne, see chapter 1.) It can even make you do stupid things just to impress your latest love object.

It wouldn't surprise us if you already knew that testosterone is also the hormone responsible for a guy's muscle strength. Without testosterone, all the weight lifting in the world won't turn you into a jacked-up action hero. Testosterone feeds your muscles, which is why you'll notice your body developing bigger and more defined muscles as you get older; it's also why men typically gain more bulk than women do when they lift weights.

Testosterone is also the hormone that's responsible for your raging libido, or sex drive. It makes you feel attracted to others and want to express that attraction physically. (By the way, although we call it the "male" hormone, girls produce it, too—in much smaller amounts—and it drives their libido as well.) As testosterone production gears up, your levels may fluctuate a bit, and it may sometimes feel as if your hormones are out of control. The truth is that they're just finding their equilibrium; it's a perfectly typical process for all of us.

Testosterone is made in your testicles' seminiferous tubules, stimulated by chemical messengers from your brain called luteinizing hormone (LH) and follicle-stimulating hormone (FSH). In early puberty, LH tells the tubules to start producing sperm, which then move to the coiled tube at the back of the testicles, the epididymis. There they gain a tail and learn to swim straight. Sperm hang out in the epididymis until you're ready for shooting (meaning ejaculation; more on that in the next chapter) because they are sensitive to heat and thrive in a temperature several degrees lower than the human body. That's why you were designed with your scrotum hanging outside: to keep your testes cool.

If you use anabolic steroids, are exposed to heavy metal (not the rock band kind, but the actual metals cadmium or lead), drink too much alcohol, or get mumps (best get that vaccine!), you can nuke your little swimmers and decrease your testosterone production. Taking a multivitamin will help keep them strong.

Sperm take around sixty-four days to make, and you start making them at puberty and end when you're an old geezer. While testosterone production naturally decreases as you get older, most teen boys have sperm to spare, with the highest level in the morning and the lowest level in the evening—which partly explains why you might feel frisky early in the morning and wake up with an erection.

Typically, boys will experience a surge in testosterone in early adolescence, and that's when you'll notice all the bodily changes described above. But the entire transition to biological manhood typically lasts several years. By age eighteen, although your brain might not be quite there yet in terms of maturity and wisdom, you're generally at full throttle when it comes to producing testosterone. The other main job of the testes is to make the sperm that will meet, greet, and mate with a woman's egg. We'll explain that process—and more boy anatomy as it relates to reproduction—in more detail in chapter 8.

Is it okay for guys to get wet dreams?

Absolutely. *It means the plumbing in your sexual system—primarily your circulatory system, which controls the blood flow necessary to form an erection—is working just fine.* But, just like erections, some guys get them earlier than others. Most guys will start having wet dreams—ejaculating while asleep—somewhere between ages ten and fifteen. Wet dreams remind us of how closely the mind and body are related. So if you find a gooey spot in the morning, it does not mean you've wet yourself. Most guys who have wet dreams (not all do) outgrow them within a few years, when their hormone levels settle down.

I've heard about erections happening for no reason, even while you sleep? Is that true?

Yep, they do happen sometimes. *It's no cause for concern,* other than if it happens at precisely the moment the teacher calls you to the front of the room to read your oral report. Of course it doesn't mean anything if you *don't* get spontaneous erections, either. But if you don't have erections at times you think you should, such as when you're aroused or while masturbating, then it is worth talking to your doc to see if there's something going on. The good news: Erections are a good measure of health, so if you are having erections, your health is probably at least in the acceptable range.

Actually, the penis is like an owl, in that it's a very nocturnal creature. The reason why men have an erectile alarm clock: Nighttime erections occur in the REM (rapid eye movement) phase of sleep, and REM sleep is more frequent just before waking up. During sleep, *there's increased blood flow to the area,* and that's what contributes to the frequency of nighttime erections. In fact, you'll probably get erections every two or three hours at night, which is actually a form of exercise for your penis.

You just said "masturbating."

Yes, we did. It's healthy and normal. Both guys and girls may feel the need for the release of an orgasm regularly, and *masturbation is a way to experience sexual pleasure without the risks associated with sexual intercourse.* None of the myths about overmasturbating are true (like hairy palms or going blind), but you are going overboard if you're masturbating in public or have rubbed yourself raw. Usually people prefer to masturbate in their beds or in the shower. Mutual masturbation means touching another's genitals and having yours touched, to give and receive pleasure. Some people feel this is much safer than sexual intercourse, which is definitely true with respect to avoiding pregnancy and many sexually transmitted infections (STIs), including HIV. Human papillomavirus (HPV), which can cause genital warts (and, in women, cervical cancer), can be found under fingernails, so it is possible that HPV transmission can occur from fingertip to vagina, or fingertip to penis and testicles, via touch after exposure to HPV on your own or someone else's genitals. This is yet another good reason to get immunized against HPV, whether you are male or female.

At what point are guys able to get a girl pregnant?

As soon as a boy ejaculates, he is making sperm that can fertilize an egg. In other words, all guys are carrying a loaded gun in early puberty, and anytime it can shoot, it can deliver sperm. So, sex, even at a young age can result in pregnancy—hence the saying, "No glove, no love," until you're ready to have kids. More on protection in chapter 8.

What are the signs of STIs in guys?

Most of the time, STIs don't have symptoms. But a burning sensation when you pee can mean gonorrhea, chlamydia, trichomonas, or another STI (all treatable with antibiotics), and burning plus tender blisters/scabs on your penis may mean herpes (treatable but once there, it stays forever). Nontender bumps can mean HPV, while nontender ulcers, or open sores, may mean syphilis or chancroid. You should see a doc about any unusual symptoms, but also make it a point to never miss your regular annual exam—more frequently if you're sexually active. A urine test can ID some STIs, and it's completely painfree. (See page 156 for a complete description.)

What bad stuff can happen to your testicles? I mean, besides getting kicked in them.

A couple of things, actually:

Varicocele: When you get too much blood flow through those vessels in the groin area, the spermatic veins can swell up so that they feel like a bag of worms; that's called a varicocele. (See diagram.) If you have a varicocele on both sides of the testes (or even one side), your sperm may overheat, which gets them swimming in the wrong directions; if that's the case, there is a medical way to fix the problem, called varicocele repair. See your doctor.

Inguinal hernias: That's when part of your intestines protrudes through a weakness or opening in the membrane that holds it in place, allowing the tissue to intrude upon the scrotum. When the bulge gets stuck, blood flow can be cut off, and that hurts. It's not an emergency when the hernia can still be "reduced," or pushed back into its normal place in the abdomen, which transiently relieves the pain. But it's called an incarcerated hernia when it can't get reduced—the bulge is stuck in jail and wants to get *out*—and usually needs immediate fixing surgically. The surgery may not require general anesthesia and the hospital stay is typically one or two days. See your doctor that day, in fact, that hour, not next week.

Testicular torsion: This happens when the testicle twists on its own blood supply, and it hurts like the dickens. If you get sudden pain in your groin or in the testicle, it needs fixing that hour, or you risk losing the testicle. See your doctor immediately. Not tomorrow.

Testicular cancer: It's the number one cancer for guys ages five to thirty. Silent but deadly, testicular cancer can grow and spread and cause life-threatening problems if undetected. But you can detect it—and get it treated—and save your own life, and the life of your testicles. We recommend that you examine your testicles once a month; they ought to feel like hardboiled eggs. If you feel something hard, like a pea or a walnut somewhere in your scrotum or in or on a testicle, get it checked by a doc.

What's the best thing to do if I do get hit in the groin area?

Ice can minimize swelling and make it feel better, but the main concern is time. If the pain doesn't subside or becomes worse after a few hours, or if your testicle swells to the size of a grapefruit, see your doctor immediately.

I hear about guys taking testosterone to build muscle. Is that okay?

The steroid hormone testosterone administered as a weight lifter's drug can cause tons of health problems, including cardiovascular complaints, testicular atrophy (shrunken testicles), premature hair loss, gynecomastia (growth of breasts), so-called 'roid rage, or steroid-induced dangerous and reckless behavior, plus all the risks of injecting drugs, such as HIV and hepatitis (liver) infection. Teenagers who abuse the hormone may actually lop a few inches off their adult height, because testosterone causes your long bones to fuse before they normally would, curtailing growth. So if some guy at the gym offers you a quick fix, that's not your best option for hormonal help; your body alone should be able to accomplish that testosterone boost, and more.

What about other supplements?

Supplements have been used for decades to build muscle. Most are testosterone derivatives, including androstenedione, or andro (the hormone that got famed slugger Mark McGwire in trouble and might possibly bar his entry into the Baseball Hall of Fame and might have contributed to his early hip replacement). Testosterone supplements *should be avoided* for all the same reasons that we just mentioned. Many weight lifters and athletes try creatine supplements, which draw water into the muscle and increase strength. The downside is that it decreases flexibility; so you can hit the tennis ball harder than Rafael Nadal, but you can't get it into any nearby court. Creatine has its own risks and must be taken exactly as suggested by an orthopedic surgeon—*not* how your best buddy at the gym told you. We do not recommend it, but if you feel compelled, you need to know whether you have healthy kidneys (a deal breaker if you don't), and we would prefer that you be safer rather than sorry.

Is there anything I can do to increase my penis size?

For boys who have baby fat or are overweight, the fatty pad right above your pubic bone can make your penis look downright small. But if *you press into that fat pad, the penis is usually perfectly normal in length.* Again, ask your doctor if you are not sure how to check or if yours is looking too small to you.

We also hear the opposite concern: "My girlfriend always says I hurt her and am too big to fit. Am I too large?" For some partners, there can be "too much of a good thing." You can try different positions to see if there are ways to be less inside during intercourse, such as with your partner on top, enabling her to better control the depth of penetration. It may also mean that your partner is not ready emotionally for sex, in which case back off and try cuddling; you can always resort to the *m* word later. (See page 139.)

Everyone else is circumcised except for me. Does that matter?

Circumcision (the surgical removal of the foreskin at the tip of the penis, usually done shortly after birth) is a cultural tradition for many individuals. Those who are uncircumcised may look just like everyone else in some countries, and be the only one with a cover over the glans (the skin at the rim of the penis where tons of nerve ending live) in locker rooms elsewhere. *Circumcision is not a medical necessity,* and some say that because the foreskin has a lot of nerve endings, it makes sex more pleasurable to keep the foreskin on. Others swear that circumcision enhances feelings by leaving the glans more exposed. There are some data that uncircumcised penises have a higher risk of acquiring certain STIs, such as chancroid (shows up as an ulcer on the penis) and HIV. If you're not circumcised, you need to keep your penis clean, because warm, moist areas can trap bacteria. When showering, pull back the foreskin and wash that area with soap and water.

It seems like I'm the last one in my class to go through puberty. Help!

There's no set time when everyone gets the testosterone surge. Being the tallest or shortest and first or last to shave all have their advantages and disadvantages, and we understand that being on either end of the spectrum can put you on the radar for teasing. If you're late, take comfort in knowing that *everyone eventually reaches puberty,* just at slightly different times. If you are worried about it, talk with your doctor about this. Some guys in very late puberty see a doctor or a pediatric endocrinologist to help give puberty a "jump start," but such treatment must be done under medical supervision, as there are risks to final height if done improperly (in other words, don't try your cousin's growth hormone—see a doctor to determine what is best for your body).

Seriously. I think I'm getting man boobs.

Gynecomastia (breast development in males) can happen in normal, healthy guys. Often, between ages thirteen and fifteen, boys get a little fatty tissue right behind their nipples. *Fat can resemble breast tissue, so if you are worried about your breast contour, try pushups, pull ups, and weight training to work your pectoralis (chest wall) muscles. Usually, gynecomastia goes away on its own.* But if you are one of those rare guys with a serious issue (meaning that you would fit in at least a C or D cup bra), you can see a cosmetic surgeon about procedures to correct the problem. Also see a doctor if one side is much different than the other.

★ FANTASTIC FIVE: STEPS FOR SUCCESS ★

1. **The best way to make sure that your male anatomy is working properly is to never smoke and to maintain a healthy diet and exercise program.** (We mean working the *rest* of the muscles in your body, not just the muscle we've been talking about.) That's because erections are controlled largely by your vascular system, and adequate circulation is influenced greatly by diet and other lifestyle choices.

2. **Check your testicles once a month.** Testicular cancer is the leading cancer among men ages fifteen to thirty-four. They should feel like hard-boiled eggs. If you notice any lumps or bumps, or the consistency feels different than the last time you checked, make sure to see a doc.

3. **Also check for varicocele** behind the testes—the blood vessels should not feel like a bag of worms. If they do, get your doc to check them out.

4. **If you experience pain in your groin or in your testicle, get seen immediately.** Testicular torsion cannot wait a few days, or even more than a few hours, as you risk losing the testicle!

5. **Discussion:** Besides the physical changes imposed by puberty, what are some of the other changes you're experiencing, in terms of your attitudes and how you feel?

What You Will Learn

◎ How the penis gets erect

◎ Female sexual anatomy

◎ How sperm and egg meet

◎ Birth-control options

◎ A primer on STIs

8

The Science of Sex

There's no doubt that sex is a hot-button topic—politically, morally, philosophically. But we're most concerned about sex from a biological standpoint. We're doctors. It's not our place to urge you to choose abstinence or otherwise but to help you stay healthy—physically and emotionally—regardless of the choice you make.

In this chapter, we're going to challenge you to think about the balance between safety and satisfaction. For many teens, abstinence ensures maximal satisfaction and safety. But face it, not all teens today are choosing to put off sexual intercourse until marriage. In this chapter, we're going to talk to you—no BS—about attraction, about sex, about pregnancy, and about sexually transmitted infections.

But before we get to the nitty-gritty of hanky-panky, we'd be remiss if we didn't point out that sex is one area in which your identity and emotions hugely influence your behaviors. In later chapters, we'll spend time exploring the brain, as well as the way that various chemicals and hormones shape who you are, what you feel, and what you do. As you can imagine, what happens under your skull is as important to understanding (and experiencing) sex as is what happens underneath your clothes. After all, the brain is your biggest sex organ. (Yep, you heard that right.) And your brain has at least as much to do with the big-picture issues surrounding sex—including if, when, why, and with whom you decide to have it—than anything else. (More on decision making in chapter 19.)

While you'll gain more insight about your sexual identity and feelings as you journey through the entire book, we believe that the first step toward an understanding of human sexuality should start with the most basic biology questions of all: What goes where? And how?

The Biology of Sex

Every day, you're bombarded with images that ooze sensuality, lust, heat—after all, sex sells. Whether it's sexy song lyrics or outrageous abs or the hundreds of images or messages that we see, hear, and think about every day, you can't escape the fact that we live in a very sexually charged culture. We see sex, we think about sex, and we read about the sex lives of the rich, the famous, the not-so-rich, and the not-so-famous. There's no denying that we're inundated with media imagery with sexual connotations. The question is, Why? What's so special about sex? For an answer, we need to go back to a nineteenth-century celebrity who was more controversial than the latest star on the cover of today's *People* magazine: Charles Darwin, also known as the father of evolution.

Evolutionarily speaking, there's only one reason to have sex: The survival of our species depends on people having babies to replenish the population. We can thank Adam and Eve and the cavemen who figured that out and passed down the info to their offspring. Along with our innate needs to find food, quench thirst, and build shelter for protection, having sex is a basic biological desire for us, as it is for all animals. On an individual level, we compete for mates because we're biologically driven to pass on our particular genes so that they remain in the population long after we've gone. While we may not have spectacular plumage like peacocks or magnificent manes like lions to attract mates, we do have ways, biologically and culturally, that help us advertise that we're interested and available. In chapter 15, we'll discuss pheromones, the chemical signals we produce without even being aware of it. In chapter 2, we talked about how our teeth and hair broadcast the state of our internal health, and in chapter 6, we noted how women act and dress more seductively when they're ovulating, or at the peak of their fertility. Beginning to see a pattern here? Whether we like it or not, our bodies and the subconscious, primitive parts of our brains drive us toward sex, sending out signals that make us attractive to others, and receiving and responding to signals from others. It's only the more evolved, logical, *uniquely human* part of our brains (located in the cerebral cortex—see chapter 9 for more details) that gives us the power to say, "Hey, wait a minute, I'm not ready," or "Yes, as long as we use protection."

Anatomy: The previous two chapters talked a bit about male and female anatomy, but we're going to go into a little more detail here, especially as the male and female sexual systems relate to, well, sex.

From an early age, you knew the basics—boys have one, girls don't. But let's take a closer look. Boy anatomy is fairly simple, because everything is on the outside.★ The male genitals consist of the penis and the testicles, two walnut-shaped balls that rest inside a sac called the scrotum. You already learned that the male hormones (primar-

---

★ Though one slang name for an erect penis may indicate otherwise, humans are among the few mammals that don't have a bone in the penis. (Many others have a bone structure called the baculum, which helps them achieve and maintain erections.) The reason? Humans have evolved to not need that bone because it's cumbersome and prone to injury, which both makes a lot of sense and explains why orangutans don't play much baseball. What's really interesting is that in exchange for not having a bone in their penises, men have been granted proportionately large penises compared to other species. Why this rare gift? Because evolutionarily, size signified fertility. Since the man's role was to ensure the survival of his species through procreation, a large penis and the promise of viable sperm attracted willing partners.

ily testosterone) stimulate the growth, division, and nourishment of sperm, which are stored in the testicles. The penis, of course, acts as the transportation system that gets the sperm from man to woman.

While we're on the subject of evolution, here's an interesting note about the scrotum: Men's testicles are actually tiny when compared to other species like chimpanzees—not that we recommend any hands-on experiments at the zoo or anything. The reason: When a female chimp is in heat and ready to copulate, she has sex with as many males as she can to ensure that she produces offspring. That child is then protected by all the adult males, since any of them could have fathered the young one. So the male testes in those species need to be large to produce large quantities of sperm, because their sperm fights with the sperm of other males for the right to get the woman pregnant. Since human men theoretically don't have to compete with other guys when it comes time to father a child, they don't need to produce a fuel tanker's worth of sperm, which means that their testes don't have to be as large. Cool, huh?

To impregnate a woman, the penis needs to be able to transition from the soft, flaccid state it's normally in to a state in which it can effectively enter a woman's genitals. The way that works is through the blood vessels of the vascular system. During stimulation, the muscles around the penis relax so that blood can be let in and absorbed by a spongy structure called the corpus cavernosum. After the blood rushes in, the veins in the penis clamp down like a dam, so that the blood stays in the now-engorged corpus cavernosum. This allows the penis to have the firmness to get inside a woman's vagina. (Side note: It's also a reason why men get erectile dysfunction if they do not take care of their vascular system—because their blood vessels aren't working properly, and the blood flow isn't as plentiful. This is a good reason to never smoke. Fifteen to twenty years of smoking can cause erectile dysfunction, also known as impotence, via inflammatory damage to your blood vessels.)

Now, female anatomy is much more complex—and that's because everything is on the inside. So here's the primer (see figure 8.1) from the outside in:

◉ Labia: the outside "lips" of the genital area; they can look different from woman to woman, and they actually evolved as a way to protect a woman's

Figure 8.1 **Sex Spots** There are many pleasure centers in the female sexual anatomy—including the clitoris, which has many sensitive nerve endings, and the G-spot, which is located in the vagina. Because of that sensitivity it also means you can feel cramps and other pains. Pregnancy happens when a man ejaculates and the sperm meets the egg. During orgasms, a woman's uterus can suck up the semen, pulling it closer to the egg.

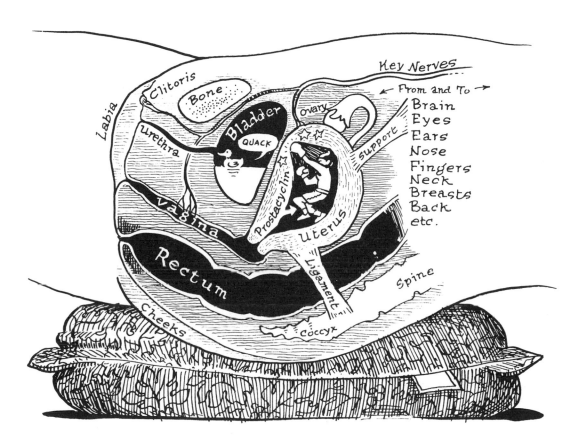

private parts. The labia may hang low, past the length of the pubic hair, or remain close to the vagina, surrounded by pubic hair. If a lip of your vagina is long enough to get caught in your panties, this is worth bringing to your doc's attention.

- Clitoris: a tiny and sensitive nub of flesh that has many nerve endings and is associated with sensations of pleasure. A woman's clitoris can become engorged with blood when excited, similar to the penis getting erect. Granted, a clitoris is much smaller, but it has just as many nerve endings, and stimulation of this area feels good to most women.

- The vagina itself: an approximately six-inch opening lined with moisture-secreting cells, made of really stretchy skin. That stretchy skin enables the vagina to accommodate a tampon or a penis, or pass a baby during delivery, ideally, with enough lubrication so that the tissue doesn't tear.

- Cervix: a doughnut-shaped tube at the end of the vagina connecting the uterus to the vagina.

- Uterus: the organ often called the womb, where a baby grows. It lies between the cervix and the fallopian tubes, in the lower part of the pelvis, above the vagina.

- Fallopian tubes: the highway for eggs (ova) from ovaries to the uterus.

- Ovaries: where immature eggs are stored and mature eggs are released from approximately once a month.

As different as the male and female reproductive systems are, it is very interesting to note that they share similarities. For instance, both become engorged with blood during sex, and the clitoris and tip of the penis are loaded with nerve endings.

When you're attracted to someone, all of the sex hormones you read about in the past two chapters get revved up, causing a chemical overload in your brain. You're feeling good, you're into the one you're with, and your instinct tells you that you want to act on those feelings. This is what we call a "hot state": when you're quite literally in the chemically induced heat of the moment. In life, as well as in sex, the best decisions are made when you're in more of a "cold state": Think the opposite of you cuddling on a couch and kissing—like, the middle of nine-thirty math class. By giving you the info you need to make smart and safe decisions about sex now, when you're presumably in a pretty cold state, we're hoping that you'll act on that internalized information when you find yourself in the hot zone. Similarly, if you choose to have sex, then you should prepare for it while you're in a cold state, by acquiring condoms, female birth control, and so forth. The flip side of this is that teens who don't receive comprehensive, accurate sex education and who have to rely on instinct alone when they're under the spell of sexual attraction are more likely to end up with unintended pregnancies.

Intercourse and conception: While there are all kinds of ways to engage in sexual behavior (kissing, cuddling, touching—even just talking!), the act that gets the most attention, for good reason, is sexual intercourse.

Heterosexual sex is basically like the simplest (and most incredible) puzzle ever created: The female has an opening, and the male has something that (amazingly!) fits pretty darn perfectly into said opening. Basic geometry, no? But what happens before—and after—that anatomical union is a little more complex. This time, ladies first.

A woman's eggs die off with age, as opposed to sperm, which even old men's bodies continue to manufacture. This lack of infinite eggs accounts for one portion of the "biological clock" that some women feel ticking in their thirties or forties, since their bodies know intuitively that the egg supply will end someday.

Once menstruation begins, a woman's ovaries release one of those eggs every three to seven weeks or so. The egg then travels down the fallopian tube, where—if there's an army of sperm waiting—it can get fertilized. Of note, while an egg must be in a fallopian tube or in the uterus for conception to occur, sperm are Olympic-quality long-distance swimmers. They can be released anywhere from directly at the cervix (the base of the uterus) to as far south as the mouth of the vagina and still reach their target. We have seen individuals who swear up and down that they did not have sex, meaning "no penis in vagina," yet the sperm still got released pointing in the right direction, just at the opening, and were strong swimmers. Another key fact: Sperm can keep swimming around looking for an egg for up to three to five days after sex, so conception may actually occur anywhere from hours to a few days after doing the deed.

During intercourse, a woman's vaginal walls secrete fluids that allow the penis to slide with just the right amount of friction to stimulate sperm release. The vagina and other areas of the body (particularly the clitoris, or pleasure gland) also are sending signals to her brain that can lead to the involuntary contraction of muscles in the body and vagina, called an orgasm. (See page 155.) While we associate orgasms with pleasure, there's a biological purpose to a woman's orgasm; an orgasm pushes the uterus deeply into the vaginal vault and helps the cervix draw in sperm, which likely increases fertility.

On the man's side, when he reaches the climax of physical and emotional excitement, he ejaculates, sending his sperm out of his penis in a spurt of seminal fluid. Semen is made up of sperm and the fluids produced by the seminal vesicle, and the prostate. Sperm is stored and matured in what's called the epidydimis, and the vas deferens acts as the tube through which it flows. A soft structure on the underside of the penis called the corpus spongiosum remains relaxed while the rest of the penis fills with blood; this allows the semen to come out during ejaculation. Interestingly, a man ships out more sperm in each ejaculation than the total number of eggs a woman will have during her lifetime; a "low sperm count" means less than twenty million sperm per shot.

Sperm are funny little creatures. It may seem that all these millions of sperm released during ejaculation are racing one another to the egg. But sperm have different roles, much like players on a football team. Some are the speedy players, trying to make it to the end zone (the egg). But others are blockers trying to prevent other sperm from making it there first. If the running back scores a goal and a love connection is made, the egg and the sperm—each made up of DNA of its respective producer—combine (this is the fertilization part) and can develop into a baby.

That's how the union works. For more info, check out www.sexetc.org. Now let's turn to your most pressing questions about sex.

The YOU Qs
You Ask, We Answer, You Decide

What makes sexual intercourse feel good?*

Male and female genitalia are both filled with tons of nerve endings, making the skin very sensitive and superprimed for arousal. On a woman, the clitoris, which lives under a hood of skin above the labia, has loads of nerve endings that feel good when touched or rubbed. But women can also be aroused simply by touching the skin elsewhere on the body (especially the breasts), through penetration into the vagina, or when the G-spot is stimulated. The G-spot, a fairly recent "discovery," is a much-argued about, highly sensitive area of the female anatomy at the top, or ceiling, of the vaginal wall. Stimulating this area can induce powerful, room-spinning orgasms in some women.

Orgasms for men occur at ejaculation, but for women, it's less clear. For women, orgasm happens when pleasurable, involuntary muscle contractions ripple throughout the body. Some women have multiple orgasms, or waves of pleasure, that can be more or less intense, last more than a few seconds, and heighten a sexual experience. Women can achieve orgasm through a variety of the methods described above, but for many, the emotional connection is the key ingredient. The brain and body are very interlinked here, with factors such as stress, fatigue, distraction, lack of trust, and tons of other brain messages potentially interfering with whether a woman achieves orgasm. On the flip side, many women do not need to have orgasms to get pleasure from sex.

Men are far simpler when everything is working well: stimulation, orgasm, done. Guys are hardwired differently, with testosterone causing great arousal prior to orgasm then a need for sleep or other recharging activity afterward.

---

* It may not always feel good, especially for women the first time, when it may involve a few drops of blood.

For both guys and girls, orgasm can be intimately linked to mind-set. If your brain is saying, "Wrong time!" or "Wrong partner!" or "Wrong way!" or all of the above, then even though the plumbing is all attached correctly, there can be a disconnect, and orgasm (and for guys, erection) may not happen. Conversely, orgasm can happen even when you don't want it to—meaning that the right nerves are being stimulated just the right way, even if your brain is saying, "Wait! Not now!" It just goes to show how complicated sex and orgasms can be.

What are the risks of STIs and what are the different kinds?

Of all teens having sex, at least one in four will pick up a sexually transmitted infection. Here are some of the majors (for more info, check www.iwannaknow.org):

Gonorrhea: bacteria that live in the cells of the cervix (in women) or at the end of the urethra (in men), sometimes causing a funky discharge. Antibiotics can clear up the infection. Left unattended in women, it can scar the fallopian tubes and cause chronic lower abdominal pain, as well as infertility. Most people don't know they have gonorrhea, so the rule is to get screened by way of a simple urine test at least once a year if you're having sex and three to six months after becoming intimate with a new partner. Have a really bad sore throat a few days after oral sex? Gonorrhea could be the culprit, causing a nasty throat infection. The bad news: Both partners need to be treated at the same time, or else it will transfer back and forth. The same goes for all bacterial STIs.

Chlamydia: This is another bacterial infection that hangs out in the urethra in the male or the cervix in the female, but it can creep up the fallopian tubes and cause big problems such as pelvic inflammatory disease, or infections in the uterus, ovaries, or fallopian tubes, causing acute and chronic pelvic pain and infertility if not treated. However, if chlamydia is treated with just a simple one-time dose of the antibiotic azithromycin (brand name Zithromax), you can avoid future pelvic pain and infertility. Visit your doctor for a urine screening test at least once a year if you're having sex, and three to six months after a new sexual relationship. The good news? Chlamydia doesn't like saliva, so it won't cause a nasty sore throat.

Genital warts: These warts are caused by a virus called HPV (human papillomavirus) that incorporates itself into the DNA of cells. Some of the more than 120 different types of HPV are linked to cervical cancer. The good news? You can now get a series of three shots between ages nine and twenty-six that can prevent several of the bad strains of HPV: Types 16 and 18 (covered by both of the available vaccines, Gardasil and Cervarix) cause 70 percent of cervical cancer and some forms of throat cancer, and types 6 and 11 (covered only by Gardasil) cause 90 percent of laser-worthy, fungating external genital warts (there are other ways to treat warts besides laser too). We feel that more coverage is better and that both guys and gals should get the Gardasil vaccine—genital warts are not fun for either sex, and a guy who carries a cervical-cancer-causing strain of HPV can pass it on to his partner. For maximum protection, you need to get all three shots before becoming sexually active; the vaccine is less effective if you already started having sex, but is still worthwhile.

In addition to cervical cancer, penile cancer, and genital warts, HPV can cause anal cancer. Anal tissue is not as elastic as vaginal tissue and can tear, providing a great entryway for infection by the human papillomavirus. Anal cancer is also more common in guys who have sex with other guys, due to exposure to HPV. It is worth getting immunized with the HPV vaccine long before you are even thinking of having sex because the doses must be spread out (the usual schedule is two months after the first one, two to four months after the second), and you need all three for maximum immunity.

Once genital warts have been diagnosed, a doc can freeze or burn off the cells with the wart virus in them. You may also be given a prescription topical cream such as imiquimod (Aldara), which kicks your immune system into high gear to fight off the virus. You apply the medication nightly three times a week, then wash it off in the morning. Imiquimod can't be used for more than sixteen weeks in a row, however. If the infection does not go away completely by then, discuss other options with your doctor; new medications are available. FYI: Even if you have the warts treated, you still carry the virus for an undetermined period of time, so protect your partner by wearing condoms during oral, anal, or vaginal sex.

Herpes simplex virus (HSV): We call herpes the gift that keeps on giving, as this virus incorporates itself into the DNA of certain nerves and then stays there forever, silently infecting others upon contact. This virus causes blisters on the lips (HSV-1) or the genitals (HSV-2). Herpes can also spread between the two areas if there is mouth-to-genital contact. You'll notice a tingling and burning, and then a blister that scabs over. An antiviral medicine called acyclovir (brand name, Zovirax) can be taken (400 milligrams three times a day, typically) to get rid of the outbreak. Other medicines are also available (valcyclovir, or Valtrex; famcyclovir, or Famvir). The virus stays in the nerve root forever and can reactivate if you're stressed or there's some kind of trauma to the area, such as eating hot foods (for mouth) or too much friction without enough lubrication (for genital ones). Some infected people never show symptoms, but they can then pass it on to someone else who gets frequent outbreaks.

Herpes can be hard on the ego. Unlike gonorrhea and chlamydia, the disease can be treated but not cured. Explaining an infection to a potential partner can be tricky. You want to tell before you do anything, but you don't necessarily want the whole world to know. So you need to be comfortable with and close to someone without having engaged in foreplay or sexual activity so that you are not telling them too late, blowing their trust. On the good side, herpes infection can serve as a natural brake pedal, slowing your relationships so that not everyone you feel close to is someone with whom you share intimate physical contact.

How do I get tested for STIs?

In terms of sexually transmitted infections, when you have sex with someone, you're essentially having sex with everyone they've ever had sex with. And that includes oral sex, because you can transmit infections via saliva and other fluids. One of the problems with STIs is that *guys and girls can be infected for years without having any symptoms*—and then infect future partners without even knowing it. Everyone who is sexually active should be screened for STIs at least once a year, and three to six months after any new partner. Most docs now use quick and painless urine tests to diagnose some STIs; in women, a doc might follow up with a pelvic exam if the test is positive (see chapter 6). Pap smears, which detect precancerous changes in cervical cells caused by HPV, are not recommended until at least age twenty-one.

Of course, the best way to reduce the risk of STIs is by not having sex and by using condoms if you choose to engage in vaginal, anal, or oral sex. If you do get diagnosed with an STI, make sure that your partner gets tested and treated accordingly. In some cases, your partner doesn't even need to be tested—you can bring him or her the medicine; ask your doc about expedited partner therapy. And if you do get an STI, don't have sex again until *both* of you have completed treatment. (Remember that Ping-Pong effect, where you bounce infection between the two of you?) Partners should both have clean tests *before* they resume having intercourse. Even if in a long-term relationship, you should be tested at least once a year—preferably every six months. After all, who knows if your partner has been faithful? If you're worried about confidentiality, know that you do have rights that protect your privacy. (See our rundown on page 403.)

What happens if you ejaculate at the opening but not *in* the opening of the vagina? Can a girl get pregnant that way?

It's not as safe as you may think; some of those swimmers could beat Michael Phelps in time to destination. *Some sperm just outside the vagina may still swim their way to an egg.* Better to aim away when it's time to shoot. And what about withdrawal? That is when you pull out before ejaculation. The problem with this method is that some of the ejaculate can sneak out, carrying sperm, before ejaculation has occurred. And those swimmers have as good a chance as any to find that egg. Ideally, condoms should always be used for vaginal, oral, and, of course, anal sex.

What are the various contraceptive methods I should know about?

First things first. If partners discuss contraception—as opposed to the boy simply assuming that the girl is taking care of it—they are more likely to adhere to it. Guys, ask your partner what form of birth control she is using, and also take responsibility by using a condom, the first contraceptive method on our list. As for same-sex sex, contraceptives aren't necessary, but disease prevention (condoms) are a must.

Condoms: They reduce the risk of STIs but are only 85 percent safe in terms of reducing the risk of pregnancy. If a condom does not break and is used 100 percent of the time, it is 100 percent effective. The problem is not with the condom, but with the consistency of using the condom. Occasionally they tear; more often, they are not used correctly. (See below.) So we recommend that couples having heterosexual sex use dual protection: a condom and one other method of contraception. This ensures that both male and female take responsibility for preventing pregnancy and STIs. For those with a latex allergy, try polyurethane condoms; they may break slightly more easily but they are just as safe against STIs as latex condoms.

The Pill: The Pill, which controls pregnancy by suppressing ovulation, so no egg is out there to meet a sperm, has the longest track record for safety and effectiveness. Taken once a day, most brands result in a menstrual "period" once a month (not a real period because you haven't ovulated—just a couple of days of light bleeding). The newest brands, Seasonale and Seasonique, were created to get women on an every-three-month menstrual cycle, which is great for gals who find bleeding a bother, are borderline anemic, get really bad cramps or migraines, or are swimmers or athletes for whom periods are an inconvenience that might impact performance. While it's all right to go long stretches without bleeding if you're on a pill that suppresses ovulation, it's not safe to get natural periods less than once every three months; if this is happening, see your doctor.

Spermicidal jelly, foam: Made of nonoxynyl-9 or other sperm-killing agents, these can be inserted into the vagina like a tampon, but unlike a tampon, they do not need to be removed, since the foam or jelly gets absorbed within one to two hours after use. These methods need to be used in conjunction with a condom for pregnancy prevention, not just applied *on* a condom. Condoms lubricated with spermicidals are still only 85 percent effective against pregnancy; you still need a second form of protection.

Vaginal contraceptive film (VCF): Made of nonoxynyl-9, the active ingredient that kills sperm on contact, VCF can get inserted into the vagina ten minutes before sex. It dissolves to foam, and VCF plus a condom provides close to 100 percent protection against pregnancy.

Medroxyprogesterone (Depo-Provera): A shot given into a muscle (intramuscularly) every twelve weeks that suppresses the release of eggs from the ovaries, thickens cervical mucus to prevent sperm from reaching the egg in the first place, and slows movement of eggs through the fallopian tubes. The main downside is that your appetite will increase, and that can lead to weight gain. Another adverse effect is potential loss of bone density, which is reversible once you stop Depo.

NuvaRing: This is a vaginal ring that you insert within six days of the start of a period, leave in for three weeks, then remove. Another one is then inserted seven days later. It secretes the hormones estrogen and progestin, a synthetic version of progesterone, both of which prevent the ovary from releasing any eggs and thicken cervical mucus. Some girls using NuvaRing develop bacterial vaginosis: a slight change in the normal bacteria that live in the vagina. Symptoms include a funny smell. Bacterial vaginosis is easily treatable with an oral antibiotic or intravaginal cream that your doc can prescribe.

IUD (intrauterine device) or IUS (intrauterine system): IUDs are small, T-shaped plastic devices that are inserted into the uterus for long-term birth control. They come in two forms, one that releases hormones (acting just like the NuvaRing to suppress ovulation) that last for five years (Mirena) and one that contains a small amount of copper and lasts for twelve years (ParaGard). Both interfere with the uterine lining, making it an inhospitable place for a baby to grow. The one with hormones does more to actively prevent conception from taking place by keeping sperm from the egg, just like the Pill, Depo-Provera, and the NuvaRing. IUDs are nearly 100 percent effective at preventing pregnancy but, like all hormonal contraceptives, do not prevent STI, so you'll need to use a condom as well.

What's the proper way to use a condom?

1. Check the expiration date on the condom package and examine it for any damage.

2. Remove the condom from the package carefully. Do not use teeth!

3. Make sure that the tip of the condom points through the ring in the direction that will allow the condom to roll. If it's inside out, it won't roll.

4. Place the rolled condom on the head of the penis.

5. Leave a half inch of space at the tip to collect semen; pinch the air out of the tip before and while rolling on the condom.

6. Unroll the condom over the penis, all the way down to the base.

7. Smooth out air bubbles. If necessary, add a water-based lubricant to the outside of the condom.

8. Enjoy your sexual experience knowing that you are practicing safer sex.

9. When pulling out, hold the condom against the base of the penis, to prevent semen from spilling.

10. Dispose of the condom carefully. Do not flush it down the toilet!

How does the Pill affect periods?

Nowadays, modern technology allows women to plan their periods; once menstruation has started and a girl is pretty much finished growing, she can use hormonal help to regulate cramps, period timing, amount of flow, and convenience of life. After her first period, a girl still has one to four inches left to grow in height; starting a birth control pill too early may slow growth a bit early, cutting off one to two of those inches. But for girls who have had a few years of periods, *the Pill and the patch can be used safely to affect menstrual timing, flow, and cramps.* Once you start the Pill or the patch, if you are on the extended cycle pill (Seasonale and Seasonique), you can plan what's called your placebo week (your week off the Pill or the patch) to be anywhere between weeks four and twelve, as in those ads for Seasonale. The Pill makers in the 1960s, who were mainly a bunch of middle-aged men, arbitrarily decided to make the Pill cycle one month, to match the calendar months. It is okay to have periods every one, two or three months, as long as you shed the lining by the start of every fourth month. So, if you're on the Pill, and your family is planning a beach vacation right when your placebo week and period are due, you can start a new pack early, then plan your period for the week after you get back. You just take the placebo week then. You don't want to cycle faster than four weeks, however; periods every other week are a drag, and this schedule might actually increase your chances of releasing an egg while on the Pill.

Won't the Pill make me gain weight?

That's a myth—one believed by many moms, kids, and even health care providers. *The Pill does not make you gain or lose, but often girls start it during their high school years, when their metabolism is slowing and/or when they have stopped participating in afterschool sports, so they associate the Pill with weight they are gaining for other reasons.* In clinical studies, women on various forms of the Pill reported no more weight gain than women who were taking inactive pills. Now, you may get to your adult-sized breasts earlier if you start the Pill in high school and use a brand containing more estrogen. Conversely, you may delay getting to your adult-sized breasts if you start with a lower-dose brand.

My mom doesn't want me going on the Pill. Your thoughts?

Your mom may disagree with your going on the Pill. Perhaps you can try to reassure her that many teens on the Pill are *not* having sex, nor is having sex a requirement for using a bit of hormonal help. *Going on the Pill is not going to change your values or change your sex drive significantly.* And your reasons for wanting to be on the Pill may be far different than an urge for sexual contact. Make sure that Mom is clear about your agenda, especially if you have no plans for sex any time in the near future. And if you do plan to have sex, you need to explain to her that it's something you've thought hard about and are acting responsibly and taking precautions so that you don't become pregnant (i.e., it's not a decision you are taking lightly). You do need to make sure that no one in the family has had blood clots or strokes, especially under age forty. If they have had clots, your doctor can order a blood test to see if you are prone to clotting. You must not go on the Pill if you smoke. The risk is fairly low—two to eleven out of every ten thousand people—and depends on which kind of pill you choose. The way you would know you might have a clot can be remembered by the mnemonic ACHES:

A for abdominal pain; the worst of your life; it feels like your appendix needs to come out now!

C for chest pain, lasting more than an hour.

H for headache, worse than a stress headache, worse than a migraine.

E for eye changes: sudden blurred vision, or difficulty seeing out of one eye.

S for severe leg cramps; it hurts just to wiggle your ankle.

If you get any of these ACHES, call your doctor and say that you are on this medicine, you are having this symptom(s), and do you need to worry about a clot. Women with type A blood face higher risks of clotting when they take the Pill, so if you have type A blood, check with your doctor about the possibility of taking two baby aspirin every day while on the Pill or other hormonal contraception. Other side effects of the Pill include nausea and depression. Most women will conceive (make a baby!) normally within a year of going off the Pill.

What is Plan B?

It is an *emergency contraceptive method in pill form that is most effective if taken within seventy-two hours after suspected birth control failure or unprotected sex*. Plan B (levonorgestrel) potentially works up to seven days after the "oops," or unplanned sexual encounter, but loses effectiveness rapidly after the first three days. (A new brand called ulipristal [Ella] is effective up to five days after unprotected sex.)

Plan B One Step is another form of emergency contraception; the difference is in the dosing. All of these methods have been used up to seven days after sex, but this is off-label use, or not formally blessed by the FDA. Each of these emergency contraceptive methods work by (1) thickening cervical mucus so that the sperm does not get past the cervix in the first place, (2) delaying release of the egg from the ovary, (3) slowing movement of egg and sperm through the fallopian tube, and (4) making the lining of the uterus not as hospitable to an embryo. The contraceptive will not interrupt an existing pregnancy and does not cause an abortion. It mainly tries to keep the little swimmers away from the egg. (A cold shower instead of sex does that even more effectively.) Though it's an emergency form that's been proven to be safe and effective, Plan B and Ella are not something that you should rely on regularly as your primary form of birth control.

Pretty much any form of oral contraceptive can be used as an EC (emergency contraceptive) postcoitally (after sex) by taking a set number of pills: for example, if it is a 20-microgram pill, five pills immediately and five pills twelve hours later; a 30- or 35-microgram pill would mean four and four. The drawback to using birth control pills as EC is that the ones that contain estrogen are incredibly nauseating at such high doses. The progestin-only versions (Plan B and similar agents) are much better tolerated and far less nauseating. Emergency contraception is available in pharmacies in all fifty states without a prescription to anyone seventeen or older and with a prescription to girls of any age. In some states, there is no minimum age. For more info on EC and help finding a pharmacy near you, go to the Emergency Contraception Pharmacy Program website at www.ec-help .org. Important note: Emergency contraception does have a 5 to 7 percent failure rate.

For boys: If you're seventeen or older, you can obtain EC from your local pharmacist without a prescription. If your partner is under seventeen and unable to get to her doctor immediately to obtain a prescription, buy it yourself—the longer you wait, the less effective it is.

For girls: If you are sexually active, ask your health care provider about giving you a packet or a prescription for EC at your next appointment. EC is not intended to be used instead of regular birth control, but if you forget to take your pill or if the condom breaks, it's good to have a dose on hand, as time is of the essence. It's kind of like bringing an umbrella; if you don't have one on hand, it invariably rains, but if you're prepared, you manage to stay protected.

How will I know when I'm ready to have sex?

Safe sex should combine meaning, pleasure, and vulnerability in a way that *makes you feel confident in sharing your most intimate thoughts and feelings.* If you're having sex but are missing a piece of that equation, you should ask yourself a few simple questions: Is this the right partner? Will he or she be there for me next month, next year, for the duration? Is there mutual trust and respect here? Can we really talk about anything? Is he or she pressuring or guilt-tripping me into having sex before I'm ready? And do I know everything about his or her past sexual life, before me?

If you're not having pleasure, it may mean that you do not yet have clear answers to some of these questions and may want to explore a healthy sexuality without actual intercourse, through touch and other senses. Or it may mean that you and your partner need to learn different techniques for foreplay, to make sure that your pleasure spots are being found and appreciated. If that's not a conversation you can have, then you probably should not be doing the deed.

★ FANTASTIC FIVE: STEPS FOR SUCCESS ★

1. **Make sex a conscious choice,** not just something that happens. If you are going to have sex, plan it, have two methods of contraception on hand if it is heterosexual sex, and for any type of sex, use condoms always to protect against STIs (at least until you are on your honeymoon). And it's okay to wait; over 54 percent of kids graduating high school have not had sex, so you won't be the last remaining virgin. Also, think about why you're considering having sex with a person. Is it because he or she treated you nicely or bought you a present,

and you feel you "owe" something? Is it because she says she'll sleep with your best friend if you don't sleep with her? Is it because everyone else is doing it? Try to figure out your motives—and the motives of others—to make sure intentions are genuine.

2. **If you are having sex, you must be mature and responsible enough to get tested for sexually transmitted infections,** so that you and your partner can be properly treated if you are exposed. And get vaccinated to prevent HPV before you start thinking about sex.

3. **Babies are beautiful.** Babies are wonderful. And evolutionarily, babies are the whole reason we're even talking about sex at all. But typically, teens are not in the best shape—financially or emotionally—to care for a baby. If you decide to have heterosexual sex, learn about the ins and outs of various contraceptive methods. Choose two. Our recommendations are on page 159.

4. **Try this:** In a group of people, split into pairs and role-play negotiating condom use for an expected sexual encounter. Variations: Try switching roles, so the guys are pretending to be girls and vice versa. Pretend that one of you has herpes; figure out how to tell, and how to negotiate yes to condoms or else no to sex. Next change the scenario so that one of you has HIV. Make sure the rules are spelled out: Everyone must be respectful, so that if someone you knew actually had that disease he or she would not feel belittled or discriminated against; make it safe to have the conversation.

5. **Chat with a friend or write in your journal about this:** Describe the differences between a hot state and a cold state. (Florida and Alaska are not the correct answers, wiseguy.) How do those two states influence your actions? Give examples of steps you can take so that decisions in one state can positively influence actions in the other state.

PART THREE

All in Your Mind

What You Will Learn

◎ How neurons develop and communicate

◎ Steps for improving memory

◎ How to take a test better

◎ The basics of ADHD

9

Brain Basics

I t's no surprise that sometimes your brain feels like an overstuffed trash can. Every-body's dumping something in it, and sometimes you just can't hold anymore. You're expected to remember math equations, history dates, the correct spelling of varicocele (chapter 7), who goes where on football play 42-blue-6, your saxophone solo—not to mention that on Thursday it's your turn to clean the bathroom.

Overwhelming? No doubt. Impossible? No way.

Your brain—your body's central processing unit—is one of the most wondrous and amazing of the body's organs; the starting place for all of life's activity. You can use it for Einstein-like discoveries or to devise an elaborate plan for a YouTube video that will spread with viral speed to far corners of the earth. Ever heard of the power of positive thought? Your brain can affect how you fight off disease, how you handle stress, and how you make decisions. And you have the power to impact how your brain functions: You can train your brain to achieve great things, or you can be self-sabotaging and defeat yourself before you even start. But first of all, brain power involves learning—hardwiring messages so that you can do something automatically, without having to put a lot of thought or effort into it. It's so complex, yet so cool. (And it's designed to handle so much material that we don't even yet know the brain's full capacity—mind blowing in and of itself.)

In the next few chapters, we're going to spend time getting you thinking about thinking. We're going to examine lots of things that affect brain function, including stress and mood. But the foundation for all our understanding of how the brain works stems from our knowledge of development and memory—in other words, how we learn.

The Biology of the Brain

In today's world, we're wired both internally and externally. Externally, we have messages zinging around faster than you can say "text." The internet has us more connected than ever before, and between cell phones, BlackBerrys, and other PEDs (personal enslavement devices), you can now find and be found anywhere. But just as hardwiring in a computer translates electronic signals into something coherent and readable and stores info on a hard drive, your brain translates all the sensory input you receive each moment into something meaningful and stores it as knowledge or memory. More important, your brain does things that computers can't do—at least, not yet—which is what makes you human and unique. It gives you the power to dream, imagine, reason, argue with your little sister, fall in love with someone at school, fall in lust with someone new on Saturday night, feel sorry for yourself if he or she doesn't reciprocate, laugh, cry, and believe.

Truly amazing, especially when you consider that most of your brain is actually just water and fat, with some proteins and carbohydrates mixed in. Despite the fact that it weighs only a few pounds (about 2 percent of your entire weight), your brain uses about 25 percent of the oxygen and sugar that your body circulates for nutrition and energy. It's a hungry little sucker, because of all that we ask it to do. (Its needs decrease greatly when you sleep.)

Brain anatomy is pretty complex, so we're just going to hit on some of the basics. In general, a brain's anatomical structures are divided into two kinds of functions: executive (intellectual-type functions that help you think and memorize) and reptilian (movement, instinct, and raw emotion). The reptilian part is called that because we really share it with reptiles; evolutionarily, this is the oldest part of the brain, located at the base and the internal core, and it controls basic reflexes, senses, and organ function. The layers that wrap around it are progressively more recent additions, so we share them with higher-level animals. The "newest" is the frontal lobe, which is responsible for that executive functioning, which sets us apart from all other species.

Your brain is connected to your body by the spinal cord. Neurons are nerve cells that transmit info between your body and your brain via your spinal cord and also transmit messages within the brain. (See figure 9.1.) You have about 100 billion neurons in your brain alone, which, if stretched out in length, would reach 30,000 miles—or across the United States ten times, or around the world at the equator twice. Each of these cells contains information that needs to be transmitted to another neuron so that your body can function properly. Cool fact: The info is actually electric, just like a computer. In the same way that electric wires are insulated in plastic, your electric wires (neurons) are insulated by a sheath called myelin, which is substantially made out of fat.

Neurons exist to transmit information, not to hold onto it. They look like mops with shaggy strings that reach out toward the handles of other nearby mops. Neurons talk with one another with the frequency of eighth-grade girls at a slumber party; a lot of information is exchanged very quickly, some of it useful and important, some of it irrelevant but still shared.

To see the way neurons work, think about baseball. The mop strings of the cells—the receivers—are called dendrites, and they're like baseball catchers; they receive the pitch sent to them from the mop handles, or axons, of other neurons. Even more important, they communicate to the other players on the field. Specifi-

Figure 9.1 **A Cool Connection** The way we process information is through the connection between neurons as they communicate messages back and forth across the synaptic junction. The more we strengthen those connections, the better we learn. If we don't use those connections, they wither away and we lose the information.

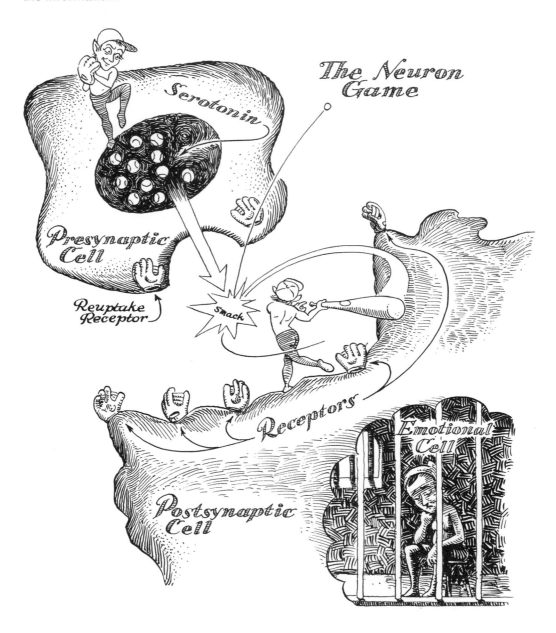

cally, the dendrite can influence how the signal is sent, received, and transmitted to other neurons. As in baseball, where the pitcher and the catcher are separated by space, so are the axons and dendrites of neighboring neurons. Neurotransmitters are the chemical messengers in your brain that, like baseballs, are tossed back and forth between neurons. When a neuron is stimulated by a neurotransmitter it has received, it in turn produces its own neurotransmitters that are "caught" by molecules called receptors on the neuron next in line to receive the information. The gap between neurons is called a synapse. Just as a pitcher and catcher can get better at tossing the ball to each other through practice, neurons can strengthen their connections by repeatedly sending the same signal across the synaptic junction. This is called hard-wiring and requires daily fat intake to myelinate or wrap the nerve in a fatty sheath that makes that neural pathway stronger and faster. For more info on how to get the right amount and kinds of fat in your diet for maximum brain power, see page 182.

Learning and memory are all about strengthening the synaptic junctions between neurons. What's really interesting is that how much you learn and memorize is influenced by a number of factors, including how early you're exposed to information (such as kids who learn multiple languages at a young age) and how interested you are in the subject. If something is exciting to you, then you learn it faster—and train those synapses to make strong connections. It's the reason why you'll probably remember every little detail from chapter 8 but may have more trouble with, say chapter 15.

Luckily, your brain is so strong that you can learn and memorize even when you're not all that jazzed about something—repetition is what works, and that's where memorization comes into play. The best combo of all for leaning is to repeat over and over something that you love to do, the way that kids who love baseball play a lot of catch, which makes them better at throwing and catching. The reverse is also true: If you don't practice a skill, you'll forget how to do it. The take-home message here is: Use it or lose it. The less you use those neurons and reinforce the connections between them, the greater the chance that you'll forget the information.

When a fetus is growing in the womb, neurons, which rely on other support cells called glial cells to be built, are created at a pace that's hard for even the finest of minds to comprehend: 500,000 per minute to reach the end result of about 100 billion neurons per baby. The importance, though, isn't in the sheer number of neurons, it's in their function. The brain is an amazingly plastic (meaning changeable) organ: It can adapt and learn. While neurons are formed after birth only rarely, the dendrites continue thickening into a dense forest of connections in response to whatever stimuli a baby is exposed to. And those connections keep getting formed—and broken—as you grow from baby to toddler to kid to teen.

So while a newborn baby might have the neurological capacity for learning violin, being a history whiz, or even developing nurturing relationships, the neurological circuitry is not yet hooked up. The neurons are waiting for the signals that will enable particular information to be processed in the brain. The more frequently the experience is repeated, the stronger these circuits grow. The less common the experience, the weaker they become, until they are eventually pruned away. The reason that the old saying "You can't teach an old dog new tricks" is largely true is because children's brains are more plastic than those of adults. Neural pathways are like freeways through the middle of cities: Once they're established, it's much more difficult to change their direction or increase their lanes. Crazy fact: Teens lose about 100,000 synapses per second.

From birth to age fifteen, the brain is expanding its connections, making new links about how to talk, how to walk, and why you shouldn't cross the street without looking. You have two peak periods where these connections are building: before age three and in these early adolescent years. Between ages fifteen and twenty-five, the hardwiring is made more permanent, as white matter (or myelin) is deposited around nerve pathways, cementing them in. The stronger the pathway, the less energy it takes to send a message.

That means you can use fewer brainwaves to make something happen, and it can become habitual, or instinctive.

Because so much of the brain's wiring becomes permanent during the adolescent years, skills or habits you cultivate during your teens are likely to last a lifetime. This can be good or bad. On one hand, you can develop a habit of daily exercise that will contribute to lifelong health. On the other hand, if you learn to be a social smoker during this time period, you're training your brain to crave a cigarette every time you relax with your friends for the rest of your life. For proof, consider that 80 percent of adult smokers started as teens. So give some thought to how you train your brain, as the habits you develop in your young adulthood can shape you positively, or haunt you in a big way, as they get etched indelibly into your brain.

The YOU Qs
You Ask, We Answer, You Decide

We're expected to learn so much in school. Any tricks for improving my brain power?

As we said, it certainly helps if you're interested in the material you're learning, but there are some other strategies you can use to help your brain soak up the world.

⊚ Switch roles. You're used to learning from teachers, but you'll actually learn better if you have to teach the information to *someone else*. Try studying with friends, becoming a tutor, or assist coaching your younger sibling's sports team. Dr. Roizen learned by practice teaching (to himself on a white board) whatever he learned in classes.

⊚ Learn some jokes. Humor can also have a valuable effect on your memory. Humor requires what the laugh doctors call conceptual blending—that is, the ability to relate the expected to the unexpected; we laugh when something surprising happens. Having a sense of humor is a sign of intelligence. Telling a joke, like being a teacher, is another way to challenge your brain. You have to be able to play mental hopscotch from one word to another to make sure that the story, joke, riddle, or pun combines a set of expected and unexpected circumstances. In other words, what happens once the guy walks into the bar? And ultimately, to tell the joke right, you have to have a fair amount of social intelligence as well—the ability to maximize the tension and mystery of the joke until the very last second.

⊚ Use visuals: One way to strengthen your mind is by flexing parts that you don't use often, such as those associated with imagination. So try this trick:

Map out a problem you have. That is, draw a picture of your issue in the middle of a piece of paper, then branch out with smaller subsections and key words related to that issue. This will help you develop more problem-solving and decision-making skills.

How about tips for actually preparing for a test?

A lot of people will tell you that cramming is bad for you, but the truth is that if your only goal is to memorize information for a test, your brain will process it better right before the exam, so there is some value in cramming. But if you want to retain the info for longer than just twenty-four hours, these tips may work better:

Chunk it. Divide up your material in small sections and take it one chunk at a time. It's easier to eat a steak in twenty-seven small bites than three gargantuan hunks.

Make connections. See if you can apply material you're learning in class to things happening in your life. When you see connections that are familiar to you, you'll have an easier time remembering the info.

Stay consistent. "Muscle memory" refers to the way that certain motions or physical activities become almost automatic over time, like learning how to balance while riding a bike. Well, your brain relies on the equivalent of muscle memory. Therefore, if you have, say, a test coming up, try to study under the same conditions in which you'll be taking the test. In other words, no music, pillows, or texting. If it's a written test, take notes with a pen or pencil rather than working on your laptop. And, it goes without saying, never study if you're high (better not to get high, period).

Don't choke. Your brain will work best when it's under a little bit of stress, but if the pressure is overwhelming, it can backfire, causing your body and brain to shut down. So embrace the fact that performing well on a test is a natural stress that we all go through, but don't do yourself in by heaping on additional stress (sleeping through an alarm, convincing yourself that your *entire future hinges on this one test*). Go easy on the caffeine, too; it disrupts sleep since it stays in your system twenty-four hours, but a cup of tea or some caffeinated beverage the morning of the test has been shown to improve focus. Just don't keep dosing yourself with more caffeine over the course of the day or you'll be too wired to sleep that night.

Test yourself. The best way to prepare is to test yourself in some form. For example, write out questions, flash cards, and so on, and try to simulate the test conditions.

Rhyme it. Try making up a song or a poem with key words or concepts you need to know. Sometimes acronyms, verses, or songs can help you retain a key concept longer than just plain memorizing it. Imagine your favorite rapper learning the material and make up your own version.

Even when I know a subject really well, I blank out on tests and get poor grades. What's going on?

It may have to do with what kind of learner you are, as well as perhaps being overly stressed, which inhibits memory and performance. Some people learn better visually, some better aurally, and some better with math. Some people are what's called kinesthetic learners, meaning that they learn better on the move. In fact, there are seven identified kinds of learners, including interpersonal learners, who work better when interacting with others—but not on a test! While you certainly can't dictate how you take a test ("Hey, Mr. Jones, can I jump rope while I answer math problems?"), it will help you to identify what kind of learner you are and embrace study habits that maximize your own natural tendencies, like creating rhymes of information if you're a musical learner or listening to books on tapes if you're an auditory learner. And for those of you who are kinesthetic learners, you can figure out which moves won't get you kicked out of class during the test.

One pearl is to try SQRW (scan, question, read, and write). This means scan the test, look at the questions to see what they are actually asking, read any text provided, and write your answer. This method also works great for doing home-work, so you can figure out before you read what they will be asking and focus on those questions as you plow through the material.

To figure out how to understand the directions on a test, try CUCC, or circle the direction words, underline the words that help you understand the direction words, count the direction words to make sure you got them done, and check off every time you complete one.

Who's smarter, boys or girls?

Let's not say smarter or better, let's say different. For instance, men are hardwired to go right to problem solving, going back to the caveman days when you needed to hunt the woolly mammoth and hurl the spear immediately just to survive. Women have better "lateralization" skills, or the ability to analyze a complex topic. It could take weeks for the cavewoman to fix the wooly mammoth seventy different ways for dinner, make clothing for the entire family from its fur and skin, turn the bones into tools, use the lining of the intestines for storage bags, and feed the family pets from the leftovers. Another way to think about it is the different ways that most guys and gals shop: The average guy goes to the store, marches directly to the shelf with the needed item, pays for it, and leaves. The average girl will browse, assess options, make decisions based on numerous outside factors, and leave after having perhaps bought the intended item but also possibly with seven other items now deemed absolutely necessary, or with nothing at all. It doesn't mean that one method of shopping is smarter or more efficient than another; there may be a bargain at a different place, making it cost effective to browse. It just means that we assess and process information differently, and if you don't recognize those differences, it can make for miscommunication and time spent with differing expectations.

So what does an IQ test measure?

IQ (intelligence quotient) tests are *standard tests of brain strength, measuring things like math, logic, and verbal strength.* Like any skill, it can be developed with some heavy mental weight lifting. Another form of intelligence is emotional intelligence (EQ), or the ability to relate to and interact with others. Both of these kinds of intelligence make a difference in your brain's overall health. Straight IQ may help you perform well on a test, but those with low IQs but high EQs may demonstrate remarkable insights with respect to people, emotions, and other realms of life.

Is it true that certain foods can boost brain power?

Here are some favorites that have been shown to give you a mental edge:

- Nuts (especially walnuts): They contain monounsaturated fats (walnuts contain omega-3 fats) and healthy protein to help keep your arteries squeaky clean, which is important for clear thinking.

- Fish: They contain omega-3 fatty acids (especially DHA), which clear your arteries and help your brain. The best brain foods from the sea include wild salmon, trout, whitefish, catfish, flounder, mahimahi, and some algae.

- Olive oil, nut oils, fish oils, flaxseed, avocados: They contain heart-healthy monounsaturated fats, which are also good for the brain.

- Spices with alpha carotene: turmeric and cumin.

Chia seeds are also great sources of omega-3 fatty acids. Boost your brain power by finding chia seeds in a health food store. They can be baked into muffins, added to yogurt or salad for a little crunch, blended into your smoothie, or used to grow those funny little chia pets you can still find in cutesy stores (no, don't eat the latter, we just think they are funny).

My friend has ADHD. What exactly does that mean?

ADHD (attention deficit/hyperactivity disorder) is a *learning disorder that develops when communication between neurons doesn't exactly work the way it'd supposed to, so ADHD sufferers have a harder time concentrating and focusing on a given task.* It's as if the ADHD brain receives information but cannot process it and file it away efficiently. This constant barrage of daily stimuli is overwhelming to the person with ADHD. When the disorder seriously impairs learning, the doctor usually recommends a psychostimulant medication to help optimize performance and concentration. Commonly prescribed ADHD meds include methylphenidate (Ritalin or Vyvanse) and combination dextroamphetamine and amphetamine (Adderall). Methylphenidate also comes in a patch form, which starts working when you put it on and stops working three hours after you take it off. This one is called Daytrana, and it's great for those who want to be able to still sleep late but be focused, without being "wired" and unable to sleep from taking their ADHD pill too late in the morning. Most ADD meds are stimulants, but two are not: Strattera and Intuniv (it may make you sleepy temporarily). If you have ADD or ADHD (ADD means no hyperactivity part but still can't focus), ask your doctor about study tricks/behavioral strategies for success as well as about possible medications. Both can help.

Which is more important, studying an extra hour or sleeping an extra hour?

You need at least seven hours of sleep nightly, so if the extra studying cuts into this, then you are *better off sleeping* so you are alert for the test, assuming you have some data in your memory bank. Sleep helps your brain store memories.

Should I quit afterschool sports to devote more time to studying?

Actually, being on a sports team teaches lots of skills. It's not just about honing your physical ability and social skills but also your ability to focus, concentrate, analyze, and so on. *Exercise also increases your brain power*, and having commitments can teach you to become more efficient and better at budgeting your time. So all in all, being on a sports team provides lots of benefits for your brain, not to mention your entire body. If you are having a hard time organizing yourself, ask for pointers from friends who seem to do this well and from teachers and/or respected adults. Learn those organizational skills early and you free up more time for yourself.

My parents always yell at me because I text and talk at the same time. I swear I'm paying attention! What's going on?

Many of us—teens and adults—think that we're pretty good at multitasking one, two, or three dozen different things at the same time. Research is beginning to suggest that kids are better at this than adults (they can switch back and forth faster) because they've grown up doing it, but ultimately the brain still focuses on only one task at a time. But biologically, *our brains can really focus only on one thing at a time with any success*, and your mind is actually switching back and forth between tasks really rapidly. So the more we try to do at the same time, the worse our performance at each individual task.

★ FANTASTIC FIVE: STEPS FOR SUCCESS ★

1. **Make sure that you eat foods containing DHA;** it's a kind of healthy fat that is essential for brain development. DHA can be found in fatty fish—specifically, in the oil. Alternatively, you can take supplements.

2. **Do whatever you can do to make learning fun,** be it studying in groups or making some kind of game out of the information you need to know. One of

the best ways to learn is by being engaged in the material you're trying to learn.

3. **Study with friends** so you can exercise teaching skills that will help solidify knowledge you've learned. Remember: Two heads are better than one. But if your friends are too distracting, either find "study friends" or go back to solo work.

4. **Discussion**: Think of a time you didn't perform well on a test. Did you do anything to sabotage your efforts? What can you do better?

5. **YOU Activity**: Get in groups of two and play the game below. Cover the right-hand column. Say the three words together, and see if you can come up with another word that's a common denominator between all of them. Time yourself to see how long it takes to come up with the answer. For example, if three words are cottage, Swiss, and cake, the common link is the word cheese. The faster you can find the link, the better. Use the middle columns below to see how you stack up against others. (For instance, in the first example, 52 percent of folks could find the connection within two seconds, while 96 percent could do it in fifteen seconds.)

PROBLEM	2 SEC.	7 SEC.	15 SEC.	30 SEC.	SOLUTION
Cottage / Swiss / Cake	52%	84%	96%		Cheese
Cream / Skate / Water	34%	76%	92%	90%	Ice
Safety / Cushion / Point	24%	51%	66%	74%	Pin
Political / Surprise / Line	7%	26%	61%	90%	Party

PROBLEM	2 SEC.	7 SEC.	15 SEC.	30 SEC.	SOLUTION
River / Note / Account	2%	29%	50%	79%	Bank
Stick / Maker / Point	1%	4%	46%	21%	Match
Force / Line / Mail	10%	27%	28%	28%	Air
Foul / Ground / Mate	2%	6%	25%	46%	Play
Pile / Market / Room	7%	20%	22%	44%	Stock
Man / Glue / Star	0%	9%	18%	41%	Super
Mail / Board / Lung	0%	5%	17%	18%	Black
Mate / Shoes / Total	0%	4%	5%	10%	Running
Forward / Flush / Razor	1%	2%	3%	5%	Straight
Shadow / Chart / Drop	0%	1%	1%	15%	Eye
Way / Ground / Weather	0%	5%	1%	33%	Fair

What You Will Learn

◎ Some stress is good for you

◎ Which type of stress can be destructive

◎ The hormones that affect stress levels

◎ Effective stress-management techniques

10
Freaking Out

The Biology of Stress Might Just Surprise You

More than likely, you don't need us to tell *you* what stress is. You've got homework, practice, parents hounding you, a social life that can drive you crazy, relationship trouble, and your little brother who keeps talking to you when you're trying to get your work done. And now you have to read this stupid chapter about stress, when you have a math test tomorrow, a paper due on Friday (which you haven't started, might we guess?), and absolutely no time to shop for new jeans before the weekend party. Gotcha.

We're not going to sit here and tell you that you don't even know what stress is until you've got bills, a family, and on and on—because that's neither fair nor accurate. Stress is different for everyone, and if you feel stressed, anxious, or angry, then it doesn't matter one lick about whose stress is more intense or justified. If you consistently feel as if you have no time, lots of pressure, and that the world is coming down on you hard, that's all that matters.

In this chapter, however, we are going to turn some of your preconceived notions about stress on their head and talk to you about what happens in your brain when you're feeling freaked out. You'll learn the difference between healthy and unhealthy stress, and some stress-management ·tactics to help you keep from spinning out of control.

The Biology of Stress

Here's the stunning fact of the day: Stress is good.

Huh? Evolutionarily speaking, stress served and continues to serve a very useful purpose. Think about it: Physiologically, stress heightens all of your biological responses, such as heart rate and adrenaline, so that you have the power and energy to deal with any problem thrown your way, be it a ticked-off reptile, an invading enemy, a natural disaster, or the fact that you have three finals, a state championship, and a summer job interview next week. During high-intensity stress, your concentration becomes more focused than a microscope, your reaction time quickens, and your strength increases exponentially. In essence, stress is what gives your body energy to handle life's big problems. Stress makes your body sharper, like a fine-tuned instrument.

So, historically, stress was good—it helped you live another day. Our cavemen ancestors dealt with stress by fighting or running like hell; that's where the term "fight or flight" comes from. Either way, stress allowed your body to deal with bad stuff.

But here's the kicker: The big difference between stress today and stress yesterday isn't the fact that cavemen didn't have teachers, homework, and chess competitions, it's that much of their stress was fleeting. They had periods of high-intensity stress followed by low or no levels of it. Think about it: no in-boxes on those cave walls. Today many of us are drowning in a sea of stress, with wave after wave after wave knocking us over. Those heightened biological reactions work in our favor for short periods, but when stress continues without any relief, they turn against us. (The major long-term stress our ancestors had to deal with was famine; they had to worry over long periods of time when they couldn't feed themselves or their families. In response, their bodies learned to store energy when food was scarce—which is why a starvation diet doesn't really work; you actually gain weight when you *don't* eat regularly. See chapter 3.)

Chronic stress can lead to lots of physical and mental problems, mess up your sleep and eating patterns, and leave you an overall mess. That's because your body can't handle being in that fight-or-flight mode all the time.

Before we talk about how stress affects us biologically, you should know that there are several different kinds of stress. In general, life's stressors can be grouped into three categories, which all have different implications for your life and for your health:

Ongoing low-level stress: You have tests, you have your afternoon job, you have obligations to your family, and you have day-to-day pressures. Life generates a constant hum of stress, no matter who you are or what you do. To expect that you can eliminate all stress is not only unreasonable but unhealthy, because your ability to respond to stress can actually make you stronger. Some people, in fact, find stress to be invigorating—so long as it's not overwhelming—as it helps them to focus their mind. Just think of how creative and productive a deadline can make you!

Nagging unfinished tasks (NUTs): One of the most influential forms of stress comes in the form of a chisel that chips and chips and chips and chips and chips and chips away at your brain cells a little bit at a time. Until. You. Can't. Take. It. *Any freaking more!* Whether it's a college application that you've been putting off or a cluttered room that your parents yell at you about every day, the stress of unfinished tasks is much more destructive than the background levels of stress from daily life.

Why? Because NUTs hang over your head, ready to pierce you when you're not expecting it.

Major life events: These are the biggies—a move, a parental divorce, a sickness or death in the family. The stats show that three major life events in a one-year period will make your body feel much worse in the following year. Consequently, it's especially important to develop coping strategies and support systems to sustain you in times of crisis.

So how does stress impact your health? Because when you're stressed, a series of chemicals that are produced in your brain travel through your bloodstream and affect just about every system in your body. Let's take a look at how your body's stress circuit works. Warning: Lots of acronyms ahead!

Your stress circuit involves your nervous system and a stress hormonal system that sounds like a *Star Wars* galaxy but actually refers to three of your body's glands: the hypothalamic-pituitary-adrenal (HPA) axis. When you're faced with a major stressor, the cone-shaped hypothalamus at the base of your brain releases CRH (corticotrophin-releasing hormone), which then stimulates your pituitary gland to release *another* hormone called ACTH (adrenocorticotropic hormone) into your circulation.

ACTH then stimulates your adrenal glands, which sit on top of your kidneys. When you're stressed, they produce the stress hormone cortisol. The inner part of your adrenal glands also produces important chemicals such as adrenaline, the fight-or-flight hormone that turns you into Superman in emergencies.

Think of this cycle of releasing hormones like falling dominos: One act leads to another. As you see in figure 10.1, these chemicals serve as your body's SWAT team during crises. Adrenaline increases your blood pressure and heart rate, while cortisol releases sugar into your bloodstream in the form of glucose to fuel your muscles and your mind. With plenty of available oxygen and glucose, you have everything you need to fight or run.

At the end of the cycle, the cortisol travels back to the hypothalamus to stop the

Figure 10.1 **Stressed Out** When we're stressed, our brains release a flood of chemicals (including ACTH through the hypothalamus and pituitary). In extreme stress, we may feel the effects of an adrenaline rush—with an increased heart rate and burst of energy. That increased alertness can help us finish our task, but of we're stressed over long periods of time, those symptoms can have a destructive effect, like increased blood pressure in our arteries.

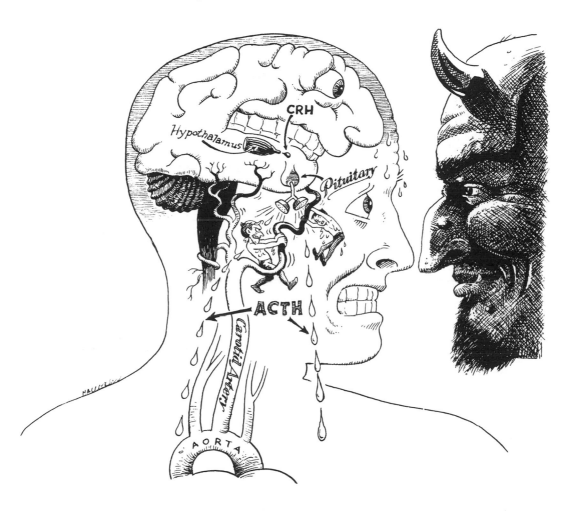

production of CRH. Stress over, hormones stop being released, body returns to normal.

But only if the stress stops.

An overactive HPA axis can make your body unable to turn off your stress response. This can happen when stress really doesn't stop (think of soldiers during wartime) or when your brain believes stress hasn't stopped (think of those soldiers at home with post-traumatic stress disorder). The result can be a flurry of health problems, including anxiety, depression, general sickness (because stress compromises your immune system), and obesity (because stress triggers the release of the hunger hormone ghrelin—see chapter 3).

It's kind of like being overcaffeinated: Your energy levels are superhigh, which helps you focus for a short period, but eventually you crash and burn because you can't sustain those levels. Same with your stress hormones: They help you focus temporarily, but then burn you out if they can't be leveled off. That's when you end up exhausted, emotionally unstable, and generally unable to cope.

Stress can be a problem not only because of the effects it can have on your mood, sleep, weight, and health, but because it may also be a symptom of other problems. Sometimes, it can be both cause and effect, creating a vicious cycle that's hard to break. Stress can bring about panic attacks, contribute to depression—it can even trigger asthma attacks. If you are having physical symptoms with your stress, it's worth considering whether you might have something more serious, like a mood disorder, which we talk about in chapter 12. If your stress manifests as an eruption of pimples every time or hives or other type of rash, it may be worth seeing your pediatrician and/or a dermatologist.

The real key to stress is learning how to manage it. Here are some of the big-picture things you can do to get a grip when you're feeling overwhelmed:

🌀 Sleep well.

🌀 Eat a balanced, nutritious diet.

🌀 Exercise daily.

⊚ Take a few minutes each day to treat yourself to some kind of relaxation activity, be it breathing deeply or taking a walk. A Twinkies feast or a Twitter fest doesn't count!

You'll learn more stress-management approaches in our Q&As below. As we said, our goal really isn't to eliminate stress, it's to help you handle it effectively when it does occur. That's ultimately the healthiest approach to dealing with your freak-out foes.

So, what else can I do to beat stress? It's not like I can just not do everything I'm supposed to when it comes to homework and stuff.

We're not advocating that you ignore your obligations, fail your science test, or ditch your friends. What we are suggesting are a few tricks to help you calm the stress hormones that may be firing rapidly at any given time. Here are a couple of tactics we like:

Play. It is important to integrate some play time into the busiest of schedules. Laughing, playing, and relaxing all decrease your stress level. That's what people mean when they say that laughter is the best medicine; it actually decreases your levels of the stress hormones cortisol and adrenaline, while distracting you from the source of the stress. Daydreaming can have a similar effect: Imagine yourself on a great vacation with your best friend and all the freedom in the world. It could be on a beach, at your favorite place in a city, or somewhere exotic and unknown. Sound like paradise? It turns out, it's more than that; that quick mental image actually improves your brain function, keeping your brain flexible and getting those creative juices flowing.

Hang out. Friends are the ultimate destressor. Research shows that one of the most vital elements in reducing the negative health effects of stress is to have strong social networks. It's mental medicine. And evidence shows that interacting with a good friend actually lowers your blood pressure and makes you more productive. However, there can be too much of a good thing, especially in today's social-network-driven world. A virtual social life, including pressure to constantly check the latest updates on Facebook, or to tweet or text back in response to each IM, can be a stressor in and of itself. Carving out face time with your friends rather than a constant barrage of Facebook posts may be a better destressor. In

Figure 10.2 **Test of Stress** Your adrenal glands are responsible for making you feel some of the symptoms associated with periods of high stress like increased heart and breathing rate. In short doses, that can help you get through the stress.

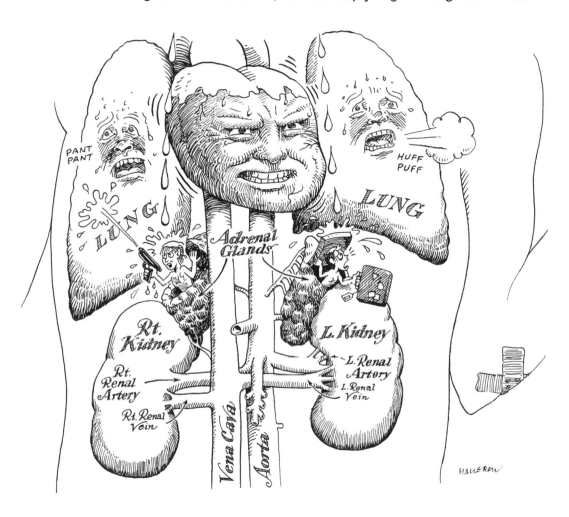

women, it has been shown that high stress levels stimulate a surge of the bonding hormone oxytocin from the brain, causing them to want to get together and have coffee—no really, the drive is for them to get together, talk, and destress. When men are stressed, they don't get the same surge of oxytocin, so there is less drive to get together and talk. Sorry, guys, you may have to cultivate other strategies to destress if your brain isn't giving you that prod to go hang out.

Try some tricks. In periods of high stress, you need to have a plan that works for you. Exercise and meditation work for some people, and both of them will help you manage chronic stress through the release of feel-good brain chemicals called endorphins. But in the heat of the moment, at peak periods of high intensity, you should be able to pull a quick stress-busting behavior out of your bag of tricks. Our suggestions:

◎ Scrunch your face tightly for fifteen seconds, then release. Repeat several times. This repetitive contraction and relaxation helps release tension you're holding above the neck.

◎ Breathe in, lick your lips, then blow out slowly. The cool air helps you refocus and slow down. If your lips get too chapped, you can just breathe in, hold for three seconds, and breathe out slowly over several more seconds. Sit up tall when you do it. You're actually getting more oxygen to brain cells that way, and giving your body a nice time out.

◎ Cork it. Hold a wine cork (don't uncork the bottle yourself, bucko) vertically between your teeth. Gently biting the cork forces your jaws—a major holder of tension (see chapter 2)—to relax. Don't swallow the cork. Please.

RELAX YOUR JAW.

I have a hard time managing all the different things I have to do. What's the best way to manage time?

While it would be a mistake for us to assume that there's only one way to work, there are some techniques that can make time management a whole lot easier. Some strategies you can try:

- **Map your day**. Though you don't have to stick to an exact schedule, you can get some stress relief if you can organize your tasks and not leave your day to total chance.

- **Break often**. Take a walk, have a glass of water, do some gentle stretches, clear your head. The few minutes you spend away from your studies will make you more efficient when you get back.

- **Enlist troops**. We know that people can be pretty stubborn when it comes to trying to accomplish goals on their own; some think it's a sign of failure if they show weakness or an inability to do a particular job on their own. But you'll reduce stress (and save time) by asking for help when you need it, as long as it's not considered a breach of trust in class or elsewhere.

I often get headaches when I'm stressed. What's the best way to handle them?

While there are several kinds of headaches, including migraines, the most common headache related to stress is called a tension headache. It used to be thought that tension headaches came from muscle tension, but it's now believed these headaches occur when fluctuations in the neurotransmitter serotonin and natural pain relievers called endorphins activate pain pathways in the brain. When serotonin levels drop, the trigeminal nerve, which comes from the brain and divides into three branches that cover the face—releases substances that cause blood vessels to become dilated and inflamed (see illustration on page 200). This inflammation causes steady pain—the feeling that your head is being squeezed in a vise—as does irritation of the nerve itself. Migraines, by contrast, usually produce sharp or throbbing pain on one side of the head and are accompanied by light and sound sensitivity and, frequently, nausea. Tension headaches can have lots of triggers, like stress, lack of sleep, skipping meals, bad posture, clenching your teeth, certain medications, and being inactive. *Don't skip meals, and make sure that you are drinking enough water;* the body needs eight to ten glasses of fluids a day to stay well hydrated. Some people also get relief by putting a little pressure behind the bones of the back of the ear. Use your thumbs and rub the area for about two minutes. Also, it's worth noting that you should avoid tight, thin head bands, which can put more tension on your head. Thicker bands (one inch or more) made of cloth are ideal. If your headaches come on daily, are persistent, wake you from sleep, or keep you from your social life as well as school, see your doctor. Over-the-counter medicines may be effective once in a while, as in one or two times a week, but if you need medicine more than that, get checked out by your pediatrician or a headache specialist (a neurologist, usually). Therapeutic massage can help, but avoid supplements and other medicines for headache relief unless prescribed by a physician.

How do I balance school, work and social life?

The older brother of our coauthor Dr. Rome gave her a piece of very wise advice when she went off to college. He told her that there were basically three categories that you could engage in each day; for her, it was academics, social life, and sports. Your three categories might be very different (academics, job, personal time, and so forth). On any day, *you can do only two out of three well. Choose wisely each day.* And if you chronically ignore one category, you may feel out of balance over time, so figure out how to work that category back into the schedule.

I get really impatient and angry when I get stressed. I know it's bad, but I can't seem to help it. What do you suggest for managing anger?

While you may think that lashing out or hitting a pillow or a punching bag helps you release tension, the opposite is true. It teaches you to develop a behavior pattern: Get mad, punch. Get mad, get even. Get mad, harbor stress until it eats away at you. Instead, do the opposite of what you'd expect. Research has found that "letting it rip" with anger actually escalates anger and aggression and does nothing to help you (or the person you're angry with) resolve the situation. In general, to cope with an emotion, you have to do the opposite. The opposite of anger isn't to withdraw or lash out but to develop empathy. So instead of swearing at your teacher for making you do homework, try to think about the twenty-some unruly kids she has to deal with all day long. And if all else fails, *bang out some push-ups or go for a run. Telling yourself to "stay calm" usually doesn't help.* Exercise actually helps lessen the effects of anger and stress.

Any foods that help with stress?

Fruits and nuts are healthy snacks with lots of nutrients. Plus, *nuts, celery, carrots, and rice cakes are crunchy, which can have some stress-reducing benefits.*

I have a friend who swears by meditation. I think it's hokey. Does it really work?

Meditation allows us to move from focused thought to an unfocused condition, which frees the mind from stress and allows creativity to grow. By reducing the "noise" in your system, you allow your full brain to develop—and it actually helps learning and reduces stress. *Transcendental meditation (one type of meditation) does provide a unique ability to quiet the mind and creates measureable changes in the architecture of the brain.* For more information and free lessons in TM, visit the website of the David Lynch Foundation for Consciousness Based Education and World Peace, at www.davidlynchfoundation.org/schools.html.

I eat when I'm stressed, but that's better than my friends who smoke, right?

A lot of us resort to unhealthy methods of stress relief—that's because they do provide a surge of the feel-good chemical dopamine that helps us feel better in the short term. It's the main reason why we get addicted to food, drugs, smoking, drinking, and other unhealthy habits. (More on the connection between dopamine and addiction in chapter 13.) The key is to know that the long-term downsides of some behaviors outweigh the short-term benefits; hey, heart disease, impotence, and lung cancer can be pretty stressful! The coping strategies we've outlined in this chapter will prove most beneficial, for now as well as over the long run. So *avoid eating, smoking, drinking, or using drugs when stressed, as these temporary fixes can create greater problems down the road.* As we suggest above, try going for a walk or run, or perhaps meditating, taking your mind off of your problem in a healthy way. And don't skip meals with stress either; too much and too little equally impact your brain power and magnify your stress levels.

★ FANTASTIC FIVE: STEPS FOR SUCCESS ★

1. **Carve out time each week for an activity *that you want to do*** that involves no other outside pressures, be it sketching, reading for pleasure, playing a few licks on your guitar, or going for a hike. Making time for enjoyable pursuits is crucial for stress management.

2. **Identify your emotions** and decide whether what you're feeling is really stress, or perhaps anger or boredom. Believe it or not, *thinking about your emotions actually helps* to lower stress levels.

3. **Avoid sugar highs and lows,** which can contribute to lower energy levels and higher stress levels. Remember, carbs get broken down into simple sugars, so you should avoid carbohydrate binges. Think about maintaining balance at every meal, making sure to sneak in some protein and fat along with the carbs; for example, a spoonful of peanut butter with those pretzels.

4. **Solo work:** Write down three of your NUTs (nagging unfinished tasks); remember, these aren't everyday stressors but ones that have been hanging over your head. For each NUT, write down three tangible strategies for getting it accomplished. Once you start eliminating the tasks on your list, you'll feel much better.

5. **Activity**

WHAT STRESSES YOU?

Circle or check what stresses you; then break into small groups and discuss strategies for helping to relieve the source of the stress.

Fear
Dying
Heights
Failing
Animals
Getting hurt by others
Not being liked by others
War
Other

Responsibility
Overload
Excessive decision making
Other

School
Exams
Work
Teachers

Friends

Other

Social

Friends

Making new friends

A romantic breakup

A friend recently moved
  away

Fitting in

Peer pressure

Being popular

Opposite sex

Pressure from a significant
  other

Sexual orientation

Other

Addictions

Drugs

Alcohol

Video Games

Social Networking Sites

Other

Personality Traits

Impatient

Aggressive, angry

Get embarrassed easily

Health

Overweight/Underweight

Appearance

Body image

Not maturing physically

Eating healthy

Other

Home Life

Brothers and sisters

Feeling jealous of siblings

Conflicts with parents

Worrying about a family
  member

Dirty, messy, or uncomfortable
  home

Too many chores and
  responsibilities at home

Too many decisions at home

Family financial worries

Lack of food

Parents separated or divorced

Parent has a new significant other
  that you don't like

Parent with not enough time for
  you or parent overly involved in
  your life

Other

Extracurricular Activities

Tryouts

Too much time spent on extracurricular activities

Not enough time for extracurricular activities

Getting to practice or activity

Being picked up from practice or activity

Your family not coming to your performance or games

Church

Afterschool job

Other

What You Will Learn

◉ Why you need more sleep

◉ The stages of sleep

◉ How to have good "sleep hygiene"

◉ Ways to fall asleep faster

11

Sleeping Duty

How to Get More—and Better—Shut-Eye

We imagine that a few chapters of this book will likely be of more interest to you than others. Chapters 6 through 8 come to mind. But we also bet our closets full of surgical scrubs that this chapter comes in a close fourth.

Why? Because sleep to a teen is like a bungee cord to an adrenaline junkie.

You want it. You need it. You crave it. You ignore buzzing alarms for it. You put pillows over your head to get three more minutes of it. You love it. Heck, you may be doing it right now.

And while parents and teachers alike may hound you because they think you're getting too much of it, the truth is that getting quality sleep is as important to your overall health, development, and happiness as just about anything else we discuss in this book. The second truth? You're probably *not* getting enough sleep. As if you needed us to tell you that.

Between school, sports, extracurriculars, afterschool jobs, homework, Facebook, and trying to have a speckle of a social life, the thing that's often the easiest to sacrifice is time in the sack. (We mean time spent *sleeping,* bozo.)

This chapter will help you understand what you can do to make sure you're getting the best snooze possible. Except for right now.

The Biology of Sleep

Sleep doesn't exist just to pass the time during Mr. B's geometry class. (Sorry, Mr. B.) Our bodies make us sleep because our brains need sleep the way guitars need strings: They can't work without it. Sleep exercises the parts of your brain that you don't normally use, in an *Inception* sort of way: Through dreams, we create alternate realities that allow us to practice problem-solving skills, open up to creative inspiration, and use our minds in ways that we may not permit ourselves to during the day.

What do we mean by this?

Not that you were around back then, but think back to classical caveman days. Our early ancestors spent each day focusing on the tasks that would keep them alive: hunting, cooking, caring for the tribe. During the day, other parts of the brain—say, the creative parts that would allow cavepeople to come up with solutions and ideas for stronger weapons or shelter—didn't get used because the cavemen and women were so caught up with living and surviving in the moment. That is, except during sleep, which is what allowed those creative parts to strengthen and grow so that they'd be fully developed when the situation arose to use them.

In a way, sleep allows your brain to lay down the code that your mind will use in the future. It gives your brain the chance to consolidate your memories so that you have a bank of information and experience available to you when you need it. Remember our discussion from just a few chapters ago about synapses and how you learn and how memories are formed? Those connections are solidified and fortified during sleep. So no matter how hard you study, how much you try to learn, how desperately you want to pass Mr. B's class (especially now that he's mad at you for sleeping through it), you have to sleep to let your brain process all of the information that you've gathered.

Sleep is also important because deep sleep increases production of a chemical called human growth hormone, which helps you maintain your healthy growth and metabolism. Obviously this is especially important for your body, which is growing rapidly.* During sleep, levels of the appetite-suppressing hormone leptin rise (for more on leptin, see chapter 3), helping you to maintain a healthy weight. And if that weren't enough, skin makes new cells twice as fast when you're sleeping as when you're awake, repairing environmental damage and healing blemishes from acne. So the purpose of sleep is not just to build your brain but also to build your entire body. Lack of sleep stresses your body and brain, leading to all of the symptoms described in the last chapter.

You may think that your occasional restless night or your shift from a good eight hours a night to lucky-if-you-get-six isn't much to worry about, since you're still managing to live okay, albeit a tad tired. The truth is that sleep problems affect 70 percent of Americans, up from 60 percent in 1990. Teens should be getting eight and a half to nine hours a night, and many don't. That's for lots of reasons—whether it's because of increased work, digital distractions, Conan and Colbert, earlier school-start times (which often aren't in sync with teens' bodies)†, or any number of other reasons. But the downsides of sleep deprivation are monumental, and not only when it comes to learning. A lack of sleep also puts you at risk for increased stress, drowsy driving, poor performance in school (and sports and your social life), mood issues, and many other problems.

And that's not even mentioning that lack of sleep has a profound effect on the

* Ever notice that when you were a little kid, you loved to wake up bright and early, and now you want to sleep late? This is a classic sign of puberty and adolescence, as your hormone cycles relating to sleep are changing.

† Schools that have moved high-school start times later when kids are more awake have noticed an increase in grades. (Yes, you can rip this footnote out and send it to your school administrators.)

way you eat: The sleepier you are, the more you crave sugar and carbohydrates to boost your energy. While that sudden rush of sugar causes a temporary spike of energy, you crash hard when it wears off. And what do you do in return? Seek more sugar for more energy. The vicious cycle continues—with the added effect of storing all those excess calories and, eventually, busting seams in your jeans.

So let's look at how we sleep. It's actually a cool biological process—and a little more complicated than just pulling the covers over your body and shutting your eyes. The way you fall asleep is through the activation of a neurotransmitter called GABA, or gamma-aminobutyric acid, for you spelling-bee champs. The reason you're not asleep right now (we hope) is that your hypothalamus—the director part of your brain—is secreting a chemical called acetylcholine to keep you alert. When you're asleep for a long time, you experience a buildup of acetylcholine that wakes you up. That's how caffeine seems to work to keep you awake, by influencing levels of acetylcholine.

In contrast, a chemical called adenosine accumulates with activity and hinders acetylcholine, so we become tired. As the day wears on, your sleep drive builds as acetylcholine and other chemicals that induce wakefulness decline. Adenosine stimulates a specific chemical reaction that causes you to sleep.

The other big chemical that affects sleeping patterns is melatonin, which is produced by a gland in the brain called the pineal gland. Our pineal gland senses when we're exposed to light, much in the way that a security-type light sensor does. (Some people call it "the third eye" because of this feature.) Interestingly, the gland is nestled way deep in our brain, far away from any direct access to light. In human beings, it likely senses blue light though special receptors in the backs of our eyes that don't actually provide vision but do dictate our circadian rhythms. (See figure 11.1.) Bedtime tip: The pineal gland—part of your brain that senses light and helps wake you— doesn't sense red light wavelengths, so if you like to sleep with a night-light on, get one with a red bulb.

When the lights go out, your pineal gland starts producing melatonin to help you sleep. The hormone exerts other effects, too, helping to control the desire for mating, lower heart rate and blood pressure, improve immune function, and relieve stress. (Fun fact: Melatonin helps bears hibernate, its levels peaking at night and

Figure 11.1 **Sleeping Beauty** The pineal gland, located deep inside your brain, is called the third eye because it releases melatonin unless it senses light; it's one of the things that help triggers you awake. The hormone melatonin is also key in regulating our sleep cycles.

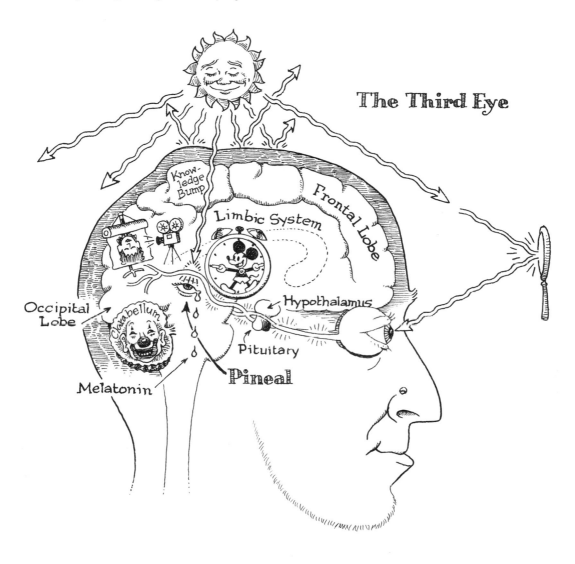

during the winter months.) As you might suspect, some of our typical nighttime habits, such as having the lights on in our room before we hit the hay, counteract melatonin production and may sabotage our efforts to fall sleep. If you're suffering from insomnia not related to lack of exercise or poor sleep hygiene, ask your doc about possibly taking a melatonin supplement, which can help get you on the right track.

Now, what exactly is a good night's sleep? While the length of sleep is important, equally vital is getting through the sleep cycle several times. The cycle is comprised of the following stages, each getting progressively deeper:

Sleep latency: the time it takes for you to fall asleep from the time you go to bed.

Stages 1 and 2: light sleep. Drowsiness as your brain is just getting into sleep. In stage 2, your brain waves start to slow down noticeably.

Stage 3: deeper sleep, which you get less of as you age because of frequent awakenings. This stage is also called non-REM sleep, or non-rapid eye movement sleep, and it is "restorative," or helps you awake refreshed when you get to complete the sleep cycle. REM sleep is a separate cycle, when you dream (see below). You cycle between non-REM sleep (stages 1, 2, and 3) and REM sleep throughout the night. If you miss out on either part, it takes a penalty out on your body and you wake up feeling like you could still pack in a few more zzzs. If you get awakened from slow-wave sleep (stage 3), you may feel groggy and disoriented, but you can wake up raring to go when stage 1 or 2 is interrupted. That is partly why "power naps" or catnaps sometimes help if they're kept to, say, a half hour or less, as you don't have time to get into that deep, stage 3 sleep.

Stage 3 sleep is the deep sleep during which you sleepwalk and sleeptalk. If you are sleep deprived, your body will jump quickly into stage 2 sleep, but you may not get to stage 3, that deep, restorative sleep from which you wake up feeling refreshed. While you need to complete a full cycle to feel more refreshed, even a quick bit of stage 2 during a catnap can make you feel better.

Sleepwalking, sleeptalking, and bedwetting are all events that can occur in stage 3 sleep. But don't worry, if you haven't had a problem with bedwetting already, it doesn't surface new just because you're a deep sleeper as a teen. Sleepwalking and sleeptalking can be highly entertaining to those around you, but with the former, make sure you are safe from falling down stairs or out of a window. Stranger events have been known to happen, some highly embarrassing, some life threatening (think balconies and second-floor windows for that sleepwalker).

REM (rapid eye movement): the deepest sleep. Your eyes are moving fast, but the rest of your body is paralyzed. It's the stage where great dreams and horrible nightmares occur. Only some voluntary muscles like some of the muscles of the eyes and diaphragm work in REM. Also, the penis can become erect, and there can be clitoral and vaginal engorgement durng this stage.

Each complete cycle (stage 1 through REM) lasts about 90 to 110 minutes, and you go through four to six of them a night. But it's important that you achieve REM sleep to feel really rested. People who have sleep problems often don't make it to REM sleep because it takes up to sixty minutes to make it to REM. If you're waking up frequently before you get to REM, then you're never getting that restorative, healthy sleep—which makes it a lot harder to stay awake the next day.

What can I do to get better sleep?

We talk about personal hygiene in a lot of contexts, such as on a date or after PE class, but most people don't talk about sleep hygiene—that is, creating the perfect sleep environment. The truth is that you need to set the perfect environment for sleep:

- A cool, dark room is the ideal environment. The temperature and darkness signal the pineal gland to kick up melatonin production and knock you out.

- There should be no laptops, no TV, no food in bed. Ideally, the bed is used for sleep; it's not an office or a restaurant.

- Add white noise. Use a fan for background noise, or one of those machines that lets you pick sounds, from the rain forest to the ocean. This drowns out other noises that might keep you up.

- Dress appropriately. The best nightclothes should be nonrestrictive and nonallergenic (both the fabric and how it's washed). Many people find it easier to sleep when it's cooler in the room, although cold feet can prevent you from falling asleep, so wear socks if necessary.

- Dim your lights a little while before bed to avoid the stimulation caused by artificial light pollution—which is all around us through TV, computers, and indoor lighting, and serves to stimulate us.

- Don't store your cell phone under your pillow. You'll wake with every text message buzz and never get any quality sleep. More important, the radiation from the phone may cause abnormalities in your brain DNA and may be one reason for the increase in brain cancer in younger cell phone users. Even better, don't sleep with your phone in your room.

Be consistent. You want quality sleep? Your body clock loves it when you follow a predictable schedule. Even on the weekends, try to rise within an hour (at most, two) of when you have to get up on weekdays, even if that means you need a power nap later. Otherwise, your body thinks you have jet lag on Monday morning and will protest big-time the interruption in time zones! Other interrupters of quality sleep: Caffeine, the most common disruptor of sleep, and alcohol, with the interruption of the sleep cycle contributing to the "hangover" that many experience. And don't forget about nicotine, which is another long-acting drug. Cigarettes smoked earlier in the day or chewing tobacco used anytime in the day can still keep you awake at night.

How can I get more sleep?

Sleep management is really about time management. (See previous chapter.) If you chronically have homework that keeps you up until midnight, but you have at least one unused study hall, find a quiet room to get even twenty to thirty minutes of something done during your free time, so that you can get to bed at a more reasonable hour. *Plan your time so that you do the task that only takes twenty to thirty minutes in that time, rather than trying to cram the project that will take two hours in a wrong-timed slot.* Find someone really organized, and have him or her help you work out a master schedule for yourself, where you build in some down time as a reward for getting the other stuff done.

What about using caffeine to stay awake? Would caffeine pills or Red Bull help?

Studies show that 75 percent of teens consume caffeine daily—and the more caffeine a teen drinks, the less he or she sleeps in the long run. Caffeine—a stimulant found in coffee, tea, and soft drinks (chocolate, too)—affects your central nervous system, and it certainly has been shown to give people energy. *It's not an answer for those who don't get enough sleep*, but a cup or two a day of a caffeinated drink may work for some but not for many others; if you can sleep like a baby, restfully, nightly, and don't get caffeine-related side effects such as headaches and irritability, you may be able to get away with some morning java. But certainly avoid it later in the day, as it lasts in your system for hours (up to 24 hours, in fact). And in the face of heart disease or a weakened heart, often caused by an eating disorder, caffeine can be a killer. You should think of caffeine pills (or other stimulants, such as many of these new-fangled energy drinks) as potentially very dangerous. It's also the reason why stimulant drugs (like ones to treat ADHD) are not an antidote for lack of sleep. The risks far outweigh the benefits. If you get the feeling that your heart is beating out of your chest (called palpitations), feel woozy, or feel faint, you should also avoid caffeine. Try decaf green tea instead, but a word of caution here, too: even decaffeinated beverages may contain a little caffeine, so if sleep escapes you, run away from even decaf coffee or tea.

Are there any foods that can help me fall asleep faster?

Warm milk will help, and a touch of cinnamon can, too. Warm milk works by allowing the feel-good hormone serotonin to get into the brain. But there's no magic food—in fact, eating right before bed can make it harder to fall asleep, especially if you suffer heartburn or reflux; it's much smarter to work on your time management and sleep hygiene.

If I go for several nights without sleeping much, can I make up for it by sleeping really late on the weekend?

Nope. Sleep isn't like a makeup test. If you do badly on an exam and Mr. B gives you a do-over, all is right in the world. You can certainly sleep more when you have more time on the weekends, but doing so won't erase all the negative effects caused by lack of sleep on the other five days. Your body tries to make up ground, but *your body works best if you get the recommended amount of sleep every night and have a similar wake-up time every day.*

My mom meditates before she goes to sleep. Does that really work?

Meditation seems to stimulate the release of melatonin to soothe your body and get you into a relaxed state that makes it easier to slip into the various stages of sleep. It's certainly much better than being on the computer or phone or watching your favorite late-night TV host.

How can I fall asleep faster?

Besides following our sleep hygiene tips above, you can also try one of these recommended remedies:

- Rub a little lavender essential oil into your skin.

- Drink some decaffeinated herbal tea, especially chamomile.

- Listen to books on tape.

- Have your parents read you a bedtime story for old times' sake. Only problem is, they may fall asleep faster than you.

What's the ideal amount of time for a nap?

We recommend *thirty minutes* (as long as it's not in class); that allows you to get some of the restorative benefits without waking up too groggy.

I can't get to sleep because I have too much to do! Help!

It's easy to spend time doing the things you know you do well, and saving the less savory tasks for later—when your brain is least primed to do them. Knowing what you're good at and what your time-draining and least fun tasks are can help you better organize your time and get you out of crisis mode. You can write on ten index cards all the categories of things you do each day or week: schoolwork, music, sports, family time, time with friends, chores, volunteer activity, and religious activity, to name a few. *Write down "must dos" and "like to dos" on the cards, and the amount of time each activity takes. Figure out how to work the "must dos" into your schedule first, with a "like to do" as a reward at the end of the "must dos."* If all of your activities take longer than you have waking hours in the day, look at your index cards and see if you can whittle down the time for each task. Do you really need two hours to practice guitar? Maybe that means band practice only on the weekend.

Want to read more about time management? Visit the website of the College Board: www.collegeboard.com/student/plan/college-success/116.html. You can also check out National Sleep Foundation at www.sleepfoundation.org.

Or, try these books:

Organizing Your Day: Time Management Techniques That Will Work for You, by Sandra Felton and Marsha Sims.

What Smart Students Know: Maximum Grades. Optimum Learning. Minimum Time, by Adam Robinson.

★ FANTASTIC FIVE: STEPS FOR SUCCESS ★

1. **Spend some time thinking about time.** The reason why many teens don't get enough sleep isn't that they're too busy, it's that they have trouble balancing all of their tasks and making the most efficient use of their time. If it helps, see a counselor or ask an organized friend to help you ID the times of your day that you can use more efficiently.

2. **Do you spend some time every day engaging in some kind of physical activity?** Make sure you're getting enough exercise. (See chapter 4.) A regular workout program can help you fall asleep, as long as you don't work up a sweat too close to bedtime. (For many people, this means be done with exercise two to three hours before you're trying to hit the hay.)

3. **It's not the spunkiest of gifts, but it's worth finding a proper pillow plus a dust mite protector.** We recommend hypoallergenic 1-micron pillow covers that zip and fit under the pillowcase and over the pillow.

4. **Purchase books on tape or a sound machine** to cut out background noise and create a routine for making you feel tired. If your family is religious, prayers also create a routine around sleep.

5. **Solo work:** Go through your bedroom at night and identify the things that you can do to make the room more conducive to falling asleep.

What You Will Learn

◎ Mood issues aren't just "in your head"

◎ The different forms of depression

◎ Why we cry

◎ What to do if a friend has suicidal thoughts

12

In the Mood

After "What's up?" and "Yo!," it may just about be the most common greeting there is: "How ya doin'?" We say it as an afterthought, as if it doesn't even matter, as if it's just an elongated form of the word *hello*. But the truth is that "How ya doin'?" may just be the most central health question there is.

That's because how you feel—in essence, your mood—really plays a role in so many other parts of your life. It affects how you learn, whether you're stressed, what you eat, how your immune system is working, how your relationships are going—everything. As you already know now, your brain serves as the hub for all of your body's functions, and your emotions are processed in your brain. As you'll soon see, emotions aren't some touchy-feely subject for psych experts. There's real biology and real chemistry behind what's going on in your brain every moment of the day that will influence your mood.

So let's look inside that brain of yours and see how you're *really* doing.

The Biology of Mood

Hormones don't necessarily go crazy in the teen years. Although some of you may feel as if you're on an emotional roller coaster, most of you may feel pretty darn okay. Both ends of the spectrum, from smooth sailing to stormy seas, are "normal," and it's equally normal to experience sudden changes in atmospheric conditions. Nevertheless, certain types of moods and changes in mood that begin to occur in adolescence can be worrisome and require attention. In this chapter, we'll outline some of the biology of emotion to help you figure it all out.

Now, you may think that hormones control your emotions, but sometimes it's actually the other way around. Emotions control your hormones, too. This happens due to biochemical changes in the brain that are triggered by emotion. Fear, for instance, is accompanied by the production of a set of brain chemicals that create the fight-or-flight response, as we discussed in chapter 10. Pleasure triggers the release of other chemicals that soothe and calm.

All kinds of emotional and mood issues involve a part of the brain called the amygdala. The almond-shaped structure takes all of the information from different parts of your brain and tags it with emotion before sending it to the cortex—the part of the brain that helps you make decisions, such as running out of a burning home. (See figure 12.1.) The amygdala assigns meaning to that smoke alarm through emotion, causing you to feel fear when you hear it. The cortex then suggests that you might consider hoofing it right out the front door.

The amygdala recognizes that there might be an emergency; the cortex decides what to do about it. So, in essence, your amygdala establishes what science heads like to call salience—that is, it chooses which stimuli or pieces of info to prioritize. The cortex is the rational part of the brain; the amygdala is the emotional part. The

amygdala controls fear and anxiety, which are at the root of most emotional disorders and big fluctuations in mood.

What's really interesting is that while the amygdala can send lots of messages to the cortex, the cortex can't do much in return; in fact, the amygdala has roughly ten times more neurons pointed toward the cortex than in the other direction. So we can't *will* ourselves to be calm just because we want to. We can't *will* ourselves out of a bad mood. And that can sometimes be hard for others to understand. Parents may tell you to just "snap out of it," but it's not as easy as that.

As we said, mood swings are normal. Some days you're happy; other days you're thrown for a loop when your cell phone freezes; sometimes you may even feel like ripping the pages out of this book, crumpling them up, and tossing them into the toilet.★

But what we really want you to be aware of is the difference between normal mood swings and some serious problems like depression. All of our emotions are really the effect of various neurotransmitters that travel in our brains. (Remember them? The chemical messengers that leap across the synapses between nerve cells? See chapter 9 for a refresher if you don't.) Feeling happy about winning the Irish step dance competition? It's chemistry. Feeling sad that your family pet died? It's chemistry. Feeling like getting cozy with your lab partner? It *really* is chemistry. Nevertheless, you still have the power to influence these neurotransmitters' effects on you, through what you eat, the ways you think, and the actions you take. For example, by using cognitive-behavioral therapy, you can train your brain to short-circuit the flight-or-fight response when confronted with something that causes you excess anxiety, so that eventually you no longer respond that way. Or you can counteract an onslaught of feel-bad chemicals by doing something that releases an army of feel-good chemicals to overwhelm them, such as exercise. In some cases, no matter how hard you may try to convince yourself to be happy, your brain may not cooperate—leaving you feeling depressed. In this case, you may need to take medication to correct an imbalance in your brain's messengers, under a doctor's supervision.

★ No, please don't do that!

Biochemical depression is a disease no different than any other; it just happens to affect the brain, so you don't look sick on the outside. People with severe depression tend to have higher levels of the stress hormone cortisol and lower levels of the feel-good chemical serotonin, leading many to believe it reflects an abnormality in the functioning of hormones and neurotransmitters in the brain.

It's good to know the signs and symptoms of depression, because if it's something that you or a friend is struggling with, you or she doesn't have to be stuck with it. People suffering from a mood disorder, especially depression, need the support of those who care about them, because often they're too ill to seek professional help on their own. Depression is diagnosed three times more frequently in women than in men. For one thing, women produce less serotonin than men and are subject to fluctuations in reproductive hormones that are linked to depression; for another, men who are depressed often self-medicate with alcohol and end up diagnosed with alcoholism instead of depression; also, men are more likely than women to deny even having a mental illness.

That can be an extra risk for guys, who have more of a chance to do something lethal—meaning attempting to kill themselves, and accomplishing that goal—when depressed. When severely depressed, many teens may think about suicide (the number two cause of death in teens), or what it would be like if they had never existed (these are what docs call "passive suicidal thoughts"). Although common, these thoughts are not normal and if you are having these kind of thoughts, it is worth seeking help. Now. Because life in the middle of depression is not as good as it gets, and it can be hard to see past the depression when you are living and breathing it. And there is a life after the depression for everyone who seeks help, at the right time, with the right team. The trick is actually asking for help or recognizing a friend or family member who is too depressed to even ask.

Fortunately, if you catch depression early, you've got a good shot at curing it. Let the problem linger, and it'll become more serious. Keep treating it with a six-pack and you'll end up both drunk and depressed—not a useful combo. Anxiety often accompanies depression but can also be a stand-alone condition. We docs like to classify anxiety and depression into different categories. Here are the ones that you should most be aware of:

Major depression: A major depressive episode lasts longer than two weeks with at least five of the seven following symptoms:

- changes in your sleep patterns, such as wanting to stay up all night and sleep all day, or just wanting to sleep 24/7 and skip the "up" part totally

- decreased interest in activities you previously enjoyed

- feelings of guilt or shame

- decreased energy that has nothing to do with changes in sleeping or eating patterns

- difficulty concentrating

- changes in appetite

- thoughts of suicide

Situational depression: This is diagnosed after more than two months with five of the seven above symptoms after someone has suffered a significant life change, such as a death in the family. Symptoms usually improve over time after the major event. If you feel it's more than you can handle, seek help.

Bipolar disorder: As you might guess from the prefixes, bipolar depression refers to people who have two different sides to their depression or behavior—that is, a depressed state and a very high-energy state.

Panic attacks and anxiety attacks: You can almost think of this as acute episodes that are born from things that normally wouldn't be a cause of stress, like feeling doomed when you get in a car. In other words, it's an exaggerated flight-or-fight response that doesn't necessarily match the situation. If you get panic attacks, you experience symptoms such as shortness of breath, an elevated heart rate, sweating or chills, nausea, dizziness, trembling, and a sense of dissociation, along with intense fear. (More below in our Q&As.)

OCD: Obsessive-compulsive disorder is a condition that is really all about unwanted thoughts, obsessions, or compulsions that, if not acted upon, create acute anxiety. A person, for instance, has a problem functioning in life unless he or she follows certain rituals every day in the exact same way. (More below in our Q&As.)

When it comes to relieving the symptoms of anxiety and depression, the biggest cure may not be in a pill bottle but in making sure that you don't stay bottled up yourself. In treating mild depression, many teens use talk therapy with a mental health professional (a psychologist, a social worker who specializes in adolescent mental health, and sometimes a psychiatrist, although some psychiatrists tend to spend more time giving out medicines than doing talk therapy; but many realize the power of talk, so teens should search for those taking a more holistic approach). Cognitive behavioral therapy, a form of talk therapy that helps you modify your behaviors and reactions to situations, used over a six-week period has been found to be 60 to 70 percent successful, and it's 90 percent successful when used in conjunction with prescribed medicine.★

How does therapy work? Probably through the release of those feel-good chemicals, including oxytocin, that are stimulated by a safe, supportive, and positive relationship with your therapist and learning new coping strategies—in other words, creating new pathways in the brain for dealing with stress.

Bipolar disorder, as we referred to above, can also involve depression, but the downs cycle with ups that get a bit *too* up. During the manic (or high-energy) phase, you have too much serotonin circulating in the brain, leading to a flight of ideas, where you can jump from one thought to the next and the next, making it difficult for the average person to keep up with you. During a manic phase, you may do impulsive things (wrong time to get a new credit card or start internet gambling) that

★ Exercise can be helpful, too, because it elevates feel-good hormones.

can run you into a bit of trouble (or debt). During the down phases, in addition to the feelings of hopelessness and helplessness associated with major depression, you may feel ashamed and humiliated about things you did during the manic phase—as in that last "hookup" when you didn't even know him or her, drank more than you meant to, and said yes to a situation from which you otherwise would have walked away. Both depression and bipolar disorder can be associated with thoughts of suicide, which should always be taken seriously. Biologically, manic depression (bipolar disorder) involves a different alteration in brain chemistry than major depression, so different medications are prescribed. As with major depression, talk therapy can definitely help, but the right medicines in both cases can be life saving.

Cyclothymic disorder is a milder form of bipolar disorder and occurs when people experience irregular, quick ups and downs, but never with deep, dark lows or wild highs. They may or may not require medication but should be followed by their doctor, as cyclothymic disorder may precede bipolar disorder (but not always). And talk therapy can also give you insight into how to manage the rapid highs and lows without turning the lives of your family and friends and your own life upside down.

Mood disorders can be deadly if undetected, and manageable if treated with coping strategies and judicious use of medicines as needed. If you or someone you care about has a mood disorder, think of it as a medical challenge to be dealt with, not as something to be embarrassed or ashamed about. Would you judge someone harshly for having diabetes? Hopefully not! Ditto for depression, or bipolar disorder, OCD or any mood disorder where biology impacts behavior. You recognize it, you deal with it, you may need to deal with it again (and sometimes again), and you keep working toward the solutions that allow you to lead a positive, productive life. (See chapter 10.)

The YOU Qs
You Ask, We Answer, You Decide

Why do I cry when I'm moody?

Just as mucus traps bacteria so that you can blow it out your nose, just as sweat is your body's way to get rid of excess salt, and just as urine and poop remove waste, tears also serve a useful purpose. We have several kinds of tears, and not just the ones that come out during an episode of *Jersey Shore*. Basal tears are produced continuously to keep our eyes moist and lubricated and to prevent damage by wind, dust, dirt, and so forth. Irritant tears are produced not when your little brother is really bugging you but when the eyes are stung by wind, sand, insects, rocks, or other foreign bodies. Both basal tears and irritant tears have the same goal: to protect your eyes.

Emotional tears come out during moments of intense feelings: sometimes joy, but more often sorrow. Unlike basal tears and irritant tears, *they carry stress hormones as a way of getting rid of them.* But are the tears caused by the stress hormones? One major hormone that increases with stress is also associated with crying: prolactin. Higher levels of prolactin are found when you experience emotional crying; as a whole, women cry more often than men (perhaps four times as often, according to one study), and also have 60 percent more prolactin. Although crying may embarrass you, it signals that you have reached a level of stress that is detrimental to your health if you don't find ways to let it out. It's okay to cry; it may be therapeutic.*

So if serotonin levels are low when I'm in a bad mood, is there a way that I can boost them?

Exercise may cause a release of natural opioids, other feel-good hormones. Skipping meals, missing food groups over the course of the day or days, and eating erratically lower your serotonin levels. *Prayer, meditation, exercise, and positive visualization* can boost serotonin. There are also foods that can help. (See below.) And heck, it's even worth surrounding yourself with some irritatingly good-mood friends to see if a little of their vibe can rub off.

So there is such a thing as mood foods?

Certain foods increase serotonin levels, such as *turkey and chocolate* (not necessarily together—yuck!). That's why people feel so good and satisfied after Thanksgiving dinner. Another good food to boost your mood is bananas, which help enhance the effects of serotonin. One supplement that appears to help anxiety and depression is the DHA (a three-letter abbreviation, not DHEA) form of omega-3 fatty acids, which is so safe that taking it should be a no-brainer. It helps make you brainier, too; 600 to 900 milligrams a day for adults makes a big difference. Carbs, especially chocolate, also boost serotonin, but if you tend toward being overweight and you eat too many without exercising enough to burn off the excess calories, you may need to go easy to avoid depression from a poor body image.

You mentioned medication. What's the deal with antidepressants?

Antidepressant drugs should rarely be given without psychotherapy (talking to a professional) because they may "activate" you before they get you feeling better, and you still need long-term coping strategies that a pill cannot provide. To

---

* New research actually indicates that a man crying is a turn-on for women, but a woman crying is a turn-off for men.

give one example, if you are so depressed that you can't get out of bed and are thinking about suicide several times a day, giving *one category of antidepressant—an SSRI, or selective serotonin reuptake inhibitor—can get you moving a week or weeks before it actually gets you feeling better.* This creates a period when you are up and moving (and now able to actually do something dangerous to yourself) without yet feeling better. The good news is that when you reach the right serotonin level, you will start feeling better, but it can take a bit of time for the drug to build up significantly to exert an effect, and that can be risky for someone who is actively contemplating suicide. If you start with talk therapy, you'll begin moving in a more healthy direction more quickly. And with or without meds, you will still need some better ways to manage stress when you are depressed, and a good therapist can help you develop those skills.

How do they work?

The most commonly prescribed medications for depression, anxiety disorders, eating disorders, and obsessive-compulsive disorder (see below) are SSRIs, including fluoxetine (Prozac), paroxetine (Paxil), and sertraline (Zoloft), which work by *allowing more serotonin to be available in your brain.* As noted above, antidepressants are not a quick fix—it can take a few weeks before you begin to feel better. During that time you need to assess your feelings and moods and have the prescribing doctor adjust the medication accordingly, but it's more of a slow fix than a quick one. SSRIs prevent serotonin from being taken up and broken down as fast, leaving it active in the synaptic spaces for a few nanoseconds longer, where it does its thing to make you feel good. SSRIs are not addicting but some patients may find them very helpful and stay on them for years, while others may be able to forgo them after a few months. They do not change your personality or make you a different person; they allow your brain's own natural serotonin to do its own thing and help you refind you. Some people may take time to adjust to these meds, getting headaches for two to ten days when they start until their brains get used to them. The headaches then tend to go away.

SSRIs do not change your personality or cause weight gain in the average person. For those with eating disorders, OCD, or anxiety disorders, they may actually take some of the anxiety out of day-to-day life, so that instead of 90 percent of your thoughts being on the stressor (eating disorder or otherwise), only 70 or 60 or 50 percent of your brain is stuck on those thoughts. On the downside, if you have bipolar disorder, an SSRI may bring out a manic phase, or being "too up" (not in a happy way, but in an out-of-body-experience kind of way).

An alternative choice is bupropion (Wellbutrin), which is safe if you don't have an eating disorder (the seizure threshold can be lowered in those with EDs). Different drugs affect different parts of your brain, which is why you should discuss changing medicines and different categories of drugs with your doc if you're feeling that the drug doesn't quite feel right or that you might need a different one. Above all, don't self-medicate—especially with drugs and alcohol—while you're on antidepressants, as that can be life threatening. Why? Alcohol and certain drugs are actually central nervous system depressants, so they put your brain and body in an even more depressed state—and make matters worse.

I think I have a friend who has OCD. Can you tell me more?

People with obsessive-compulsive disorder are compelled to follow patterns and rituals or demand perfection in themselves or their surroundings. In its mild form, OCD can be a good thing, leading you to dot the *i*'s and cross the *t*'s on your homework, keep your room clean, and stick to an exercise routine. But when obsessive-compulsive tendencies go overboard, you have OCD—kind of like the hamster who can't get off the spinning wheel even to the point of passing out. The person with OCD may take twelve hours to complete a school project that should have taken three hours, because he has to do it just so. Or she may wash her hands so frequently that she rubs the skin raw. Eating disorders such as anorexia nervosa can bring out OC tendencies around food; for instance, the person may feel compelled to cut up food into so many bites, or have other extreme rituals about food or body. The person with OCD and an eating disorder kind of gets a double whammy, since when her brain gets starved of oxygen and nutrients, the compulsions become even more powerful and harder to ignore. With OCD, SSRIs keep your serotonin working long enough to break the cycle of repetitive thought. Someone with OCD may not need an SSRI all the time, but when the disorder is getting the best of you, and the rituals and fixation are interfering with your regular life, an SSRI can be lifesaving.

Everyone has thoughts of suicide, don't they? I mean, that's normal, isn't it?

Having thoughts of suicide, unfortunately, is somewhat common, but it is not normal and is the brain's warning signal to get help *now*! Suicide is the second leading cause of death for teenagers (car accidents being first). *If you are having thoughts of self-harm or considering killing yourself, or even just wishing that you didn't exist, seek help from a mental health professional immediately*—be it a psychiatrist, psychologist, social worker, or counselor—to help you develop stress management strategies and to see if you could benefit from medication. (Of the four types, only a psychiatrist, an MD, can prescribe psychoactive medications.) And if a friend or acquaintance has mentioned thoughts of suicide to you, tell an adult immediately, even if you've been sworn to secrecy.

Why are we so concerned? Obviously, suicide means death, yet teens often attempt suicide as an "I'll show you" to parents, friends, exes, bullies, without fully realizing that they won't be around to enjoy their tormentors' reactions. Or they think they'll draw attention to their needs by taking what they think is a sublethal dose of a toxic drug or leaving a note so someone will rescue them in time, but often miscalculate the risks involved and end up killing themselves, even if they really didn't mean to.

We know how hard it must be, but you really need to tell an adult about your thoughts—a parent, doctor, counselor, teacher, mentor, social worker—anybody who can get you immediate help. Those thoughts need to be taken seriously, and there is always help available. If you can't say the words out loud, send a text or an email, with a warning, *"Read This Now: This Is Serious."* Don't expect even the most clued-in parent or doc to be able to read your mind; make your messages simple and clear. "I am feeling like I want to kill myself [or substitute whatever other phrases describe how you are feeling]. I need help—now!" If all else fails, suicide hotlines, staffed by trained professionals, are available and can be reached by contacting the National Suicide Prevention Lifeline at 800-273-TALK or online at www.suicidepreventionlifeline.org.

I've had an anxiety attack before. What can I do?

Anxiety attacks can happen when your fight-or-flight response gets activated at an inopportune time, meaning that there's no saber-toothed tiger to run away from. You feel like your heart is racing, you start to sweat, your pupils dilate, and you feel as if you're ready to jump out of your skin. What to do? *Self-relaxation techniques, self-hypnosis, and other mind-over-matter strategies can help.* You can literally talk yourself down, or slow breathe yourself back into a relaxed state.

I have a friend who's a "cutter." She says she does it to relieve stress. What can I do to help?

Cutting, or self-mutilation, can lead to a brief adrenaline surge and a kind of mental "numbing." Some people report feeling dissociated from the pain and relieved of their stress for that moment, but then the pressure builds up, driving the person to try cutting or other self-harm again to get another "fix." Self-mutilation causes the release of natural painkillers called endorphins that can cause a high, like a runner's high. The result is very similar to drug addiction. If you have a friend who cuts, try to talk to her directly about it. You can say that you noticed the cuts or have seen her make them, and it scares you, as you have heard it is a sign of inner pain and can be a pretty addicting habit. If she gets mad at you, you can remind her that you are commenting only because you care, just as you would feel compelled to try to help her if she had developed a heroin habit. Cutting can be a cry for help and sometimes a prelude to attempting suicide, so *if she ignores you, it is fair game to call her family, tell the school counselor or a trusted adult advisor, and/or her doctor,* sharing your concerns and what you have observed. Again, if she gets mad at you, you can say that it is worth being on the receiving end of her anger rather than enduring the pain her death or continued self-destruction would cause.

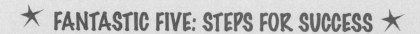

★ FANTASTIC FIVE: STEPS FOR SUCCESS ★

1. **Exercise can be a great mood enhancer** because it helps boost levels of serotonin and endoprhins. Make sure you're staying active—at least thirty minutes of physical activity a day. It's good for your body and brain.

2. **Stay connected**. Having strong relationships with friends and family not only improves your mood but also can help you when times are tough. We know you like texting and IM-ing, but make sure you also get plenty of face-to-face time, too.

3. **Don't be afraid to ask for help**. Repeatedly, if need be—until you get the help you need. And getting help for a friend who is depressed will allow you to have that friend for much longer.

4. **Solo work:** If you suspect that you're mired in depression, ask yourself these questions. Answering yes to more than two of them for more than two weeks in the last month may be a sign that you should talk with your doc about depression.

   Are you unsatisfied with your life?

   Do you get bored a lot?

   Do you often feel hopeless and/or helpless, like there's nothing you can do to feel better?

   Do you feel too blah to venture out with friends or family?

   Do you feel worthless, like nobody appreciates you?

5. **Discussion:** If you knew that a friend was considering suicide, what would you and your classmates do about it?

What You Will Learn

◎ The chemistry of addiction

◎ The difference between physical and psychological habits

◎ How to ID an addiction

◎ How to treat an addiction

13
Hooked On . . .

When we say the word *addiction,* your immediate thoughts may revolve around alcohol, drugs, cigarettes. Indeed, these vices are surely the unholy triumvirate of destructive addictions, because getting hooked on any of them will wallop your insides and your outside.

But we'd like you to take a step back and think about other things that might possibly have you—or your friends—addicted. Diet Coke, lip balm, texting, Facebook, red M&M's, video games.★ Any of them sound familiar? We thought so.

★ Yes, there is much research showing that teens can get addicted to video games, and it can lead to consequences such as depression and anxiety. The recommendation is no more than two hours of screen time a day for high schoolers and no more than an hour a day for middle schoolers.

But here's the thing: The line between habit and addiction can be a fine one. What's the difference between doing something you enjoy and overdoing it to the point of addiction? How do you know when you've gone too far? Why is one person's passion another person's ticket to Nail Polish Anonymous?

They're all great questions—ones we'll explore here, as we talk about how your brain and body work in terms of turning innocent habits into full-scale addictions.

The Biology of Addiction

Addiction is a complex phenomenon, but it all starts in the place you might suspect: your brain. Technically, what happens is that a substance (or behavior) actually creates physical changes in the brain related both to neurotransmitters (the chemical signals that relay messages from cell to cell within your central nervous system) and neural pathways (the connections between neurons that we talked about in chapter 9). Those changes make you think—deep-down believe—that you're starving for that substance or behavior and that you'd die without it. Now, that's not true, but the brain believes it is. How?

In most cases of addiction, you begin to crave something that has caused your brain to release dopamine, one of the key neurotransmitters that signals your brain to feel pleasure. Your body then craves more of that substance or experience because it makes you feel good. That leads you to form a habit, where you keep repeating the behavior so that you can keep feeling that hit of dopamine. Unfortunately, as you become used to that experience, your body starts to make less dopamine, so you often need more of that experience to get the same hit of dopamine.

At the same time, by repeating the behavior over and over, you're also creating strong neural pathways that "memorize" the behavior and make it automatic. Your brain goes through rapid growth during adolescence, so these pathways are more likely to become permanently etched during this time. That's why trying cigarettes at sixteen is more likely to addict you than if you tried them at twenty-six, not to mention why cigarette companies spend so many marketing dollars trying to attract young customers.

Let's take a comparatively harmless habit: biting nails, for example. You start to do it because touching your fingers to your mouth is innately soothing, because it reminds your brain of all the pleasure it got from sucking your thumb or fingers when you were a baby. The action stimulates a rush of dopamine, which causes pleasure, and a rush of oxytocin, which reduces your stress level. (Any oral stimulation—smoking, thumb sucking, and so on—releases oxytocin.) After doing this for a while, a habit is created so that you automatically bite your nails any time your stress-o-meter so much as hints at rising, even before you're conscious of it. This is why it can be so hard to break an addiction: By the time you're fully aware that you're doing the action, your brain and body are already engaged in a dance of expectation and fulfillment, and it can be enormously difficult to stop a cycle that's already in motion.

You can also look at food as a good example of how addiction works. Say you're stressed. Stress activates chemical pathways that affect both your brain and body: You feel anxious, your heart races, you begin to sweat. If, in fact, you're not being chased by a saber-toothed tiger and don't need to be on hyperalert, your body will naturally seek a way to calm that stress response. People do it in different ways, but many folks choose to do it with food (especially carbohydrates), which, in addition to activating the part of the brain that calms you down also switches on the brain's reward center. After that initial feel-good hit wears off, you'll reach again for the same food that made you calm and relaxed: comfort food. Now substitute tobacco, or alcohol, or sex for the word *food*, and you can see how addictions are often born out of a stress-busting behavior.

Some people are genetically predisposed to addiction. It appears that their brains are programmed to get a greater kick, or a greater "hit" of dopamine, from certain chemical stimuli, such as alcohol or nicotine. Some guys say that the pleasure from their first beer was such that they knew they would not be able to go without. But make no mistake: It appears that all of us can become addicted to many things, and the earlier in life you try them, the more addicted your brain seems to get.

For a behavior to be classified as an addiction, there have to be some destructive results associated with it. You can be addicted to reading, for example, but as long as it doesn't interfere with the rest of your life—including your social life—it's not a problem. The harmful effects can come in physical forms (such as the consequences of most classic addictions, like smoking, alcohol, even food). But they also can come in the form of emotional or social problems; for example, your friends no longer want to hang out with you because you put on that lip balm every, oh, twelve seconds. If you're addicted to something, you'll do just about anything to fulfill that need, even if it's not in your best interest. In some experiments, drug-addicted lab animals self-administered the drugs to the point of death. The reason is that dopamine and other neurotransmitters involved in addiction stimulate the emotional center of your brain, which, when it comes to controlling behavior, is a lot more powerful than the logical part of your brain.

Addicted people don't merely *want* whatever it is that has them in its clutches; they *need* it psychologically and/or physically. Cravings can be emotional (you want something because it feels good *or* because it blocks out something that feels bad) or physical (your body needs, say, caffeine or nicotine). If not fulfilled, physical cravings can lead to symptoms of withdrawal. On the mild side, you may experience a headache if you skip your daily morning coffee. On the severe side, people in withdrawal from severe drug addiction often need to be hospitalized with their vital signs closely monitored, sometimes for weeks or months, while their bodies reequilibrate.

Why is it so hard to stop? Because of the complexity of the physical and emotional parts of addiction. Many people with addictive behaviors reinforce those behaviors because they soothe them when they're in pain. In a way, they act as a form of stress relief (a reason why some people smoke when they're under pressure), and the answer to removing the triggers for the addiction is to learn other ways of managing stress. But your brain and body also have to wrestle with the conflict between a short-term payoff and long-term adverse effects such as cancer and wrinkled skin from smoking. (More on this in chapter 19.) In some cases, it may be necessary to take a short course of medication to help break the cycle of addiction, or wean off of a chemical dependency through a substitute, like Nicorette gum instead of cigarettes. Talk with your doctor if you think you need medical support.

Addictions are really just Band-Aids that don't address the root cause of the problem, which is why it's important to identify the underlying stresses that may be fueling your addiction and take a good look at our stress-management techniques in the Q&A that follows.

You Q&A
You Ask, We Answer, You Decide

So how do you know if you have an addiction?

It's sometimes difficult to diagnose an addiction because the addicted person may have social and psychological problems that overshadow the addiction itself. Depending on the severity of the addiction, it's common for the addict to develop social, school, family, medical, and legal problems—think of the person who flunks out of school and turns out to be abusing drugs. But the way we test for addiction is by asking a series of questions.

There's a formal series of questions called the CRAFFT Screening Tool, adapted from adolescent medicine and addictions expert Dr. John Knight, to screen for alcohol and drug addiction. It works equally well for other addictions, like Facebook, as shown below. Feel free to sub in whatever potentially addictive substance or behavior you're concerned about. If you answer yes to any of these questions, it can be a sign of a habit becoming an addiction.

1. Has anyone ever told you that you have a problem with Facebook, or that you should cut down on your time on Facebook?

2. Do you wake up and immediately feel like you need to check Facebook or have a Facebook fix?

3. Has being on Facebook ever caused you problems in the rest of your life (like caused you to not study enough for a test or fail to finish a paper)?

4. Have you ever chosen being on Facebook instead of another pleasurable experience, like hanging out with friends or family?

5. Have you ever missed a normal vital part of daily life to be on Facebook, like joining your family at the dinner table or taking a shower?

What's the difference between impulsive and compulsive behavior?

Impulsive behaviors come in many forms: impulse buying, like what you might do if you walked into a grocery store *starving*; or an impulsive choice of a risky behavior, like, "Hey, everyone is jumping off that bridge into the river, I should try it, too!" Hopefully, someone has checked to make sure the water is deep enough below with no rocks. Impulse control disorders occur when impulsive behaviors get the best of you. They are characterized by:

◎ an increasing sense of tension or excitement before committing an impulsive act;

◎ pleasure, gratification, or relief when you actually commit the impulsive act;

◎ possibly regret or guilt following the act. (This part doesn't always occur; it depends on the situation and the consequences.)

Impulsive behavior is about making decisions in the moment, while compulsive is about doing it over and over. In both cases, you may not have dealt with the underlying stress that's triggering the behavior.

Both impulse control and compulsion may be involved in creating an addiction. Initial use may start impulsively, but once addiction sets in, the process of seeking the substance or the behavior to prevent negative feelings, stress, or withdrawal between episodes can serve as the compulsive part.

What are the most common addictions you see in teens?

The most common addictions are *(1) alcohol, (2) cigarettes and smokeless tobacco, (3) marijuana, (4) video games,* and *(5) Facebook,* in that order. People tend to forget about chewing tobacco and snuff, but it is just as addictive and dangerous to your health as cigarettes. The nicotine in tobacco causes the addiction, while the hydrocarbons that you suck in are potentially deadly, causing over a dozen different forms of cancer, as well as the serious respiratory ailment emphysema. Furthermore, chewing tobacco and cigarette use is hazardous to your skin (wrinkles), sex life (impotence and poorer quality orgasms), heart, and brain.

Marijuana is physiologically and emotionally addictive, but because of the growing movement to legalize it for medical use, many people assume that it is safe for the general population. In the smoked form, you get the toxic effects of the hydrocarbons of the smoke (one shared joint or blunt used to contain the same amount of carcinogens as four cigarettes). You won't get hydrocarbons from eating pot brownies, but with today's marijuana, each blunt may be more like a whole pack's worth of cigarettes.

Alcohol is tricky. Despite being legal and socially accepted in many cultures, especially ours, it can be addictive and have dangerous consequences in the portion of people who have low tolerance or who carry a genetic risk for alcoholism (about 17 percent of the American population). Unfortunately, you can't test for that gene beforehand, although you can get a clue from your own family history. Has anyone in your family struggled with alcohol or substance abuse? How about depression? Knowing that should help you figure out whether to avoid drinking completely or to proceed with caution. For those who have already tried drinking, here's a question: Have you ever blacked out from overimbibing? Blacking out means that you were awake and functioning while drinking, but after sobering up, you don't remember all the details. *Danger! That's a hallmark of carrying the alcoholic gene.* Passing out means that you drank more than your system could handle, and your body went to sleep to protect you. Unfortunately, if you drink enough to pass out, your body may "protect" you by slowing down respiration to the point of coma and death. If you're ever in a situation where someone has passed out after drinking alcohol, waste no time in calling 911 and getting help—it's better to admit that the two of you were drinking and face punishment than to lose a friend. While you're waiting for the EMT, take immediate steps to make sure your friend can breathe. If he's vomiting, position him on his side so he doesn't swallow his vomit. And call 911 to walk you through CPR if you don't know it.

As for another most common addiction we see, involving phoning, texting, and practically living on the internet, some teenagers just can't stop. You may not have this, but check out your parents. Do they answer their BlackBerry messages at dinner? Or is there ever a sacred time when that call just goes unanswered, as it should? Feel free to educate them on the addictive nature of the internet. In your life, does your IM-ing, Facebook time, or texting interfere with sleep, schoolwork, other activities, or your mood? Do you feel stressed or depressed if you can't get to your Facebook account or text your friends? Or if no one has texted you back? Do you feel compelled to check repetitively, even if not much time has passed since your last text? Do you limit activities in order to continue IM-ing or tending to Facebook? Can you keep yourself from texting? For how many minutes, hours, or days?

What are the steps to take if I'm addicted to something?

First, see if you can quit cold turkey. Just stopping abruptly often works for those in the early stages of an addiction, as it's more like breaking a bad habit at that point. But once your brain has been hardwired to crave the substance or behavior, you may need additional help.

If you try to quit yourself but can't, seek help. Start with your doctor and/or your school counselor, to seek information on how to quit. Your parents may also be great resources, unless of course, they are using themselves.

If you think you can just use a little bit, think long and hard about the short- and long-term consequences. Other helpful hints: Find friends who don't use. A change of scenery or a change of companions can do wonders for discovering healthier ways to spend your time, energy, and money, and help remove you from the environment that can trigger a specific addiction. There's evidence that a young person's network of peers is a powerful determinant of his or her behaviors; it's hard to overestimate the influence that friends can have. That is why one of the strengths of Alcoholics Anonymous (AA), Overeaters Anonymous (OA), and other successful antiaddiction programs is that they provide a new peer group; instead of hanging out at the same old bar, you go to group. As a chronic disorder, addiction requires long-term treatment that is usually measured in months and years.

Several medications that have been shown to help. Some, like anticraving medications like bupropion, work by—you guessed it—reducing the cravings and thus lessening the chance that you'll want the substance.

What's detox?

It's basically a *form of treatment that removes you from the toxic substance to which you're addicted.* Detox can be very useful, but physical withdrawal produces lots of discomfort, so substitutes may be employed to ease the transition. For example, nicotine patches are often used when someone tries to quit smoking, allowing him or her to gradually wean from nicotine without the adverse symptoms that can occur from stopping a multipack habit cold turkey: diarrhea, irritability, stomach upset, headache, and sleeplessness or too much sleep. For heroin and narcotic withdrawal, detox is most safely done in a treatment setting, to help with the acute physical and emotional consequences of withdrawal. A substance abuse specialist can prescribe medicines if needed.

Any good tricks to help when you're addicted?

Don't say no. Just say yes to a healthier option. Here's what we mean: When your brain reads a sign that says No Smoking, your brain actually sees only the word *smoking,* thus reinforcing the message to smoke. It's like a reminder: *Yes, cool! Smoking! I like it!* It's your brain backfiring. Instead it's better to look at (and think about) cues such as chewing gum instead of "no cigarettes," or "fruits and vegetables" instead of "no peanut-butter pie."

Use distraction. When you are most tempted to give in to that old habit, instead call a friend, read a book, do some homework or household chores (yes, we're parents), or shovel a neighbor's walk. (Doesn't work in Florida, but it's great for those living in more northern climates.) Random acts of kindness can be particularly helpful.

Find a hobby. If you relied on smoking to keep your hands occupied or to keep yourself from (fill in the blank: overeating, gambling; whatever other addiction you might have), find other ways to keep your hands and brain engaged. For instance, when you are tempted to reach for a cigarette, try origami, or making a paper airplane, or playing with Silly Putty, or some other means of keeping your hands busy.

Think big money. Figure out how much your addiction costs you, and keep a running tab of money saved as you leave behind your addiction.

Is it possible to be addicted to something that's good for you?

Absolutely. *You can be addicted to reading, so that your dopamine system and pleasure centers get just as activated by a good book as by any other addictive substance.* You can also be addicted to foods that in moderation might be really good for you but in excess could get your body into trouble. Read: too much of a good thing. The same goes for physical activity; you can get a natural high from the endorphins that get released when you exercise regularly enough and hard enough. But there is such a thing as too much of a good thing with exercise; *orthorexia* refers to exercise addiction and an obsession with healthy food, or compulsive exercise to the point of ill health, without sufficient energy intake (food, liquids) to support the energy expenditure. Exercise addiction can be deadly, if the person's body is burning its own tissues for fuel—especially when it gets severe enough to cost heart muscle. Less serious, but still problematic, are overuse injuries—strains, tears, inflammation—to joints, muscle tendons, ligaments, and other connective tissues as a result of obsessively pushing the body too far.

My mom says I'm addicted to my phone. Is that possible?

Yes. See above for the internet addiction part. *If you find yourself IM-ing, tweeting, texting, game playing, and so on, and becoming irritable or bothered by any interruption, you may need to cut back.* Don't sleep with your phone in your room. (See page 214 for the reasons why.) And look at our other addiction-busting strategies throughout the chapter.

How can I quit smoking?

Your options:

⊚ The NicoDerm patch delivers nicotine through your skin to help you manage the physical cravings while you put down the cigarette. Gradually you'll lower the level of nicotine delivered through the patch so that you no longer experience the cravings. The patch comes in different strengths, and most people smoking a pack a day start with a 21-milligram patch applied each morning and taken off before putting the next one on. After two months (the manufacturer says weeks, but we have seen much more success when the patch is used for two months), the person can move to a 14-milligram-a-day patch, the starting point for those folks smoking half a pack per day. The 14-milligram patch is continued daily for two months, then the person goes down to a 7-milligram patch until the urge passes altogether or often two more months, for a six-month total. Many people can quit in six to eight weeks, but we prefer six months on the patch, in combination with walking, phoning or texting a buddy daily, and taking the anticraving pill bupropion (brand name Zyban). We typically prescribe a low dose of 100 milligrams twice a day. If you get itchy at the patch site, a little over-the-counter hydrocortisone cream will usually make it stop. Sometimes, though, you might have to switch to a different brand of patch, since it's the specific adhesive used to make the patch stick that brings about the itchiness. For those prone to insomnia, remove the patch at night. *Or* you might want to keep it on. You'll have to discover by trial and error what works for you, as some people have problems sleeping with the patch, while others find it difficult to enjoy a restful night without it. You'll need a doc's prescription for the bupropion.

⊚ Nicotine gum can do the same thing as the patch. Pop a piece and chew until you get a peppery taste, which tells you that the nicotine has been released. You can then park it between your gum and lip, and chew it whenever your nicotine level starts to drop. People will chew a piece of gum instead of each cigarette they'd smoke, and can slowly wean themselves off it over time by switching to regular gum when the cravings start subsiding. As a bonus to the nicotine, the gum also gives you something to do with your mouth. Nicotine gum comes in 4-milligram and 2-milligram versions, with those smoking at least a pack a day starting with the higher dose, and less frequent cigarette smokers using the lower dose. Here's what we tell people trying the gum who are heavy smokers:

⊚ Chew a piece of gum each hour for six weeks.

⊚ Next chew a piece of gum every two hours for three weeks.

⊚ Then chew a piece of gum every four hours for three weeks.

⊚ Don't chew more than thirty pieces a day of the 2-milligram gum, or twenty pieces a day of the 4-milligram gum.

⊚ Chew slowly until you experience that peppery taste, which takes about fifteen chews.

⊚ Then put the gum between your cheek and gum until the peppery taste has disappeared. This may take a minute or longer.

⊚ Start chewing again whenever you notice no peppery taste, then park it again.

⊚ Get rid of the gum when you can't get any more peppery taste, usually after thirty minutes or so.

Nicotine inhalers deliver a finite dose of nicotine, just as asthma inhalers deliver a fixed dose of asthma medication. The difference is that the nicotine inhalers are often used to mimic the hand-to-mouth habit of smoking, with low nicotine levels delivered to the buccal mucosa of your mouth (that skin by your gums). Most smokers use the inhaler for about three months and then taper their use over another three months. This method can be irritating to the skin on the inside of your mouth, nose, or throat, and may cause a little stomach upset or cough. These side effects go away when you stop using the nicotine inhaler.

Nicotine sprays are another option, with eight to forty inhaled doses per day, but not more than five inhalations per hour. Each dose delivers 1 milligram of nicotine. Most smokers use this method for three months. Asthma sufferers should avoid nicotine sprays, as they can make the chronic lung disorder worse. General side effects include coughing, sneezing, watery eyes, and nasal irritation.

Bupropion (brand name Zyban, if in higher doses) is a pill that can be started two days before the quit date, then taken for eight to twenty-six weeks while the person attempts to quit. This medicine works on the brain's receptors to decrease nicotine cravings while improving mood and preventing the weight gain that people often experience when they quit cigarettes. Don't take bupropion if you have an eating disorder; it can cause seizures. Bupropion is given at a daily dose of 100 milligrams for three days, then morning and evening for eight to twenty-six weeks. This medicine gets released slowly. This drug should not be used without a serious discussion with your doc in individuals with seizure disorders, as it can lower the seizure threshold. It also should not be given to people with brain tumors or to those taking MAO (monoamine oxidase) inhibitors—a type of antidepressant. Adverse reactions include headaches, dry mouth, insomnia, tremors, and skin changes.

When you combine an extra thirty-minute walk for thirty days before and every day after quitting and add thirty minutes of weight lifting every week after you've quit, we find that sixteen- to twenty-five-year-olds gain an average of six pounds and three pounds, respectively, in the first month. The men end up two pounds heavier after six months and the women two pounds lighter. The weight gain often comes from enjoying the taste of food again and from substituting food in the mouth for a cigarette in the mouth, out of habit.

(Nicotine patches and gum are not approved for use in people under age fourteen—and Zyban is not approved for quitting smoking in people under eighteen—but neither are cigarettes. We strongly recommend you get help from a medical professional to kick the tobacco addiction.)

But can't smoking help me lose weight? And won't I gain weight when I quit?

Contrary to what some people believe, cigarettes do *not* speed up metabolism. But they do not help you lose weight because you cannot taste food. When you eventually try to quit, you will run the risk of gaining weight as many people substitute food for cigarettes and end up eating more than their energy needs would demand. The trick? Don't start smoking in the first place, so you don't need to worry about quitting. This strategy is far simpler and a lot less expensive. If you're already a smoker, then try all the strategies above.

★ FANTASTIC FIVE: STEPS FOR SUCCESS ★

1. **Identify any addictions you may have.** If you have a mild or full-blown addiction, the first step to beating it is admitting you have a problem.

2. **Avoid toxic environments and temptations.** Surround yourself with people who have healthy habits and avoid situations that have the potential to trigger your addiction. To help change addictive behavior, remove yourself from environments that trigger your cravings. For instance, if impulsive overeating is your downfall, don't walk or drive past the Dunkin' Donuts; take the slightly longer route home.

3. **If you are addicted to something, seek help and find a buddy to help you.** The lure of addiction is too powerful to go at recovery alone.

4. **Solo work:** Think about a healthy "addiction" (for example, reading, playing a musical instrument, chess) that you could substitute for an unhealthy addiction. Does it trigger any negative addictive behaviors? (For instance, playing music only when you are high.) Figure out how you can substitute healthy ones for harmful ones.

5. **Discussion:** Do you know someone who's addicted to something? What strategies would you use to help him or her?

The Drug Deal
Learn the Ins and Outs of What Makes You High and Low

The Drug	The DL
Alcohol	Many use alcohol to ease anxiety or to self-medicate if they don't feel good about themselves or feel depressed. The downside: Alcohol is a depressant, so that the temporary camouflage of one's feelings does not help and, in fact, can lead to lower self-esteem, lower education and job potential, and poor choices that you wouldn't have made otherwise. Studies show that guys who started drinking by age thirteen are 5.5 times more likely to become alcoholics.
Marijuana	The active ingredient is delta-9-tetrahydrocannabinol (THC), which works on cannabinoid receptors in the brain, including the hippocampus and the cerebellum. The latter area helps your sense of balance, which is why a pot smoker's reflexes are off (as are his driving skills) when he is high. Chronic use of marijuana blunts your short-term memory, making it hard for you to remember simple things. Chronic users also may experience long-term memory loss, lack of motivation, poor sperm development (the little guys may swim sideways or in the wrong direction), and gynecomastia (breast development in guys).

The Drug	The DL
Nicotine	Nicotine is absorbed not just by your lungs but also through the membranous lining of your gastrointestinal tract, mouth, and gums. Smoking just one cigarette delivers 1 mg to 3 mg of nicotine to your system; this is quickly absorbed by the nicotinic acetylcholine receptors in your brain. But it's not just the nicotine that's hazardous to your health; you also absorb tar, carbon monoxide, radioactive polonium, benzopyrene, and other toxins and hydrocarbons that cause inflammation in your body. Long-term effects include prematurely aging skin; decreased enjoyment of sex due to impotence and decreased orgasm sensation; memory loss; risk of cancers of the lung, mouth, bladder, breast, and numerous other sites; emphysema; heart disease; and many other ailments. The nicotine is the addictive substance, but the hydrocarbons you inhale when smoking or absorb when using smokeless tobacco are what damage your body.
Inhalants	Inhalants are chemicals that you breathe in (called "sniffing" or "huffing") to get a buzz. The problem is that they interfere directly with the flow of oxygen to your brain by way of the bloodstream, and when used frequently, can actually kill off brain cells. Inhaling nitrous oxide, also known as laughing gas, can result in so little oxygen delivered to the brain that the user has a seizure (called "rabbiting," because the person falls over and may shake his legs like a rabbit). This can lead to brain damage or death.
Uppers	Stimulants make you feel restless and agitated, dilate your pupils, and make your heart race so that you feel you can leap tall buildings in a single bound. At the same time, your blood pressure can rise dangerously high, your heart can race to the point of generating chest pain, and you can temporarily lose your appetite; that is, until you come off the drug, at which time you may eat to make up for lost meals. During and after using, you may not be able to sleep, and if you take stimulants chronically, you may feel confused, depressed, and paranoid, as well as experience hallucinations, or sensations that are not actually happening. Stimulants cause sudden death, as your heart can be overstimulated to the point of cardiac arrest. Stimulants also rob you of cells in the enjoyment centers of the brain over time. Examples: cocaine, crack cocaine, amphetamines, methamphetamines, prescription and OTC diet pills, ADHD medicines.

Ecstasy	Also called X, Eve, the love drug, and other names, this drug is known as MDMA in medical circles and acts like both a hallucinogen and a stimulant. Psychedelic effects include sensory enhancement and distorted perceptions, often without overt hallucinations. Physically, the heart races, pupils dilate, blood pressure goes up and body temperature rises, triggering potential dehydration and possible heat stroke. Users can get confused and paranoid, depressed, or anxious, and may even suffer panic attacks. Use can cause muscle spasms, followed by muscle breakdown (rhabdomyolysis). The way ecstasy works is by sending a surge of the neurotransmitters serotonin and dopamine into your brain. The serotonin part makes you feel so euphoric that you love the wall, your neighbor, your neighbor's dog, and so forth. The dopamine makes you feel no pain, so you can be dancing on a broken ankle for hours without realizing it. In the long term, ecstasy can kill neurons, literally creating holes in your brain.
Downers	Use of these depressants—benzodiazepines (chill pills), barbiturates (downers), methaqualone (Quaaludes)—can cause central nervous system sedation, pinpoint pupils, disorientation, slurred speech, and a staggering gait. Chronic misuse can bring about respiratory problems, low body temperature, coma, and death. You can also see the opposite of the intended effect when used for a long time: Instead of chilling, the person gets hyper, easily excitable, and, if using methaqualone (Quaaludes), disinhibited.
Hallucinogens	These are drugs that cause hallucinations, distorting your perception of reality. Some hallucinogens also cause rapid, intense mood swings; for instance, from intense pleasure to even more intense fear, also known as "a bad trip." These drugs disrupt the interactions of nerve cells and the neurotransmitter serotonin.

For more detailed descriptions of these and other drugs, see www.nida.nih.gov.

PART FOUR

Who Are You?

What You Will Learn

◎ How we form perceptions about ourselves

◎ The science of mirror neurons

◎ How to work through identity issues, sexual
and otherwise

14

Discovering You

What makes you *you*? Good question, isn't it?

Oh, we know all the basics: name, age, gender, hairstyle, clothes preferences, favorite music, and so on. And, yes, all these things are a part of your identity. Actually, *everything* is a part of your identity, including many of the things that we talk about in this book, such as issues of appearance, what kind of relationships you have, your body shape, how you handle stress, and everything in between. In a way, this book is really not only about improving your health but also helping you to find your way during these formative years.

That's why we'd like to take a little time to discuss just that: your identity. We'll explore how you find out who you are—not just on the surface but deep in the pit of your soul. Of course, a short chapter isn't going to solve every issue, nor will it solve every mystery, because, one, identity is a pretty vast subject, and, two, it's not static—you're expected to change, grow, and develop throughout your lifetime.

What we'd like to do here, however, is give you some things to think about, especially in terms of our favorite subject: you.

The Biology of Identity

You know what's funny? Most of the pop culture world has it exactly wrong when it comes to trying to figure out the teen psyche. Conventional wisdom tells us that adolescents are more troubled than an engineless car. Right? That's all we hear: raging hormones, out-of-control mood swings, lots of angst, conflict with family, irrational, emo.

That's just the way it is, they say.★

But is that really true, that adolescence is inherently a time of storm and stress?

No.

New studies show that about 80 percent of adolescents don't go through the so-called teen turmoil; they relate well to their families and peers, and they are pretty comfortable with their cultural and social values. And that's good news, because relationships and values provide the foundation for how you establish your identity.

Speaking biologically, adolescence is undeniably a time of transition, in terms of how your brain develops, your body develops, and your psyche develops. At this time in your life, it's perfectly normal to try out different personalities and roles, defining for yourself what feels comfortable and what does not. You may try a new hairstyle or hair color, a new wardrobe, a new club or activity, a new group of friends. But underneath it's important to have a strong sense of self; otherwise you run the risk of

---

★ By "they," we mean what you tend to see and hear in the news—the reports of teens in trouble or doing bad things. It's not newsworthy to report on someone who gets along with her parents, earns decent grades, and holds an afterschool job.

losing your individual identity and becoming a shadow of your peers, or withdrawing from others.

So, then, the question is: How do you develop that core identity?

There are three ways that young people develop into adults, and they're all interconnected. Although you can take different pathways, all potential pathways influence one another:

- **Biological processes** produce changes in your physical nature and include genes inherited from parents, brain development, height and weight gains, changes in motor skills, and the hormonal changes of puberty.

- **Cognitive processes** refer to changes in your thinking abilities, intelligence, and language. Putting together a sentence, memorizing a poem, mastering trigonometry, imagining what it would be like to be a movie star, and solving a crossword puzzle all involve cognitive processes. Tempted to jump out a window because it looks like fun? Your executive function, or frontal lobe processing, would help you figure out whether it is a first-floor window and safe or whether it's a recipe for a broken leg (or worse).

- **Social and emotional processes** involve changes in your relationships with other people, changes in emotions, and changes in personality. An infant's smile in response to a parent's touch, an adolescent's joy at seeing a favorite band perform on stage, your relief when your classmates stop calling you your least favorite nickname, or the trauma of getting cut from the team all reflect the role of social-emotional processes in development.

All three processes make up who you are, and all can work together to help refine your personality traits and define your core values as you move forward in life.

What may surprise you, however, is the body part that ties all of this together: your eyes.

Now, we don't mean that in the literal sense, Mr. Blue Eyes. We mean that your eyes really serve as the bridge between you and the outside world. Sound a little heavy? It may be, but let us explain.

When it comes to identity, your vision of yourself comes in two forms: how you see yourself and what you see in others.

A lot of us tend to think that our eyes are video cameras that record life as it is, and our brains process the world through fact—this is that and that is this, blue is blue and red is red. If that sounds like a line from Dr. Seuss, we apologize. But the reality isn't so simple. The minute our eyes see something, our brains attach meaning to it, and that meaning is influenced by countless things, including our previous experience, the environment we grow up in, what our parents taught us when we were young, as well as our current state of mind. What we think we see is heavily influenced by what we expect to see given our past and present circumstances.

Just as our perception of the world around us *is* our reality, so is our perception of ourselves, even if nobody else sees the same thing. The classic example is of a person who thinks she's fat when not one other person on the planet would think that. It doesn't matter what you tell her; she literally *sees* herself as fat. Or how about the zit that looks like a volcano to you but is hardly noticeable to anyone else? Just about every adjective you can use to describe yourself—whether it's based on your appearance or your personality—is based on your own perception, not some universal truth. This can be a little mind bending, to be sure, but the interesting thing is that it means you can change your reality by changing your perception of it. Remember how hot you used to think that guy in Spanish class was, and now you think he's a total dork? We rest our case.

Now, keep in mind that your feelings play a huge role in how you see yourself. For example, if your cup is naturally half empty, meaning that you're generally pessimistic rather than optimistic, you can consciously change that lens and work at seeing things in a more positive light. It can be easy for some and a hard-learned skill for others.

Try this activity: List something that is getting you down, and try to find a positive spin. For instance, "I'm going to flunk this test, so I might as well not study," can be changed to "I'm not going to do well on this test if I don't study, but I might do okay if I work on these areas today and try to master it." This power of positive thought helps shape how you want the world to see you—something our buddies at HealthCorps call the "Brand of You."

Think of Tiger Woods: His brand has changed from star athlete to the star of tabloids, and he has lost some of his big clients due to that tarnished reputation. How do you want your brand to appear? A stupid choice might not cause lasting harm, but it can sure set you back. Find ways to be true to yourself, with dignity and pride in your own natural strengths. Can't think of your own strengths? Ask family and friends what they value most about you. You can also broaden that to asking a favorite teacher, a respected coach, a family friend, or a best friend. Write down all their responses, so that you can pull the list out and remind yourself of those positives when you're going through a rough spot.

One way to think about your identity is that it's your sense of reality about yourself. As you can imagine, it's not just your own actions and behaviors that influence your identity, but it's also the interaction and relationships you have with other people. Having negative relationships oftentimes gives us a negative self-view, and vice versa. Relationships start at home. If you've been told since day one that you are stupid and ugly, that can kind of rub off, and you start acting stupid and ugly—even if you really are wonderful. If your teacher calls you a derogatory name in class, it can make school feel unsafe and not enjoyable —and certainly not a great place for learning. On the other hand, if you know that your best friend thinks you are the best thing since iTunes and always has your back, it makes that nasty teacher's words a bit more tolerable.

We all crave belonging. We crave groups. We crave approval. We crave community, whether it be in the form of friends, teams, bands, clubs, or any other group dynamic. And some teens tend to try out a lot of different groups: Which one feels better? Which one makes you feel like you? Or is your group the "anti-group"? Are you the person who prefers to stand alone, fly solo, do your own thing, without regard to who may be around? Is Solitaire the brand you want to market for yourself? Or is that just how it feels, not necessarily your choice? If the latter, figure out safe places to explore group dynamics. And if you can't think of anything, try community service—a universal group-maker, as you all share the same mission of trying to help a cause or improve others' lives. And you might actually like how it makes you feel to help.

Evolutionarily, there's a reason why we need groups: Way back when, anyone who wasn't part of a group didn't survive. And there's also a reason why our ancestors felt compelled to separate from their parents and families and move into other groups: to ensure that they wouldn't mate with a sibling. This need to separate from family and join a group still happens today, especially in the teen years.

Why is this so important? Because your groups can define your identity—one, because of that filtering process we talked about (your perception of who you are is based on your experience); and, two, because your natural, biological reaction is to take on the traits and behaviors of those in the group where you're spending your time.

How? Through a cool phenomenon involving specialized brain cells called mirror neurons. (See figure 14.1.) Here's how they work: Someone does something around you (yawns or crosses her arms), and you pick up on it and reflect back the same action. Mirror neurons—tiny, neurological video cameras—record life as it happens. They play a big part in how children learn, but they can also influence your actions and behaviors later in life, too. When you see a person performing an action, mirror neurons fire in various areas of your brain, making you want to mimic that action.

The cool thing is that mirror neurons don't fire only in response to yawns and other inconsequential bodily blurts; they also react to emotions, generating empathy. When you see someone touched in a painful way, your own pain areas are activated; when you see a spider crawl up someone's leg, you feel a creepy sensation. Social emotions such as guilt, shame, embarrassment, and lust are based on the uniquely human mirror neuron system. It's what allows you to connect with other humans—and transcend your differences

So what's the takeaway? As you might imagine, because of your mirror neurons, part of your identity is formed by the actions of people you spend time with (and likewise for the people who hang around you). While it's clear that one of life's joys is interacting with diverse groups of people, you also want to surround yourself with people who you suspect share the same values as you, because you'll help reinforce one another's identities through your actions, words, and even emotions. That's one of the reasons why your parents have such a strong interest in who you friends are.

Figure 14.1 **What We See, What We Do** Mirror neurons process what we observe in the world so we mimic that same action; they're why we yawn when we see others doing it. Mirror neurons play a big role in how we establish our identity in that we tend to engage in the same behaviors as the people in the groups around us.

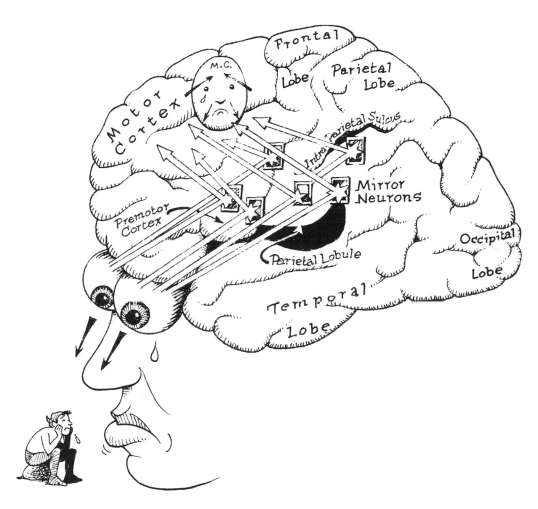

It's good to try on different hats, as long as when you choose to settle into a group you do it with integrity and careful consideration.

Especially at a time when your brain is still growing and soaking in information about the world, one of the biggest steps for figuring out who you are is simply to recognize that your identity is influenced by many things, and one of your jobs is to figure out where *you* feel like *you* fit.

The YOU Qs
You Ask, We Answer, You Decide

I don't really know who I am and what I'm about. What can I do to sort that out?

Part of the journey of finding out who you are involves *finding what we like to call "your authentic being"*—that is, the core of who you are beyond your basic personality traits. We can't answer that question for you, but we can give you two bits of advice.

One, find your passion. We don't care whether it's music or sports or art or surfing or photography or science. Find it, feel it, join others who share your passion, and pass it on to others who are open to it. It's a wonderful process trying to find the thing (or things) that jazz you to the bone and that you look forward to the days you get to do that. When you come across yours, you'll know it. And you'll be a changed person because of it.

Two, carve out some time to help someone else. There are few feelings in the world that surpass that of knowing you've helped someone—maybe mentoring a younger student or volunteering with your family at a local charity event. It feels good and *is* good. So good, in fact, that some researchers have found that the effect of giving is similar to the so-called runner's high, prompting a stream of the feel-good substances called endorphins. It doesn't matter if you don't have cash to spare; everyone can give the gift of his or her own time and involvement. If you need ideas, ask your school guidance counselor or some other adult you trust for volunteer opportunities. It can be a one-time deal, a simple hour out of your time, or a bigger energy investment.

My peers seem to have a life plan. I have no clue. What do I do?

Many teens don't have concrete plans for what they want to do when they grow up. Some kids have the luxury of going to college, studying whatever they want, and trying different things. Many more kids feel the need to be a bit more focused before they get to college so as not to waste precious family finances. And some feel that they don't even want to finish high school. (If you need incentive, consider that the difference in earning between a person with a high school degree and someone without is more than $10,000 a year.) It's normal not to have exact goals when leaving high school, but having a goal of getting *to* college is a great start and has lots of benefits, like more flexibility of job choices and greater lifetime earning potential.

So if you don't know what you want to do, try to focus on where you want to go to college as a first step. Do you like a big city? Small city? Rural setting? Do you want to be a big fish in a small pond, or a small fish in a big pond? Do you want college to be the same size as high school, or so big that you will never know everyone? If you want to see some familiar faces but still have the chance to meet new people, try a medium-sized school, one with 4,000 to 6,000 people. If you like the unknown and can stand a larger crowd, try a large state school (Ohio State versus Michigan, anyone?). Do you want a school more academically focused or one with more opportunities to get involved in extracurriculars? Do you want a lot of requirements telling you what courses you have to take, or do you want more freedom to decide? Some colleges have lots of mandatory core courses, while others have minimal requirements.

Not ready for college? Take a year off, but do something productive, like volunteer for HealthCorps or travel and learn a language, or take a class in a new discipline that has always interested you.

The good news is that even if you don't know what you want out of school yet, *learning what is not right for you gets you a lot closer to learning what is right for you*. Can't afford a four-year college at this time? How about working a job—or jobs, as the need requires—and taking a course or two at the local community college? Even if it takes more years to finish, you still end up a college graduate, with higher earning potential. Real-world work experience can make you more focused in your choice of classes: Want to run that hair salon you've always dreamed of? You'll likely need a business course, perhaps one on marketing, and certainly one on how to balance your accounts.

You talk about groups? How can I find a good one? And how will I know it's right?

What do you like to do? What defines you? Are you half Latino and half African American? Join both groups and savor the best of both cultures. If someone wants you to be all of one group, and nothing of your other half, figure out if that is desirable or unrealistic for you. Do you like all sides of yourself? What are attributes of both sides of your family that you cherish and respect? Can't find any? Think of caring adults with whom you can identify and "adopt" aspects of them to help you sort out which group works for you.

In school, groups often share a passion: cooking, French, robotics, sports, scouting, and so on. Out of school, groups can be formal or informal. *We advise finding groups where some or all of the interaction involves face time—those mirror neurons don't respond to text.*

There are also groups that bring together people who have shared a common trauma, such as the High Five Club for five-year cancer survivors (at Cleveland Clinic Children's Hospital), the Alopecia Areata club for those who have had a medical illness that caused them to lose all their hair, Al-Anon for family members of people with alcoholism. These groups can help turn a potentially negative experience into one where the pain is shared, along with the joys of the present and future. Service groups make you feel good, which has a positive impact on your looks and well-being, because if you feel good on the inside, your outside tends to radiate that energy in a good way. And there are also groups that are linked together through religion and/or church. The point is: Many groups out there provide the deep emotional connections between people who share passions. Chances are, you'll find yours—it usually just takes a little looking.

I feel terrible about myself. I do not feel worth much. What can I do?

Many people go through a phase of being overly self-critical. Some people, such as comic Woody Allen, devote a whole lifetime to it. Being overly self-critical can wreak havoc on your self-esteem, but there are a few things you can do to combat this.

1. Think about your best friend (and if you don't have one, think of someone you admire). List three things about them that you really like.

2. Now do the same thing about yourself. And you can't say there is nothing you like. Think about traits that you definitely have, such as your ability to be a loyal friend, or your ability to stay focused on one thing—even if that one thing is being negative about yourself. Think how great that focus could be if you could just get it stuck on something positive!

3. Write your positive qualities on yellow stickies and place them strategically in your room, in the kitchen, on the bathroom mirror, and other places you're sure to see them.

One of the ways that people develop and reinforce low self-esteem is by mentally telling themselves they're not good enough or smart enough or handsome/beautiful enough, and so forth. Drown out that negative self-talk with positive self-talk. Create a mantra, or a saying that you repeat over and over to yourself, either aloud or in your head: *I'm attractive, I'm funny, I'm a great guy.* It may be hard at first, but keep doing it anyway. After awhile, this positive affirmation will replace the negative self-image you've been carrying with you.

I'm struggling with my sexual identity. Any advice here?

Your sexual identity means whether you are attracted to guys, girls, both, or neither. Think back to the last time someone got your heart going pitter-patter and literally took your breath away. Was that person a guy? Was it a girl? Could it be either, depending on the person? Heterosexuality means being attracted to the opposite sex. Homosexuality means having a same-sex preference, and occurs biologically in at least one out of ten people. Bisexuality means feeling attracted to either gender, and may occur in as many as one-third of young adults as a phase, if not forever. Being asexual means you are not attracted to anyone and have a relatively low sex drive. This can come with overstress, some phases of chronic disease, and with certain medicines, and usually is not a permanent state.

Many people dabble in different sexual identities before they figure out which gender attracts them. Some individuals are raised in an environment where only heterosexuality is "tolerated," with other sexual preferences seen as immoral or unnatural. In fact, homosexuality and bisexuality have been around since prehistoric times with some of the greatest ancient literature glorifying same-sex preferences (ask your classics teacher—or Google—about Sappho and the Isle of Lesbos).

Some people have what's called gender dysphoria, meaning that they feel trapped in the wrong body. Even if this is so, you can still be attracted to guys, girls, or both. So, you can be a girl, feeling like you should have been born a guy, attracted sexually to girls, guys, or both. Confusing? It can be. If this describes you, it is worth talking this out, ideally with a counselor or doctor well versed in issues of gender identity and gender dysphoria (which means unhappiness or discomfort with the gender you have been assigned) so that you can come to a resolution that plays to your strengths, allows you to be comfortable with whoever you are, and leads to a healthy sexuality, no matter what your preference.

A lot of high schools now have support groups for LGBTQ (lesbian, gay, bisexual transgender, questioning) kids. If you can't go public and join a group, perhaps seek out and confide in an older person from outside your family. Be careful what you write on the internet or who you "friend" on Facebook, especially if you're not ready to be outed just yet. The internet is public space. For more info, check out www.itgetsbetter.org, www.lambda.org/youth, or www.glsen.org.

How do other brands affect my brand?

Teens and tweens mean Big Spending to many businesses: the cosmetic industry, sporting goods, junk food, to name a few. You're seen as the next potential nicotine addict, the next potential buyer of an iPad, or a Droid—or anything, really—and you can use that power to shape society. If you hear about a business that seems shady, look it up on the Better Business Bureau website—and then use Facebook, Twitter, and other social media tools to spread the word. But make sure that your facts are accurate before you hit the send button! And you should be just as careful with what you wear, because *nonverbal communication is often more powerful than what is said in words.* Clothes, hairstyles, piercings, and tattoos are part of the overall message you're sending about yourself, and you want to make sure the message is the right one—for The Brand of You.

★ FANTASTIC FIVE: STEPS FOR SUCCESS ★

1. **Surround yourself with peers who are aligned with your values.** That doesn't mean that everyone has to be the same—who'd want that?—but there's a great magnifying effect that happens when people are together. In simple terms, bad can feed into more bad, and good can feed into more good.

2. **Work on smoothing out any conflicts you have at home,** or take the Zen approach and learn how to let issues roll off your back. Conflict with parents can feed into your stress about your identity. It's not always easy, we know, but a strong family support system will help you find yourself, too.

3. **Learn to take a compliment.** Don't be Teflon and bounce it back off you. Let it stick, by saying a simple "Thanks!" when someone gives you one. You don't need to compliment them back, or anything else. Practice just the words "Thank you." Your self-esteem will rise when you learn to let these unsolicited compliments stick.

4. **Solo work.** Ask yourself what you want your Brand of You to be. Define it. What kind of logo would you have?

5. **YOU Activity.** Taking the following emotional intelligence test, which will gauge not only how smart you are but also how well you have a handle on your emotions.

The Emotional Intelligence Quiz

1. You're on an airplane that suddenly hits extremely rough turbulence and begins rocking from side to side. What do you do?

    A. Continue to read your book or watch the movie, paying little attention to the turbulence.

    B. Become vigilant for an emergency, carefully watching the flight attendants and reading the emergency instructions card.

    C. A little of both A and B.

    D. Not sure—never noticed.

2. You've taken a group of four-year-olds to the park, and one of them starts crying because the others won't play with her. What do you do?

    A. Stay out of it—let the kids deal with it on their own.

    B. Talk to her and help her figure out ways to get the other kids to play with her.

    C. Tell her in a kind voice not to cry.

    D. Try to distract the crying girl by showing her some other things she could play with.

3. You had hoped to get an A in a course, but you have just found out that you received a C– on the midterm. What do you do?

    A. Sketch out a specific plan for ways to improve your grade and resolve to follow through on your plans.

    B. Vow to do better in the future.

    C. Tell yourself it doesn't matter how you do in the course and concentrate on classes where your grades are higher.

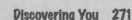

D. See the teacher and try to talk him or her into giving you a better grade.

4. Imagine that you're a salesperson calling prospective clients. Fifteen people in a row have hung up on you, and you're getting discouraged. What do you do?

   A. Call it a day and hope you have better luck tomorrow.

   B. Figure out what's wrong with you that is getting in the way of making a sale.

   C. Try something new in the next call and keep plugging away.

   D. Consider another line of work.

5. You're a student leader in a group at school that is trying to encourage respect for racial and ethnic diversity. You overhear someone telling a racist joke. What do you do?

   A. Ignore it; it's only a joke.

   B. Report it to the principal and ask that the person be reprimanded.

   C. Speak up on the spot, saying that such jokes are inappropriate and will not be tolerated in your group.

   D. Suggest to the person telling the joke that he or she go through a diversity-training workshop.

6. You're trying to calm down a friend who has worked himself into a fury at a driver in another car who has cut dangerously close in front of him. What do you do?

   A. Tell him to forget it. It's no big deal.

   B. Put on one of his favorite CDs and try to distract him.

C. Join him in putting down the other driver, as a show of support.

D. Tell him about a time when something like this happened to you and how mad you were—until you saw that the other driver was on the way to a hospital emergency room.

Answers to the Emotional Intelligence Quiz

So far, there's no single, accepted paper-and-pencil test—like an IQ test—to measure emotional intelligence, but there are situations in which it is possible to say which response is the most emotionally intelligent. How can you tell which response is best? First, you need to know the basics of emotional intelligence. Briefly, emotional intelligence means:

★ Knowing your feelings, and using them to make decisions with which you can be comfortable.

★ Being able to manage your emotional life without being hijacked by it—paralyzed by anxiety or swept away by anger.

★ Persisting in pursuing your goals in the face of setbacks.

★ Empathy: reading other people's emotions without their having to tell you what they're feeling.

★ Handling feelings in relationships with skill and harmony.

With those principles as a guide, here are the answers from psychologist Daniel Goleman, who developed the concept of emotional intelligence. This is not an emotional intelligence score, but rather a guide to raise awareness about this skill. For more info, see www.morethansound.net (above test by Scholastic and Cengage).

1. A, B, or C. Choosing D reflects a lack of awareness of your normal response to a stressful situation.

2. B is best. One of the best ways to help people who are upset is to get them to understand what is upsetting them, what they are feeling, and what they can do to change the situation or make themselves feel better.

3. A. One characteristic of emotional intelligence is self-motivation—the ability to formulate a plan for overcoming obstacles and frustrations, and to follow through on it.

4. C. Optimism, another mark of emotional intelligence, leads people to see setbacks as challenges they can learn from, and to try new tactics rather than giving up, blaming themselves, or becoming demoralized.

5. C. The most effective way to create an atmosphere that welcomes diversity is to make it clear in public that you do not tolerate offensive expressions. Instead of trying to change prejudices (a much harder task), keep people from acting on them.

6. D. One of the most effective ways to calm rage is to distract the angry person from the focus of the anger, empathize with his or her feelings and perspective, and suggest a less anger-provoking way of seeing the situation.

What You Will Learn

◎ The science of attraction

◎ The power of nonverbal communication

◎ How to identify healthy and unhealthy relationships

◎ How to manage peer pressure

◎ How to work through parental conflicts

15

That's a Good Connection

Unless you decide to pack up, hike into the woods, and live on berries, water, and elk meat, then chances are you're going to spend a heck of lot of your life with others. Lots of others. You have your family, your love interests, your friends, not to mention your classmates, your teachers, your teammates, your pets, and the hundreds—if not thousands—of other people you'll interact with as the years go by. While at times hitting the woods may sound pretty appealing, there is something to be said for civilization, and we do get a sense of fulfillment when we contribute to it, whether by sharing our talents and skills or by developing relationships with organizations and individuals in our communities.

Sometimes those relationships are wonderful; sometimes they hurt more than a thumbtack in your ear. Some relationships are in person and some exist through the blogosphere, Facebook, and Twitter. Sometimes you have relationships with people you don't want to have them with, and sometimes you want relationships with people who'd rather go to the dance with their Xbox than be with you. So it's no wonder that your connections with other people—romantically and otherwise—can be the source of some of your most serious stresses. As a result, the whole notion of relationship health is actually important to your own health and happiness; the better your relationships, the better your health and the stronger your emotional state of mind.

In this chapter, we're going to take you through the science of how you're attracted to people, what happens to your body biologically when you do find a connection, and even how you use your body to communicate to the people you care about most.

The Biology of Attraction and Relationships

Chances are, at this point in your life, you've changed relationships just about as often as you've changed shoes. That's okay, and that's expected at your age. You should hang out and go out with lots of different people (as long as you treat them all respectfully and vice versa). But did you know that what makes you attracted to someone in the first place is actually a chemical process in the body?

And we're betting that you might not even be able to guess what part of the body we're talking about. It's not the heart. It's not even the body parts we covered in chapters 6 to 8. It's actually your nose.

Say what?

Yep. Attraction, at least at the very basic level, has everything to do with odor. Now, we're not talking about the kinds of odors that should send you straight to the shower; we're talking about microsmells—called pheromones—that are like dog whistles of the body. They're so subtle that you can't detect them consciously, but they're powerful enough to influence decisions about attraction.

These chemical compounds are emitted by both men and women from near sexual organs and other places you sweat, like your underarms. When you sense some-one else's pheromones (you can't smell them—you pick them up unconsciously), your brain goes on high alert, telling you to either start making heavy eye contact or to evade at all costs. Our bodies are hardwired to seek pheromones, which are produced by each of us and our potential mates. They actually bypass the logical part of your brain and go right to the part that controls emotions: your amygdala. And it makes total sense why you can't really control *who* you like; you like who you like partly because the chemicals in your body have found a match that stimulates your emotions to get, well, that tingly, butterflies-in-your-gut feeling.

Women produce different, more attractive pheromones when they're ovulating and most fertile, prodding them to go forth and multiply, which is the whole point of life, evolutionarily speaking. What's even more mind blowing is that pheromones are designed to help you attract and be attracted to someone with a different genetic makeup than you—basically to keep you from wanting to marry your brother or sister. It reflects our instinctual need to diversify the population; it's evolution's reminder that, hey, when you marry your brother or sister, your kid comes out kind of weird.

Here's how they work: Pheromones float through the air and stimulate nerves in your nose. The nerve signals are carried to your brain and trigger complicated chemical reactions that ultimately end with a question such as "Wanna hang out?" Recently, scientists have become extremely interested in this system. They suspect that the pheromone system starts with nerve cells in a pair of tiny, cigar-shaped sacs called the vomeronasal organ (VNO), where the signals are first picked up. (See figure 15.1.) Located just behind the nostrils in the nose's dividing wall, the VNO is a pretty primitive structure. Nerve zero begins in the nose and ends in the brain area that deals with sexual feelings. Because this nerve is important in the sex drive of other animals, researchers have theorized that it plays a big role in our drive to have sexual or physical relationships with other people.

While the chemical reaction that causes you to be attracted to someone is out of your control, that doesn't necessarily mean that you'll fall in love with that person or that you'd even connect with that person on any kind of deep level. But if that attraction does develop into something deeper, your body actually changes. Not just in the tingly way that you feel when you're in love, but in a hormonal way, too.

Figure 15.1 **Animal Sense** One of the most powerful odors humans give off is one you can't even consciously smell: Pheromones send out subtle signals to potential mates about attraction. We sense them through a nerve called the VNO (or Nerve Zero) and they play a role in determining who we find attractive.

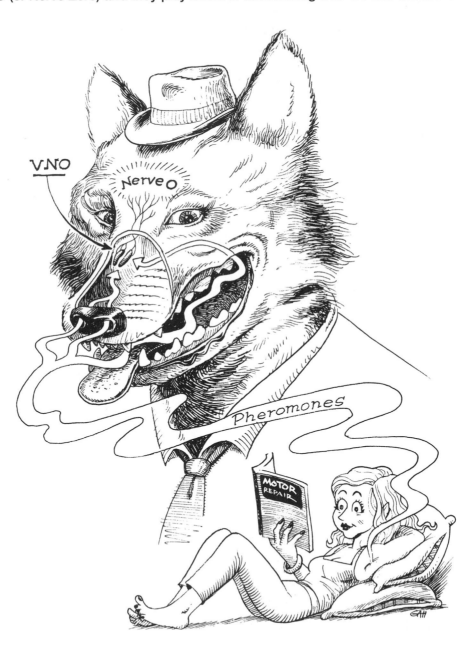

It's true: MRI images show that two parts of your brain—the caudate nucleus and the ventral tegmental area—light up like a movie marquee when you're in the romantic phase of love. (See figure 15.2.) Why? Because of the love potion ingredient called dopamine, which also happens to be the addictive substance we talked about in chapter 13 that's released by sugar, sleep, heroin, and tobacco. When you're in love and nurture that relationship, your brain pumps out this feel-good chemical. Dopamine drives reward-seeking behavior or craving and increases your brain cells' release of the euphoria hormone serotonin, so the better you feel, the more you want. That's why you want to spend every minute with that person—you literally become addicted, not to the person but to the experience of being in love: Your body wants more, more, more, more dopamine through that connection.

Dopamine and serotonin are high when you're in "romantic" love, which explains why when you're without your loved one, you become lovesick. Being lovesick actually makes serotonin levels drop 40 percent—down to the same level as people with obsessive-compulsive disorder. Being in love, by contrast, triggers the increase of happy chemicals, including serotonin, which is why we feel happy when we're in a good relationship.

As is characteristic of other addictions, you develop a tolerance to dopamine over time, which is why relationships can lose some of their luster after a while. Healthy relationships aren't always great, but if you're always feeling bad, that's not a good sign. That's why feeling unhappy in a relationship might be a sign that it's not a healthy relationship. But hormones don't only play a role in our romantic relationships; they also come into play when we're developing or nurturing relationships with family and friends.

There's also another hormone in particular we want you to be familiar with: oxytocin. It's a powerful chemical that makes you feel intimacy and community, it's what bonded you to your mother when you were born and also what makes you feel a sense of comfort and belonging—when, for example, you sing at church. When we're in good relationships, romantic and otherwise, we release oxytocin, which suppresses the stress hormone cortisol, and that is part of what helps us feel good. It's why you want to be with your best friend, why you feel good sitting in the classes of teachers you like, and why (yes, you can admit it) it matters to you that your parents

Figure 15.2 **This Is Your Brain in Love** Feel-good hormones like dopamine and oxytocin contribute to that in-love feeling you can experience.

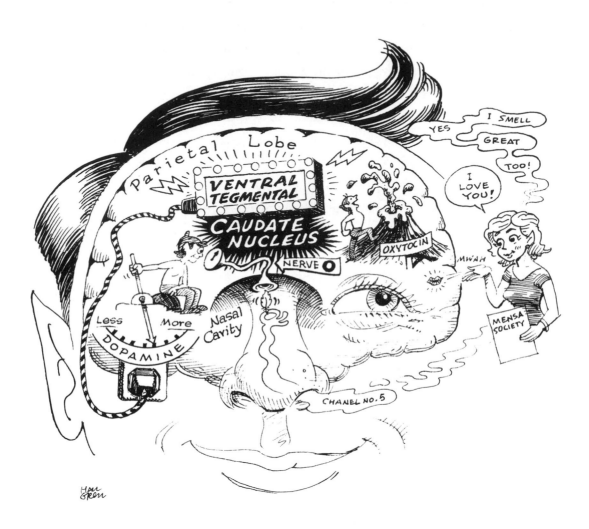

care for you so deeply. You're connected. This oxytocin-mediated feeling of being connected to other people is one of the most important chemical processes that goes on in your body. Being connected to others—family, friends, and so on—has been shown over and over to be a vital component for maintaining not only a healthy sense of self but also a healthier body, particularly because of the stress-reducing effects of relationships.

In addition to chemistry, a lot of what bonds two people together are the things you know about: common interests, personalities that just click, the fact that you and your best friend went to kindergarten and have been hanging out together ever since. What we talk about and what we do together become the shared experiences that strengthen relationships throughout our lives.

Nonverbal Communications

A big part of how those relationships grow and thrive (or don't grow and don't thrive) is through communication (or lack of it). What we say to others (or don't say), of course, is a large part of communication. There are healthy and unhealthy ways to communicate, and we'll cover that below, but many people don't pay much attention to one of the most important aspects of relationship communication: nonverbal.★

Nonverbal communication is a huge component of human interaction; our minds have the ability to understand the feelings, desires, hopes, and intentions of others through signals such as facial expression and body posture. You get home late, and your parents don't say a word but have their arms folded firmly across their chests? You're in deep doo-doo. Girlfriend looking longingly at your best friend? Uh-oh. Without a word being spoken, we can read other people and often accurately assess which of the six basic emotions—happiness, anger, surprise, disgust, sadness, fear— they're expressing.

★ How many of you remember Ursula in the *Little Mermaid,* the octopus-like witch who takes Ariel's voice and tells her explicitly how to Get Her Man? She sings: "You have your looks! Your pretty face! And don't underestimate the importance of *body language!*"

These six emotions are hardwired in our brain, meaning that we all have the ability to operate the facial muscles that communicate those feelings, and the meanings of these expressions transcend cultures. However, a teen's brain isn't as readily equipped to interpret nonverbals as an adult's. So they are at risk of "misreading" faces, cues, and body language in general. When you show a bunch of adults a picture of a person who is afraid, 100 percent of adults recognize fear on the person's face—and on MRI scans, their brains light up in both their limbic system (the center of raw emotions) and their frontal cortex (the decision-making part). In contrast, only half of teens identify the emotion as fear, mislabeling it as anger, confusion, and a variety of other emotions. The point: It's easy to misread somebody else's nonverbals, and yours can be misinterpreted, too. So you need to try to pay attention to both verbal and nonverbal cues in relationships—and not assume something about another person, which can be damaging to your relationship. That's why characteristics such as tone of voice are so important in how you interact (and why misunderstandings can so easily happen in today's world of texts and instant messaging). If you're having a serious talk with someone you care about, it's always better to do it face-to-face. (One reason why you shouldn't break up with someone via text!)

If your relationships—with friends, parents, significant others—aren't working out the way you want them to, think about what your body language may be saying about you, and what the nonverbal cues are that you may be reading or misreading. Do you look someone in the eye or avoid eye contact? Do you cross your arms when someone is talking to you, a sign that may make you look defensive? Does your mom or dad pat you on the shoulder when they tell you that you did a good job on your test?

All of this is to say good relationships should increase your feel-good hormones. The flip side is that when your instincts tell you a relationship is not healthy, you should pay attention to these feelings. You should feel good about who you're spending time with, because, for one thing, you'll become like them (remember mirror neurons from the previous chapter?), but even more important, because close relationships ultimately lead to a happier and healthier you.

The YOU Qs
You Ask, We Answer, You Decide

How will I know if I'm in love?

Pheromones will clue you in that this is a person you are attracted to, but it can be hard to tell the difference from being "in lust" versus "in love." Do you have anything in common? Anything to talk about? Or is it pure animal attraction? When you are in love, *you feel at your best with the object of your affection; you feel that you can be yourself (not pretend to be someone you aren't) and be valued for it.* A "soul mate" is someone with whom it's safe to be vulnerable; you can share your feelings and intimate thoughts without fear of ridicule or betrayal. It is someone you trust, someone who will treat you with respect all the time, not just some of the time. If some of these things are true but not all, you may be in lust, or even in love with the wrong person. Look further for the right person.

I really like the person I'm seeing, but we argue all the time. What should we do?

Almost all people have differences of opinions—in fact, life would get boring otherwise. How you handle an argument can make or break a relationship however, and not all of us get great role modeling at home on this one; remember, nonverbals contribute a lot to communication. In an argument, is your significant other belittling you? That's a bad warning sign and can do awful things to your self-esteem. Does he or she threaten or hit you? That should be a relationship deal breaker. People may modify their habits, but that one is a learned behavior that is incredibly hard to change. You can't divorce your parents, but you sure can choose what sort of behaviors you tolerate in a significant other.

Does your partner listen and let you get your viewpoint out? Do you afford him or her that respect and courtesy? This is a learned skill, and a useful one. *Just like learning to play a sport or musical instrument, it definitely takes practice,* as it is not intuitive to most of us when the stakes are high and our emotions are turned up in volume.

Here are some simple rules for argument engagement:

◎ What do you want to get out of the argument?

◎ What do you *not* want to have happen?

◎ What does your partner think? Try to listen first, before responding, and make sure your partner knows that his or her viewpoint has been received loud and clear. A good way to communicate this is to reflect it back, "What I'm hearing you say is . . ." Put yourself in the other person's shoes before speaking.

◎ What can you agree on?

How do you know if you're in an abusive relationship?

Red flags of an abusive relationship include *irrational and jealous accusations, stalking behavior, threats of violence*—basically, one partner exerting control over another through direct or indirect threats. A guy might tell a girl which friends she can go out with; a girl might threaten a guy that she's going to leave him if he doesn't buy her a new outfit or if he talks to his ex-girlfriend. Although guys can be the victims in abusive relationships, statistically, more guys beat up girls than vice versa. Girls may be just as hurtful, but with words more frequently than with fists. Both physical and psychological abuse can inflict significant damage and have no place in a healthy relationship, whether it's hetero or same-sex.

Healthy relationships are ones of mutual respect; for instance, you never criticize a friend in public and always have his or her back. Unfortunately, many young people stay in abusive relationships because they fear being abused, think the partner will change, or even because they think they'll never find anyone else. We know it can be difficult, but part of growing up is learning how to set boundaries—and this goes for both romantic relationships and friendships (which can be abusive too). No should always mean no. And if you are not sure how respectful a partner or friend may be of your no, do not get yourself into private situations with him (or her)—and keep your clothes on!

And what about peer pressure? How can I tell if I'm giving in to peer pressure versus making my own valid decision?

Peer pressure is when another person or a group pressures you to do something that may not reflect your own wishes or values. The pressure can be subtle: an unspoken understanding that if you don't take a drag on that cigarette, you will become persona non grata in this social circle. Or it can be overt, as when everyone at the party starts chanting "Chug! Chug! Chug!" and won't stop until you do. Many people put their friends' needs, whims, and demands above their own. Sometimes this can be noble and altruistic, as in doing something nice for a friend who is going through a hard time. But at other times, the requests may do you more harm than good. *The trick is knowing which is which—and keeping yourself out of harm's way while being able to take some safe risks.* Peer pressure occurs when you throw that rational side of you out the window at your own expense—and sometimes with life-threatening consequences. Case in point: Imagine a fatal drunk driving accident when you should have known better than to let that friend drink and drive, but all your friends were drinking and driving, and you didn't want to be a killjoy, so you went along with the crowd.

If faced with a situation where you may be experiencing peer pressure, here are a couple of hints. If a friend wanted you to jump out of a window, would you do it? When you find yourself in a risky situation, ask: Is the request logical? Does it make sense? Would you do it without the friend being there? What are the downsides of your choice? The upsides? Is it a safe risk? It is okay to say, *No! I value life more!* or just say no to peer pressure. In fact, sometimes you will gain more respect for not making the stupid choice, but there's no way to know that in advance. Sometimes this is easier thought out in retrospect. One hint: If your heart rate flares, it's probably a sign that you're nervous as well as excited, and maybe you need to take note of that sensation. When making decisions, it is best to take a deep breath and make sure that your decision is right for you, rather than making one on an impulse. Oftentimes the answer is an early exit: If you can see where a situation is leading, maybe you'd be better off leaving rather than waiting to see what happens next.

Parent trouble. Big-time. They just don't get me. What can I do?

Well, they're probably a little bit frustrated (they don't want you to grow up too fast), a little bit sad (they know that you are growing up), and quite a bit anxious that you avoid the pitfalls of adolescence so that you can go on to be a happy, healthy adult, which is every caring parent's dream for his or her child. That said, there are certainly some communication styles that work better than others if you want to keep things smooth between you. Some ideas:

- If you fight a lot, it helps if you and your parents can give yourselves a timeout similar to the ones they may have given you when you were a kid. Surely you remember: when they removed you from a situation so that you could calm yourself down. This timeout allows all of you to *step out of the heat of the moment and really think about what you want to discuss.* Taking yourself out of the hot state we talked about in chapter 8 into a more rational cold state will work better for all of you. You may not always get what you want, but they'll be more likely to understand your point of view if you can strip away the emotion and/or attitude that often comes with arguments.

- Pick your battles: It's not in your best interest to argue over everything, and you'll be more effective if you make your case when there's something you *really* want at stake. And try to be sensitive to stresses in your parents' lives: Don't raise a touchy subject when they're rushing off to work or have just come home from a draining day taking care of your sick grandmother.

- The best way to get "stuff" or "privileges" is not to make demands or tell your parents that everyone else is going to the [name pop star] concert and they're being unfair by not letting you go too. Rather, offer to earn what you want, and you'll earn your parents' trust at the same time. Is there a set of weekly chores that you can do, such as taking out the garbage or washing the dishes or walking the dog or doing the laundry? Taking on household chores puts credit in the parent bank that you can draw on later. Also, never underestimate the power of manners. A little friendliness or even asking your parents about their day can go a long way toward understanding one another and maybe even bring you closer.

◎ If you just can't see eye to eye with your parents, seek out another adult who can give you the support you need without all the emotional baggage—perhaps a relative, teacher, coach, employer, guidance counselor, or spiritual leader. It's important for you to have mentors and good relationships with adults for many reasons (including enjoying the benefits of oxytocin).

Where do I find friends who would be a good fit for me?

What are you passionate about? Are there clubs in school or groups outside of school that support that passion? What about finding people at a temple, church, mosque, or other religious organization? Common values can provide a good basis for a friendship. Another surefire way to make friends is to unify around a good cause, such as a community service project. *Doing something for others actually can get your own feel-good neurotransmitters going,* giving you a surge of serotonin and dopamine.

Also, take a step backward in order to take a big look forward. In five years, where do you want to be? What do you want to be doing? Is the group you are trying to be best buddies with going to be on that same path? Will they help get you there? Sometimes having a long-term goal can help you find your crowd.

One of my teachers has never liked me. What can I do to mend the fences without looking like a kiss-up?

Be positive. Do your best. Turn in your homework on time. Save the wisecracks for a different class, or even better, off campus. *Don't sit next to the biggest troublemaker in class*. Unless it's assigned seating; then you're in trouble. You can ask the teacher if you can be moved to sit next to someone less distracting. Or you can learn to tune the troublemaker out.

What's the difference between a coach who's just being tough and one who's crossed the line?

A coach who's being tough sets high expectations for you and believes in your ability to meet those expectations. A coach who crosses the line can come in different forms: the verbally abusive kind and the physically abusive kind. *Inappropriate coaches resort to bad parenting strategies: name calling, insults, and verbal and mental abuse.* Inappropriate physical abuse can be contact of any kind. That includes anything sexual between coach and player, as well as hitting, beating, or slapping a player. If that's happening, help yourself and your teammates: Tell the school principal, or guidance counselor, or another school official, and make sure that your parents know. If you don't speak up, you're putting other kids at risk of being abused as well.

My parents sometimes criticize me about my tone of voice even though I don't say anything wrong. Why can't they deal?

Think about your nonverbals—gestures, eye rolls, even the way you fold your arms. *Every nonverbal move or action goes a long way toward communicating your emotions to others.* When you consider that 90 percent—*90!*—of our communication is conveyed nonverbally, you realize that how we gesture can be as powerful as what we say. The two parts of the brain that control this kind of communication are the amygdala and the cingulate gyrus, for those of you keeping score.

What do you recommend be done about bullies at school?

Always enlist your friends—there's support in numbers. And maybe your parents. You should talk to your parents—not so that they'll step in, necessarily, but so they can give you some strategies that will work for you. If you fear being beaten up, enroll in some martial arts classes to gain some skills. If you fear name calling and lack of respect, you'll actually get more respect in the long run if you stand up to the bullies. Another strategy: Ignore the bullying and try to project a feeling of self-confidence. Most bullying is done to get some kind of reaction, and most bullies won't pick on those who project strength.

If these solutions don't work, you may need to get adults involved to put an end to a problem that can have some damaging long-term effects. We know it can be hard to approach adults about bullying, because you may fear being ridiculed, but *find your courage.* You may prevent some other kid from being beaten, or even killed, by helping to raise school awareness that your school is not currently a safe place. Use the power of your voice to tell about what's really going on. Also note that most bullying occurs when there's no supervision, so the easiest form of prevention is to be with others (peers and otherwise) when you're moving around. Recent attention has also focused on the bystander—another casualty of bullying, but one with the opportunity to make a huge impact. If you're the bystander, intervene in a proactive way: Get help, tell a teacher, adult, or policeman. Call 911. Don't just stand there, do something! Doing nothing allows the bully to take something from you, too—by leaving you powerless at the sidelines. Take back your power. Take a stand. And end bullying.

What about cyberbullying?

Cyberbullying, aggressive or insulting behavior in electronic form, is invisible and potentially deadly. New data show that one out of four adolescent victims of cyberbullying fear for their safety. Kids have committed suicide over cyberbullying, and adults have not been guilt-free in this either. *If you (or someone you know) are being cyberbullied, get him help*—that could mean changing his Facebook account, telling adults, even reporting harassing behavior to the police (who can help with restraining orders if need be, for textual harassment). Change your internet use patterns, or help a victim change her patterns. That can mean changing your Facebook address and only friending people who are actually nice to you and whom you know personally. You can change from Yahoo to gmail or vice versa, go online at different hours than you previously did, and not respond immediately when someone is being hostile. In fact, never hit Send in the middle of strong emotions—if the emotions are negative, hostile, or angry, it is always better to cool down before hitting that button.

My parents always tell me to "be safe" online. What exactly does that mean?

Well, for one, it means that there are a lot of crazy people out there who like to prey on the innocence and perhaps naiveté of some younger folks—meaning that they change their identity to try to establish an online "relationship" that could potentially lead to an in-person (and thus, dangerous) meeting. *But it also means that the internet is forever, and you should protect your reputation, too.* Posting some pictures of you doing goofy things might be fun now, but not so much when trying to get a job. Keep these tips in mind:

- Don't give out your personal information on Facebook or anywhere else in cyberspace. You do not need to share what school you go to, where you live, or any personal info.

- Don't upload photos that you would not want your grandma, college guidance counselor, school principal, or future employer to see. The internet is a tattoo that cannot be removed.

- Don't email when angry. Really!

- Don't friend someone you don't know personally. Do you really want a stalker on your site?

- Don't involve yourself in sending porn, which is prosecutable. That means no sending a breast or bottom shot to a significant other, a best friend, anyone—ever!

- Report harassing behavior. If it doesn't feel right, tell your parent, school guidance counselor, or another caring adult.

🌀 Seek help if you are feeling bullied or harassed online.

🌀 Be conscious of what Brand of You appears on your Facebook or other social media site.

What about pets?

We know all the good things that pets can bring to our homes—stained carpets aside. *But they can also improve your self-esteem and health.* Owning a dog, for example, lowers stress levels, *and* it can get you outside for a walk. But *walk* when you walk your dog; please don't walk and text!

FANTASTIC FIVE: STEPS FOR SUCCESS

1. **In any argument or conflict, try to remove yourself from the hot state** in which emotions may make you say things you really don't mean. Give yourself a timeout and agree to discuss the conflict when both sides have cooled off. It's a strategy that will serve you well now and all of your life.

2. **Find a mentor you admire and respect;** it can be a coach, a teacher, or an older sibling. The value of having someone close to you who can lead by example is a powerful one.

3. **Take a walk.** With a friend, your mentor, even your parents. (Egad!) Spend a little time working on relationships outside the context of the digital age's texts and tweets.

4. **Solo work:** If you're in a relationship, use the following list to try to identify what kind of relationship you may be in. Then think about both the positive and negative aspects of being in that kind of relationship. If it helps, write out a few of your thoughts about it.

- Romantic: Partners are thoughtful toward each other; they make an effort to make each other feel special and happy.

- Explosive: Arguments escalate, communication is offensive, strong emotions and strong reactions.

- Shaky: Trust issues, may involve betrayal or infidelity.

- Dependent: One partner feels incomplete without the other person.

- Loyal (good and bad versions):

  - Good: Monogamous, supportive partners are faithful to each other.

  - Bad: One partner refuses to leave the relationship even though it is clear that it should end.

- Adventurous: Fun couple, laughs a lot, takes part in fun activities together, has a strong friendship.

- Friends with benefits: not a committed relationship, but it revolves around physical intimacy.

5. **Discussion:** Your friend is in an abusive relationship but doesn't see it. How could you approach her to make her think about it and protect herself?

PART FIVE

In Sickness and in Health

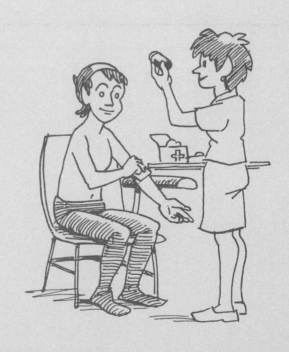

What You Will Learn

◎ How immune cells work to fend off invaders

◎ The different kinds of bodily invaders

◎ The best ways to prevent and treat sickness

16

Ill Feelings

Understand Your Immune System to Stop Getting Sick

We don't care if you're a teen, a toddler, or a dog who broke into a bag of biscuits. Nobody likes getting sick: the coughing, the aching, the chills, the runs, the view of the toilet bowl, or the umpteen other symptoms that can mess you up. Real bad.

All you feel like doing is curling up in bed, tucking your head into your chest, and sleeping for the next seventy-two hours. (Okay, maybe you feel like snoozing that long most of the time; see chapter 11.) Unfortunately, it's a fact of life that you are indeed going to experience some spells when you're feeling like a tank ran you over, pinned you up against a brick wall, and then revved its engine just for kicks. Unless you plan to live your life hermetically sealed in Saran Wrap, you're eventually going to encounter a germ and catch something.

Luckily, our bodies are built to handle this illness trauma. We actually have a biological defense system that's designed to fight off sickness—so that you can go back to your lovely life of algebra, swim practice, and g-chatting. By understanding how this microscopic army works, not only can you shorten the time that you're out of commission but also you can prevent some of the nasty buggers from ambushing you in the first place.

The Biology of Immunity

When you think of defense systems, you may think of sports, or maybe your dad questioning a potential boyfriend. Protect your valuables, defend your territory, allow nobody to score. But when it comes to immunity, think of the way that a military or security operation would protect its turf. Your many immune cells all perform specialized duties that, together, keep your most precious possession safe: your body. So let's take a look at how the immune system works.

Your body's immune cells are a little like your taste buds in that they know exactly what they like and what they don't. Typically, they like the other cells in your body, and they're not exactly keen on foreign interlopers. So when visited by a germ, such as the bacteria that causes strep throat, or even the bacteria that causes a pimple to sprout, your immune system recognizes it as a foreign substance, just as a guard would notice an unwanted intruder on a surveillance camera. *Not supposed to be here,* it thinks.

When the white blood cells of your immune system spot the foreign invader, one type of white blood cell—called a macrophage—finds the germ, engulfs it, and digests it, sort of the way a security guard would stop and question an intruder. Okay, the security guard really doesn't *eat* the intruder; he just kind of digests the purpose of why the intruder is there.

But the work isn't done yet. The intruder is just being called in for questioning, so that your body can determine whether it's a real threat or not.

To do that, the macrophage gets on its walkie-talkie and calls for backup. The message, the chemical equivalent to *"Help! Help! Intruder! Pimple forming on tip of nose! Prom's tomorrow night!,"* is an SOS to other cells, which respond by traveling through the bloodstream to the area in question. That's why wounds are red: It's the new blood supply.

While the other immune cells are en route, the macrophage takes down information about the foreign cell it has engulfed, so that the immune system can recognize it. Essentially, that information is what either puts the foreign substance on your body's Most Wanted List or waves it through security, as the macrophages let other cells know what to attack and what to ignore. As all of this information is being relayed, the backup immune cells are starting to arrive on the scene of the infection. They'll look for that mug shot to identify and obliterate harmful invaders.

This ID process is a crucial first step, because, when working correctly, it allows your body to fight the enemy and not unleash friendly fire on your own healthy cells. By the way, that's what an autoimmune disease such as thyroiditis is: when your body's cells turn on one another.

As you can see in figure 16.1, the immune cells attack in different ways, and your body has different kinds of attackers: T cells and B cells. The T cells directly attack and digest the offending culprit, while the B cells create substances called immunoglobulins that act as neutralizing defense mechanisms to tag the organism for immediate destruction. Both work together to destroy the invader.

Immune system battles leave the germs dead, but also kill the T and B cells, leaving a pool of waste—better known as pus—behind. The reason the immune cells self-destruct, in a process called apoptosis, is to ensure that those killer T and B cells don't attack your healthy cells. This waste builds up pressure under the skin, creating redness from new blood supply lines coming to battle and pus from the white blood cells responding to the scene. This is why an infected hangnail gets all red, hot, and swollen. In the case of a pimple, the waste material rises to the surface; it's the process that would happen to form the pimple. The white you see on the pimple is the remnants of an amazing immune process. By the way, systemic infections can cause fever,

Figure 16.1 **Immunity Granted** The complex immune system works a bit like your body's security guards. Some cells identify invaders, some question the invaders to make sure they shouldn't be there, and then some are in charge of getting them out of your body. The fallout of that operation often comes in the form of such pleasantries as nausea, mucus, fever, and other bodily symptoms.

which is also part of the body's defense system because it denatures enemy protein. And GI viruses cause symptoms like nausea and vomiting, which are your body's ways of eliminating the unwanted guest.

Your immune system is housed in various areas of your body, like police precincts. While invaders such as viruses and bacteria can break through the typical entranceways (mouth, nose, genitals, skin) and go anywhere they want, your security system has only a couple locations in your body. They are:

Thymus: It may sound like the name of a mythological Greek god, but the thymus is where your T cells mature. When you were a child, your thymus, which is located in front of your heart, was actually the size of your ticker. It shrinks dramatically as you age, until we can barely find it in eighty-year-olds. Presumably, this shrinkage is because you need a stronger immune response as a child, since you haven't yet been exposed to many of the viruses and bacteria that can make you sick.

Bone marrow: It would be unwise to house all of our protector cells in one area, so the bone marrow throughout the body produces the young generations of immune cells that go to battle. In particular, it stores the B cells, which mass-produce antibodies—the small molecules that ram themselves into the side of bacteria and virus-infected cells.

Spleen: Chances are that the only time you've ever heard a spleen mentioned is when a TV doctor said someone needed one removed. But the spleen, a fundamentally important immune organ, is the Starbucks of your body—it's where all the T cells get together and talk to one another. In a sense, it's a hub of immunity, where blood flows and information can be exchanged about infections that need fighting.

Lymphatic system: Remember your first sore throat, when your mom or doctor felt around under your jaw? The reason they were poking around there was because they were looking for swollen lymph nodes. Your lymph system is like the paddy wagon of your body: It hauls off all the waste material from the infection and drains it from your system. The lymph system maintains hubs throughout your body—under your jaw, in your armpits, in your groin, and many other places (see enlarged version at right). So if you infect a fingernail, for instance (Stop biting them, would ya?!), the closest hub—say, in the elbow—swells with white blood cells. One by one, they figure out where the infection is and go out to fight it. Then the remnants of the infection flow into the lymph drainage system and are recirculated to the heart.

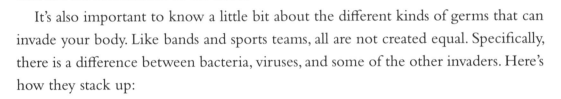

It's also important to know a little bit about the different kinds of germs that can invade your body. Like bands and sports teams, all are not created equal. Specifically, there is a difference between bacteria, viruses, and some of the other invaders. Here's how they stack up:

Bacteria: We can't live without bacteria—they help us digest food, they add nutrients to our food before we even eat it, and good bacteria help keep out the bad bacteria. The human body contains two to five pounds of outside bacteria; nearly five hundred different kinds have been identified as living on the surface of the skin alone. But like songs and reality-show characters, there are as many bad kinds as there are good kinds. Bacteria, which are single-cell organisms, are neither plant nor animal. They're actually very prehistoric organisms that lack the subtle architecture of human cells—namely, they don't even have a nucleus (the brain of our cells). In terms of size, about 1,000 bacteria fit into 1 square millimeter: about the thickness of a dime. Bacteria have the ability to replicate themselves, and that replication is what causes an infection. They replicate with amazing speed, creating as many as 100,000 offspring in one day. The result, like pimples or strep throat, can be treated with antibiotics designed to kill the bacteria. (A throat culture or rapid diagnostic test often can determine whether a sore throat is caused by a bacteria or a virus.) Bacterial infections can also be sexually transmitted, as in the case of chlamydia—one of the most common bacterial STIs, which actually has no symptoms in 75 percent of people who have it. The worry with many bacterial infections is that, if left untreated, they can cause more permanent damage to your organs. Untreated chlamydia can cause permanent scaring of your fallopian tubes leading to infertility. Uncontrolled strep infections can lead to abscesses in the tonsil and associated breathing problems, as well as rheumatic fever, which causes long-term damage to the heart, kidneys, and joints.

Viruses: The way many people distinguish between bacteria and viruses is that bacteria respond to antibiotics, while viruses don't. (Some viruses respond to antiviral medications such as oseltamivir—Tamiflu—to combat influenza and certain antiviral medications for AIDS, for example, but most viruses simply run their course without treatment.) But their main differences lie in their structure, size, and function. Bacteria are complex cells that have the ability to replicate themselves, while viruses are about one hundred times smaller, much simpler on a cellular level, and don't have the tools to replicate themselves. They need your cells to make babies, and, boy, do they use your cells! Viruses, which can be transmitted from hand-to-hand or mouth-to-mouth contact (the common cold) as well as sexually (HIV, HPV), need to spread in order to survive. When a virus attacks one of your cells, it essentially hijacks it, booting out your DNA and substituting its own, then commanding your cellular machinery to make millions of virus clones to send all throughout your bloodstream. (It's similar to how email viruses commandeer your address book and send messages to all of your friends.) The most common virus is the common cold, which is actually caused by several different families of viruses. Even though some bacterial infections do cause upper-respiratory symptoms, most cases of the common cold are not caused by bacteria—thus making antibiotics useless against the fight. In fact, taking them unnecessarily only weakens your immune system. If the illness persists, you might attract bacteria secondarily as a result of the virus weakening you; the typical sign of a secondary bacterial infection is producing unusually thick, colored mucus or sputum from your nose or throat when you cough or blow your nose. Two interesting viruses that never go away are the herpes simplex I virus, because it hides out from the immune system in neurons and can be triggered by things like stress and sun (see page 158); and chicken pox, or varicella, which also hides out in neurons and can return decades later as shingles.

Parasites: Parasites need another organism to live off of, so they require something from you to survive and to replicate themselves. A tapeworm, for example, lives in your intestine, eating the same food you eat—and it can grow up to twenty-two-feet long, or about the height of a two-story building. Lice are another charming example. Parasites are most common in unsanitary food and poor water supplies and are responsible for four billion cases of diarrhea around the world every year—bad news for everyone.

Fungi: Fungi, which are about one hundred times bigger than bacteria, are actually a primitive vegetable; they're small plants without chlorophyll that can't make their own food but can get it from other organisms, like your toenails. Some fungi we eat, like mushrooms and yeast in bread. And since their natural enemies are bacteria, they naturally produce antibiotics like penicillin that we can take to protect ourselves. But some can also cause ailments such as athlete's foot and vaginal infections, both of which can be treated with medication that kills the infection-causing fungus.

As you can see, the immune system is a pretty incredible biological process that controls if you get sick and for how long—and largely dictates how you feel and how quickly you can recover when you do get sick. But there are some things you can do to minimize the damage.

The YOU Qs
You Ask, We Answer, You Decide

Why can't I take antibiotics for a virus?

The vast majority of viruses do run their course and exit your body via the portholes most associated with blowing, sneezing, and coughing. *Most antibiotics—when taken for viral infection—can actually have a negative effect.* What happens is they kill off the good, commensal bacteria that keep the bad bacteria in check, so you actually end up more vulnerable to bacterial infection in the end. While it may have some sort of placebo effect by making you feel better, it's actually not helping you—and may even harm you, unless you get a bacterial infection on top of your viral one. One way to tell the difference between bacterial and viral infections: Bacterial infections usually produce thick green, brown, or yellow secretions that you cough or sneeze out; viruses can also cause secretions, but they're usually not as thick or dense or productive (meaning cough-out-able).

How come I have to take ten days of antibiotics when I feel better after a few days?

You'll probably be surprised to learn that antibiotics aren't really designed to make you feel better, though that's a darn nice side effect. They're designed to kill or incapacitate the enemy. So while you may feel better in two or three days, it's important to take the whole course of antibiotics—even if it's ten days or two weeks—*to make sure that the drug has killed all of the enemy.* If you take medication for only half its course, you may have weakened the remaining bacteria without having finished them off. And weakened bacteria actually come back stronger than before, and the new generation of bacteria may be resistant to the antibiotic, so now you won't have any weapons to use against it. When you're fighting persistent little suckers like bacteria, you need to land the knockout punch. By the way, antibiotics can kill not only the bad bacteria but also the good critters. After you finish the course of antibiotics, you can eat live-culture yogurt to repopulate your intestines with healthy bacteria, or better yet, try probiotics in pill form, which help populate the good bacteria in your gut. Choose a formulation that will survive your stomach acid, like Culturelle or Digestive Advantage or Sustenex.

So what's the best way to prevent getting sick?

Bribes, high-fives, and love notes aren't the only things that pass from hand to hand. Germs do, too. Stop a second and think about how many things you touch that other people have touched immediately before you: sink faucets, door handles, gas pumps, money machines, railings, other people's phones or hands, the cash register tape, and your sandwich. It's the most common way that infections can be passed: You touch someone or something, then your hand touches your mouth, nose, or eye. Turns out that the typical American touches his face with his hands more than fifty times an hour. The best thing you can do to prevent spreading (and receiving) germs is to *wash your hands regularly.* Soap and water will separate bacteria from your hands, and keep them from entering your system the next time you touch your mouth or nose. In times when sinks are hard to come by, it's a good idea to stash some antibacterial gel with you. Rub in a dime-sized squirt to kill bacteria. Also, make sure to cough and sneeze into the crook of your elbow, not your hands—that way, the germs won't spread when you touch something afterward. Next on the list is to manage stress, get great sleep, eat healthfully, exercise regularly, and enjoy chicken soup.

Are there foods that I can eat to stop me from getting sick?

Between your T cells, B cells, and other white blood cells, they pretty much have things under control and keep your body secure. But it never hurts to call in reinforcements in the form of specially trained nutrients that have been promoted to the rank of immune booster. The best nutrients for keeping your system secure:

Vitamin C: Take 500 milligrams twice a day every day to boost your immune system, so that it can produce more bullets to kill the invaders. You can take it in supplement form (pill, liquid, chew, and so on), as well as through foods such as oranges and other citrus fruits, 100 percent natural orange juice, tomatoes, and bell peppers.

Yogurt: Live-culture yogurt contains lactobacillus acidophilus, a healthy bacteria that makes milk become yogurt and fights off fungal infections. Better yet, try probiotics in pill form. They work by helping to prevent the overgrowth of fungi that shouldn't be able to grow in your body. Another great fungicide: garlic.

Flavonoids: The vitamin-like substances work like vitamins but aren't essential for life. Flavonoids seem to allow your immune cell memory bank to maintain the memory of old foes longer and more intensely and thus improve the performance of your immune system. Some suggestions of foods high in flavonoids: onions, cranberries, broccoli, tomatoes, apples, strawberries, oats, grape juice, and red wine (*after* you're twenty-one!).

My parents always say that OJ and chicken soup are the best foods for sickness. Are they right or full of it?

Trust Mom here. Everybody seems to have his or her own remedy for what helps cure a cold, but the truth is you can't really cure a cold; you can only speed up its course. And there have only been a few things that have been shown to really have an effect: chicken soup, vitamin C, and zinc lozenges (not zinc inhalers, as they seem to cause permanent loss of smell). Take 2 to 3 grams of *vitamin C* as soon as you feel a cold coming on, then another 1 to 2 grams every few hours for the first thirty-six to forty-eight hours. The mechanism here is unknown, but fights the infection faster. If you start after the first twenty-four to thirty-six hours, it does nothing. The difference is a two- or three-day cold rather than the standard three days to get it, three days to keep it, and three days to get rid of it. Chicken soup activates gamma interferon, which gives your immune system enough of a boost to better fight off infection. So, Jewish penicillin (another name for chicken soup) *is* good for you. Also, pumpkin seeds contain zinc—one of the minerals that's been shown to help reduce the average length of the common cold.

Why does my nose run in the winter?

You have small hairs called cilia that continually carry secretions up your nose toward your sinuses. The temperature in your nose is usually around 80 degrees Fahrenheit. (Put down the thermometer; trust us on this one.) But *it can drop during cold weather, thus paralyzing these hairs.* When the cilia cannot beat fast enough, the secretions drain down with gravity, and your nose runs.

What are the germiest things in my house?

Anything that gets *touched by a lot of people:* think door handles, phones, remote controls, computer keyboards. In addition to washing hands and disinfecting your door handles, phones, and remote controls, here's something you can do that you may not have thought of to help prevent the spread of germs: Before you flush the toilet, shut the lid. That will prevent microscopic germs from spraying up and out, eventually blanketing items on the nearby sink—including your toothbrush.

How do vaccines work?

Vaccines contain weakened, dead, or partial viruses or bacteria that stimulate your body to *develop antibodies to the specific virus that causes disease.* If you then become infected with that real virus, your body will immediately recognize it and send off its army to attack and destroy the invaders. Most vaccines are given to babies, toddlers, and children under ten, but here are a few vaccines commonly given during adolescence that you should be aware of. (Just remember—always get your vaccinations after a full night's sleep and several days of perfect food choices and daily multivitamins; never get a vaccine when you're already sick and your immune system is compromised.)

- Tdap (widely known as tetanus shot): recommended at eleven years old, then sixteen, twenty-one, and every ten years after that (and if you cut yourself with a dirty object, like a nail, if it's been more than five years since you've had a booster). It also protects you against pertussis, or whooping cough, which has come back in epidemic proportions because not enough people are getting their immunizations on time.

- Gardasil: for boys and girls ages nine to twenty-six, protects against four of the more than 200 strains of the human papillomas (HPV). The ones it targets can cause genital warts as well as cervical, throat, penile, and anal cancer. Immunity against HPV requires three doses and is most effective if given before age fourteen and before the onset of sexual activity.

- You should also have vaccines against MMR (measles, mumps, rubella), hepatitis A, hepatitis B, and meningitis, as well as the Varivax vaccine against chickenpox if you didn't receive them as a baby or child.

- Flu shot: Every year. Good for everyone, especially if you have asthma or another immune-related issue. You need the shot, not the nasal spray if you have asthma (the squirt is a live virus vaccine that could trigger your asthma).

★ FANTASTIC FIVE: STEPS FOR SUCCESS ★

1. **Practice good hand hygiene. Wash your hands or use anti-bacterial gel.** Often. The most common way germs are spread is through hand-to-hand contact (and then touching your mouth or nose). Washing away the germs regularly will help minimize the damage.

2. **Get plenty of flavonoids** (see list above)—they're great strengtheners of your immune system. Also, orange and tomato juice and citrus fruits are particularly good sources.

3. **Don't use antibiotics if you have a virus.** They can actually have a negative effect. If your parents are pushing for a prescription from your doc, educate them about why antibiotics won't work

4. **Solo work:** make a list of all the things you touch every day that other people also touch. Think about these places and use a squirt of antibacterial gel afterward.

5. **Discussion:** We've had avian flu (from birds), swine flu (you guessed it), and monkey pox (yes, it causes a rash worse than small pox and is contracted from imported animals). The next outbreak hits a town near you. How do you keep yourself safe?

What You Will Learn

- How the respiratory system works

- The basics of allergies and asthma

- The best breathing techniques

17

Breath of Fresh Air

A Primer on Allergies and Asthma

Most of us take breathing for granted. It's something that we do without even giving it a second thought (like spelling *you* as *u*). Unless, that is, you're a tuba player, play sports, are getting chased by a shark, or sit down next to your crush.

But for some people, breathing isn't second nature. For those people—those who suffer from asthma and allergies—heavy breathing can even be life threatening. In this chapter, we're going to explore how allergies and asthma work; though they're not entirely similar, they do have some overlapping biology, which makes them related.

Even if you don't currently have either of those conditions, it is smart to understand a bit about how your lungs work and how you can take care of them. With every breath you take, your lungs breathe in oxygen and breathe out carbon dioxide and a lot of other waste gases. Beautifully simple, wonderfully efficient. In Chinese medicine, lungs serve as the orchestra conductor for the entire body, setting the rhythm from which everything else follows.

No matter our age, health, or activity level, we can all learn to breathe a little easier.

The Biology of Breathing

Breathing isn't as simple as it looks. Let's look at the process—and how it falters when allergies and asthma are involved.

You probably have a good image of the way your two lungs look on the outside, but on the inside, they work a little differently than you might suspect. While you might imagine that they function like balloons in that they expand when air is inhaled, it's probably better to think of your lungs as large sponges. They're light and fluffy when filled with air, squished when the air is squeezed out of them, and they get bogged down when they get wet (as they do in some diseases) and, in those cases, don't exchange air very well.

While your lungs may act like sponges, they look like an upside-down tree—with the trunk being your trachea, or windpipe. (See figure 17.1.) When air enters your nose and mouth, it travels down your trachea, which then divides into two airways—or bronchi—that feed into your two lungs. Like tree branches, those airways break off into four, then eight, then hundreds of thousands of little airways in each lung. Those airways are your bronchiole tubes. At the end of each bronchiole is a tiny sac called an alveolus. Think of alveoli as leaves at the ends of the branches. Healthy lungs have hundreds of millions of alveoli. Each alveolus is covered with a thin layer of fluid that helps keep it supple and open as well as by tiny capillaries that surround it like a fisherman's net. Blood flowing through those capillaries absorbs oxygen

Figure 17.1 **Breathe Free** The diaphragm muscles at the bottom of the rib cage help the lungs expand to allow oxygen in and contract to push carbon dioxide out. Not only will practicing deep breathing a few minutes help improve your respiratory system, but it's also a great stress reliever.

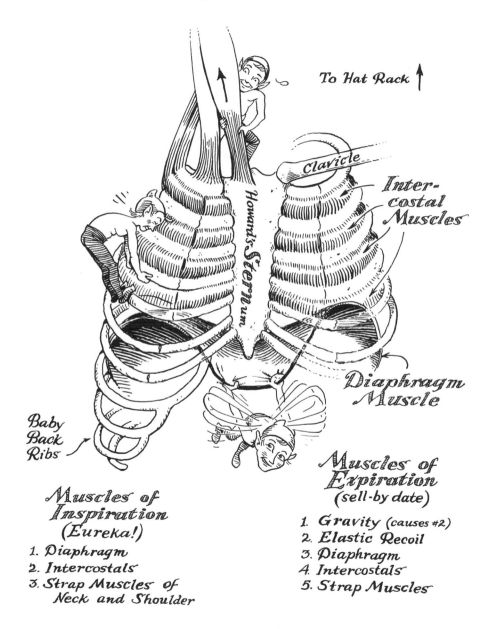

To Hat Rack ↑

Clavicle

Inter-costal Muscles

Howard's Sternum

Diaphragm Muscle

Baby Back Ribs

Muscles of Inspiration (Eureka!)
1. Diaphragm
2. Intercostals
3. Strap Muscles of Neck and Shoulder

Muscles of Expiration (sell-by date)
1. Gravity (causes #2)
2. Elastic Recoil
3. Diaphragm
4. Intercostals
5. Strap Muscles

through the moist membrane of the alveolus and passes carbon dioxide out into the lung so it can be exhaled.

To keep the gas exchange flowing smoothly, your lungs have to be maintained in good working order. Your bronchial tubes bear the main responsibility for cleaning out your lungs. Typically, they're like a four-year-old's birthday cake: covered with mucus, which traps dirt and germs. Your airways are also lined with millions of tiny hairs called cilia. These act like little brooms that sweep up to your mouth and nose all the stuff that's caught in your mucus. They're fast-action sweepers, like high-speed windshield wipers—constantly moving back and forth to clear your lungs of nasty stuff that makes its way in with every breath. Cigarette smoke kills cilia, destroying the very mechanism that's meant to protect your lungs from toxins. And that's probably the least bad thing hot air from cigarette smoke or even electronic cigarettes does to your body.

The last part of your lungs that's especially important for healthy breathing is the musculature around them. Your diaphragm is a large, flat muscle at the bottom of your chest cavity that allows the lungs to expand. We'll talk about proper breathing in a moment, but it's important to know that the movements of breathing are like other movements in your body. They're all controlled by muscles. Using your diaphragm, you can develop techniques to help you breathe more fully.

Allergies: Allergies can come in several forms—contact allergies through skin, food allergies, and airborne ones. Allergies are an overreaction of the immune system to outside invaders called allergens (see previous chapter). The pathway that airborne allergens, such as dust and pollen, travel is via the lungs, and many of the symptoms that are associated with allergies also involve the respiratory system (like runny nose and coughing).

Your nose acts like an air filter, keeping out large toxins as best it can. Unfortunately, dust and dander can sneak by, despite its best efforts. When an allergen enters the body, the body tries to protect itself by producing antibodies called immunoglobulin E (IgE). That sets off a chain reaction in which IgE sends a signal to allergy cells (called mast cells) to release chemicals that fight the allergen. When those chemicals (some are called histamines) are released into the bloodstream, they produce inflammatory reactions throughout the body, not just at the site of invasion. It's those reactions that trigger the itchy eyes, the runny nose, and the hives, among other effects.

A hypervigilant immune system moves from code green to code red as soon as it's exposed to certain (more often than not otherwise harmless) foreign substances such as dust or pollen. The allergic process kicks in, the cells start attacking, and you start feeling the symptoms. In the case of allergies, the cells pull out Uzis rather than BB guns to fight a minor pest. This kind of overreaction also causes damage in the form of allergic symptoms, which may include hives, itchy eyes, or a skin condition called eczema.

Asthma: Asthma is a kind of allergic reaction that's manifested through the respiratory system. Look at the diagram of the lungs and imagine what happens if you turn on a spigot and there's a sharp squeeze in the hose. The water can't get out of the hose and stays bottled up at the point of obstruction. It's the same thing that happens when you have decreased airflow: The hose feels squeezed and air can't get out. That's asthma. In patients with the disorder, the trouble isn't with getting air into the lungs, it's with getting air out, and it feels like a vise is squeezing the bronchus. The squeezing comes from the inflammation, which blocks the flow of air, and also from the constriction of smooth muscle in the area, which further blocks the area. During this time, the muscles in the area become red, swollen, and more likely to go into spasm—which constricts the bronchi to trap air in the alveoli (the squeeze in the hose), which causes the plastic-kazoo sound of trying to force air through the small opening.

How does it get to that point? Sometimes the blockages are triggered by an allergen (which can trigger the inflammation response), and sometimes they may be triggered by such culprits as cold air, exercise, and stress.

Once the squeeze in the hose is straightened, the water is released easily. In your airways during an asthma attack, once the obstruction is cleared—most often, through medication—air is released, and you can breathe smoothly again.

More than fifteen million Americans have asthma, and one-third are under eighteen. Asthma is a complex disease in that it can be caused by a mix of factors, including environment (like dust mites, house dander, mice, and cockroaches), lifestyle (where you live dictates air pollution levels), genetics (kids have at least a 25 percent chance of developing asthma if their parents have allergies and asthma), obesity, and exposure to secondhand smoke. All of those things may compromise your immune system and contribute to the development of asthma. It's important to note that even if you have a genetic predisposition for asthma, you can control the symptoms and the disabling effects that come from the chronic inflammation secondary to acute attacks.

Even if you don't have one of these lung-related conditions, chances are that you will find a time when you are thinking about your breathing—perhaps it's during heavy exercise or if you're in a stressful situation. While much of the discussion below is focused on specific conditions, you will find some general advice about how you can keep your lungs and entire respiratory system working in perfect form.

The YOU Qs
You Ask, We Answer, You Decide

If I get shortness of breath, does that mean I have asthma?

Actually, shortness of breath can come from a bunch of different factors. If you are out of shape, your lungs may work just fine, but you still get winded easily. If you have pneumonia, the fluid in your lungs can interfere with air exchange, making you short of breath; in addition, you would feel achy and likely have a fever and a cough.

If you truly have asthma, we can diagnose it via pulmonary function tests, or PFTs. Some pediatricians perform these right in their offices, while others send you to a pulmonologist, or lung specialist. During a PFT, you breathe out as hard as you can through a tube, kind of like blowing out a lot of birthday candles at once. *If you have asthma, you don't breathe as effectively, even with your best effort.* If your doctor performs a test called a methacholine challenge, he will have you breathe in a medicine that will make your airways twitchy (that's the methacholine) and then blow through the tube. Immediately afterward, he'll administer a medicine that will relieve the twitchiness if you have asthma, causing a great improvement in your PFTs. If this test is positive, it means you've got asthma. But have no fear: Olympic athletes can have asthma and still compete and win. The trick is to treat your asthma optimally and to prevent those airways from becoming twitchy in the first place. With properly treated asthma, you can still run fast and jump high. It should not be a deal breaker for any activities if you are doing right by your lungs, such as taking the appropriate meds and not smoking or otherwise inflaming your airways.

So there's a right way to breathe? Please explain.

Most people breathe the way they dance: They *think* they know what they're doing, but they really don't have a clue. Stop right now for a second and focus on your breathing. Now look down. See anything moving? Probably not. That's because most people typically take very short, shallow breaths; the kind that simply come from your chest. For you to really improve your lung function, you need to practice taking deep, whole breaths.

Remember what makes the lungs move most? Your diaphragm. That's the muscle that pulls down to give your lungs room to inflate, so they expand with oxygen. To learn proper breathing technique, you could take yoga lessons—where people focus as much on their breathing as they do on their ability to scratch their heads with their toes. Or you could just lie flat on the floor, with one hand on your belly and one hand on your chest. Take a deep breath in through your nose—slowly. Lying on the floor at first when you practice is important, because if you stand up, you're more likely to fake a deep breath by doing an exaggerated chest extension rather than letting your lungs fill up naturally. *Imagine your lungs filling up with air; it should take about five seconds to inhale. As your diaphragm relaxes, your belly button should be moving away from your spine. Your chest will also widen—and maybe rise ever so slightly—as you inhale.* When your lungs feel full, exhale slowly—taking about seven seconds to let all the air out.

Okay, so now you know how to breathe deeply, but what will it get you, besides stares in study hall? A lot, actually. For one, deep breathing through you nose helps transport nitric oxide—a very potent lung and blood vessel dilator that resides in your nasal passages—to your lungs, making your lungs and blood vessels function better. Taking deep diaphragmatic breaths (see below) helps your lungs go from 98 percent saturation of oxygen to 100 percent saturation of oxygen, and that little 2 percent can sometimes make a big difference in how you feel. Another

benefit is that it helps improve the drainage of your lymphatic system, which removes toxins from your body. (See page 303.) Of course, it also helps relieve stress—the deep breaths act as a minimeditation. Shifting to slower breathing in times of tension can help calm you and allow you to perform at higher levels both physically and mentally.

Our recommendation: Take ten deep breaths in the morning, ten at night, and as many as you need when shooting free throws or before a big test.

What do you do for an asthma attack?

An asthma attack—a period of time when it's extremely difficult to breathe—may last for several minutes or even up to a few days. Severe attacks can be fatal, but that doesn't mean you need to live in fear. In fact, many treatments can help asthma patients enjoy life performing all of their normal activities. First, you'll want to try to avoid the things that trigger the attacks, and/or use medicines prescribed by your doctor to prevent asthma attacks in the first place. These preventive medicines include inhaled steroids and anti-inflammatories such as Singulair (montelukast). Steroids are the librarians of the respiratory system; they prevent symptoms from occurring by telling your airways to be quiet and by reducing the inflammation in the area.

You'll also be prescribed medications to open your airways during an attack; these are the "rescue" medicines. One of the more common categories of rescue medications are bronchodilators: inhaled medications that relax the muscles in your airway so that the airways becomes larger, making room for more air to pass through. They're usually taken via an inhaler with a spacer attached, which you need to be taught how to use. Your doctor should help you develop a tailor-made asthma action plan, so that you know exactly what meds to take for prevention and for rescue, as well as when to seek emergency medical attention. Think of an asthma action plan like a traffic light: So long as the light is green, you can do everything, with no problems. Yellow means step up the plan, trouble is ahead, proceed with caution. Red means acute asthma attack, and you likely need your inhaler, a call to your doctor, and/or a visit to the emergency room if you can't reach your doctor. The goal is to stay in the green light phase, and if you have an asthma flare-up, never let it get to red light phase. If you need emergency room visits, it is likely that your asthma is being undertreated, and you need to see your regular doctor to revise your asthma action plan.

What's the best way to treat allergies?

The good news is that you don't have to suffer with allergies; you can take various over-the-counter allergy medicines, such as Claritin (loratadine), Allegra (fexophenadine), or Zyrtec (cetirizine), that keep your body from releasing histamines, the substance that triggers the whole allergic cascade of events. You can also use a nasal steroid, with two squirts to each nostril every morning. Brands such as Nasonex (mometasone), Beconase (beclomethasone), and others work just fine for this. Many people go for the quick fix with a nasal decongestant such as Afrin (oxymetazolone). This kind of medicine constricts the blood flow temporarily to your nose, but then it rebounds back, bigger than ever, causing more drippiness for the allergy sufferer. In other words, *don't go for the quick fix; go for the medicines that will stop the problem before it starts.* Many people need more than one medicine to keep their allergies in check: for instance, a nasal steroid plus a histamine blocker. Sometimes even this isn't enough; that's when you resort to other measures (like removing rugs and not sleeping with pets in the room, or perhaps not even having pets) and make a trip to the nearest store that sells hypoallergenic dust mite protectors for your pillow and mattress and box springs. These zipable covers go under your pillowcase and sheet cover, to keep the poop from dust mites from sneaking up your nose just to irritate you. With any severe allergies, often to peanuts or bee stings, you may need to keep an EpiPen on hand. This is a shot of epinephrine (adrenaline) that's delivered to help open up your airways in the event that an allergic reaction causes your throat to close if you're going through what's called anaphylactic shock.

If I have a raspy voice, does that have anything to do with what's going on in my lungs?

Hoarseness can signify actual changes to your vocal cords, the things that guard the entrance to your trachea. It's especially true in those who shout often or speak loudly. *When you constantly strain your voice, or when you smoke, you irritate the vocal cords and form scars on them.* These overgrowths can develop into polyps, which usually are not removable by surgery. This is where the ounce of prevention is worth far more than the pound of cure. If you have a chronically raspy voice, it may be worth asking your pediatrician about whether or not you need to visit an otolaryngologist, or ear, nose, and throat doctor; it may also be a sign of reflux. And by all means, stay away from cigarette smoke (and all other kinds of inhaled smoke). One homemade remedy: Pineapples—fresh, canned, or in juice—can help reduce raspiness, probably due to an enzyme they contain, bromelain, which can help soothe vocal cords.

You're not going to tell us that smoking causes lung cancer?

Seems like you—and the entire rest of the world—already know that. You know the damage it causes, you know the health risks (smoking is associated with just about every major health problem, including death), you know that it's bad. *So we don't think you need a lecture* about not even starting in the first place.

FANTASTIC FIVE: STEPS FOR SUCCESS

1. **Practice healthy breathing.** There's a real art to involving your entire respiratory system, including the musculature around the lungs. (See page 321.) It will not only help your overall breathing but also your stress levels, and even your skin tone.

2. **Avoid allergens that can trigger attacks.** It might take some work to ID what things cause you to have allergies. However, the best way to avoid the symptoms isn't to medicate but rather to avoid the triggers.

3. **Have an asthma action plan.** If you don't have one and you have asthma, ask your doctor to help you create one.

4. **Solo work:** Having specific relaxation techniques not only helps prevent asthma attacks but it also can defuse panic attacks and other stressful moments. Basically, you're training your body to behave because your mind tells it to. See if you can come up with mental imagery or a mantra that help you get into a relaxed state of mind.

5. **Discussion:** One of your classmates has asthma. What are the steps you should take if she has an attack?

What You Will Learn

◎ How food is digested

◎ How your kidney works as a filter to flush toxins

◎ Toilet-related problem and solutions

18

Teenage Wasteland

What You Flush Away Can Give You Serious Clues About Your Health

If you're like most teens, you spend a lot of time in the bathroom. Most of that time, you may be combing, brushing, washing, obsessing, not to mention scores of other *-ing* words that are better left behind closed doors. Well, we want to open that door. Not to invade your privacy, not to be gross, and not just to get in a few crappy toilet-humor jokes.

The truth is that if you strip away some of the stigma surrounding your waste products, you can actually learn a heck of a lot about the state of the most magnificent biological system there is: your body. That's because what happens in your digestive and urinary systems greatly influences your overall feelings and attitudes toward life. That's right. In fact, here's something that will both blow your mind and give you the heebie-jeebies at the same time: The same chemicals found in your brain that affect your emotions are also found in the lining of your gut. Yup. It's like your bowels are your second brain (perhaps where the phrase "bleep for brains" came from).

With that, please allow us to sneak a peek into the collective stalls of the world and give you a little insight about the things that everybody produces and elementary school boys love to joke about: Your waste.

The Biology of Waste

Poop

You're already advanced enough to know the basics of digestion: You eat, you poop. But the journey food makes from table to toilet is actually a great travel tale, which will give you some perspective on both your eating habits and the general health of your body. On your gastrointestinal interstate, there's only one entrance: your mouth. During every trip, your food hits a symbolic three-pronged fork in the road:

- Either it will be broken down and picked up by your bloodstream and liver to be used as energy.

- Or it will be broken down and stored as fat.

- Or it will be processed into waste and directed to nature's recycling pot: the porcelain junkyard.

Here's how the system starts: Before a morsel even reaches your mouth, your body has a radar gun to let you know that food is coming—powered by such physiological cues as sight and smell. In response to that sensory information, glands in your mouth start to secrete enzymes into your saliva to break starch into sugar. Then the cells lining the stomach release acid to help prepare for the incoming goodies.

Now, don't underestimate your tongue as a player in this whole process. Back in the day, people relied on our senses of smell and taste for survival. If something tasted good, then it was safe, and if it tasted like dinosaur dung, then it could be poisonous. We do the same things. We rely on our smell and our tongue for information about food. That information is sent to the brain, which then sends messages to our forks: keep eating or stop eating. That message largely comes from our five tastes (sweet, sour, salty, bitter, and umami, which recognizes the inherent deliciousness in foods), but it also comes from what we smell. Some researchers say that three-quarters of how we "taste" foods actually comes from how we smell them, which is why food tastes bland when you have a cold and are all congested.

Once you make the commitment to chew and swallow, food travels down your esophagus. Think of that as the ramp onto the main digestive highway, which begins with your stomach. The main component of stomach acid, hydrochloric acid (HCl), is so strong that it is used to remove rust from steel. HCl breaks down proteins into component amino acids and kills wayward bacteria. It would eat away the lining of your stomach, too, if you didn't have a protective coating of mucus. When people suffer from reflux or heartburn, it's because the acid from their stomach is burbling up into their esophagus and irritating the tissue there. Stomach ulcers occur when the mucous coat is breached and the acid begins to eat away at the stomach itself. Antacids, which are commonly taken to relieve heartburn, neutralize the pH of stomach acid so that it is no longer corrosive.

After food spends some time in your stomach, it will be released into the duodenum, the first part of your small intestine, and then move into the small intestine. (See figure 18.1.) The small bowel secretes a hormone called cholecystokinin (CCK), which stimulates the vagus nerve connecting all the different parts of your digestive system to your brain. The vagus tells your brain you are full and instructs your stomach to slow its emptying—if your stomach is full, you can't easily eat more.

Figure 18.1 **Eater's Digest** The food you eat goes on a great journey through many different organs—starting in your stomach, colon, and small intestines, where a magic mix of hormones and bile start your digestion. Excess calories get stored as fat (especially in an organ called the omentum).

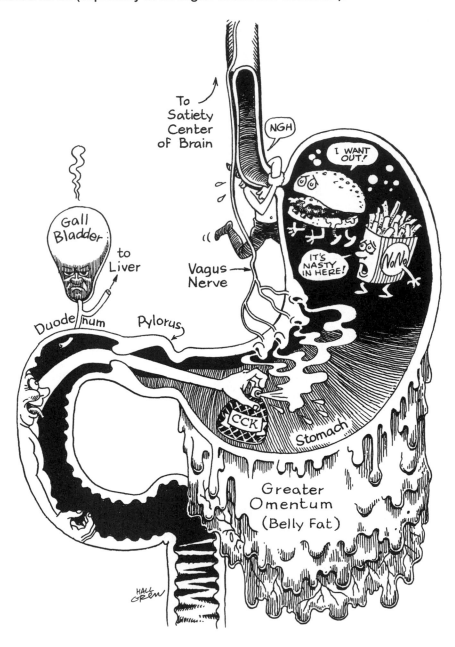

In the small intestine, food has a head-on collision with bile, a thick green digestive fluid that's secreted by the liver, stored in the gallbladder, and released into the duodenum. After fat is broken down into smaller particles, these tiny particles interact with bile to help form a compound that is easily absorbed by the cells of your body. Bile surrounds the fat in your meal so that it can be better digested and absorbed.

At the bottom end of your small intestine, food hits the ileal brake—another signal that you're full. At this juncture, a traffic signal called the ileocecal valve slows the passage of the soup-like contents from the small bowel to the large intestine and prevents waste from the colon from traveling back up into the small intestine. The squeezing required to move through this valve is reduced naturally by some foods (such as both insoluble and soluble fiber, which makes the transit across the valve slower so that you stay fuller longer), since your body feels that you're still digesting and not ready to evacuate those foods yet. Very little absorption of nutrients occurs in the colon, so once the food passes the ileocecal valve, not much more happens except that you reabsorb water while consolidating the waste you've formed. Waste moves through your colon until it's finally sent out of your body and flushed away. In an ideal world, that end product should have the shape of the letter S—not pellets, not paste, but a long, curvy shape that mimics the shape of your colon. That's indicative of a healthy digestive system—that you're eating well, and are consuming enough water and fiber to help food move through your body efficiently. If your poops don't have that shape (yes, you should look), you could be having problems with constipation or other digestive issues. (See below.)

Pee

Poop is just one way of removing waste. You read about your lungs in chapter 17; they exhale carbon dioxide, a respiratory form of waste. Your kidneys remove waste from your blood.

Kidneys are made of little units called nephrons. Each nephron functions separately as a minifiltration plant, filtering bad stuff or unneeded stuff from the blood. Drugs such as marijuana, cocaine, steroids, and narcotics (the frequently abused painkiller oxycodone, for instance, better known by its brand name, OxyContin) get filtered out here, which is why they're detectible in a urine test. Water and good stuff like most amino acids and glucose get reabsorbed, and the bad stuff moves from the nephron into one of two collecting tubes called the ureters. You have one ureter attached to each kidney, and they both dump into the bladder, the storage tank for urine. When it gets a full sensation, the bulb-shaped bladder sends a message to your brain, and voila! You get that little song in your head, "Gotta go, gotta go, gotta go," and if it's an inopportune time, you get to do the wiggly little potty dance—or just keep your legs crossed for that extra class period.

Your kidneys keep your body's salt levels in balance. They also play a role in regulating blood pressure by keeping your fluid levels in balance. As they're cleaning your blood, your kidneys sense when you need to make more red blood cells and send a message to your bone marrow via a hormone called erythropoietin (EPO for short). Remember that vitamin D you need to absorb calcium? The kidneys are where it gets activated and ready for use.

In addition to regulating salt levels in your blood, your kidneys also help to regulate your blood sugar. In general, your body wants to hold on to as much glucose as possible, as it's too valuable as an energy source to flush away. So normally the kidneys absorb glucose back into your blood after it passes through the nephrons. However, if your kidney is overwhelmed with too much sugar, it will dump the excess into your urine, making it smell sweet. This is what happens in diabetes; the scientific name for the disease is diabetes mellitus, with *mellitus* meaning "sweet as honey" in Latin. In type 1 diabetes, the pancreas is unable to ship out adequate amounts of insulin, and in type 2, insulin is not able to move as much glucose as is needed into your cells. In both, the kidneys get rid of all that extra sugar. How can you tell if you have diabetes? Easy: You start needing to pee like a racehorse—that's your body trying naturally to get rid of all that sugar—and you're constantly thirsty because you're sending out all this pee. If you experience these symptoms, ask your doc about diabetes.

By the way, your urine should be clear or a pale yellow; that indicates you're well hydrated. If it's a deep yellow, like concentrated lemonade or Mountain Dew, or even orange-brownish, then it means you're not getting nearly enough water.

Figure 18.2 **Gutting It Out** Food pulls over at various spots in the intestinal tract. Here are the rest stations where nutrients are absorbed:

Stomach: alcohol

Duodenum (first part of the small intestine; takes off from the stomach): calcium, magnesium, iron, fat-soluble vitamins A and D, glucose

Jejunum (middle part of the small intestine): fat, sucrose, lactose, glucose, proteins, amino acids, fat-soluble vitamins A and D, water-soluble vitamins like folic acid

Ileum (last part of the small intestine; leads to large bowel): proteins, amino acids, water-soluble vitamins like folic acid, vitamin B12

Colon (also known as the large bowel): water, potassium, sodium chloride

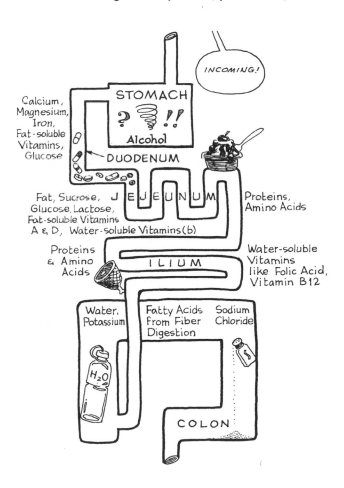

The YOU Qs
You Ask, We Answer, You Decide

How often should I be pooping?

You're considered normal if you're pooping once a day, three times a day, or even once every three days—*as long as you're not having cramps, pain, diarrhea, or have odd-shaped poops.* If you're feeling like you're not pooping enough and really straining to go, you should drink more water or add fiber to your diet to get things moving. You can also eat certain foods to relieve constipation. We affectionately call it the CRAP diet: cherries, raisins, apricots, and prunes. And there's such a thing as too much fiber; if you eat tons of salads and fiber-containing foods, but not enough of the other food groups, such as fat or protein or both, you can also get constipated. Constipation is nature's way of telling you that you are missing something in your meal plan (what you eat each day).

My stomach just doesn't feel right some of the time after I eat. What should I do?

The first step is to try to figure out if a particular food might be the culprit. The best way to do that is through the *food-elimination test.* What you'll do is completely eliminate certain groups of foods, one at a time, for at least three days in a row, although sometimes the elimination of a food takes two or more weeks to show its benefits in terms of how you feel. During that time, take notes about all the different ways you feel: your energy level, fatigue, and how often you go to the bathroom. Think about what makes you feel better or worse. Here's the order we suggest in terms of eliminating foods: gluten-containing wheat products (including rye, barley, and oats; see our G-Free Plan below), dairy products, refined carbohydrates (especially sugar), saturated fats and trans fats, and artificial colors. The latter are tough to get rid of because they're in practically everything. But don't get rid of all fats; your body still needs thirty to fifty grams of healthy fat a day.

I have a milk allergy. What can I do?

You first need to consult a doc to see if it's a true allergy or an intolerance. Here are some ways you can help manage it, if it is decided that you shouldn't be having milk products:

- Milk is one of the easiest ingredients to substitute in baking and cooking by using an equal amount of any of the following: water, fruit juice, or soy or rice milk.

- Watch out for hidden sources of dairy. For example, some brands of canned tuna fish and other nondairy products contain casein, a milk protein.

- In restaurants, tell your server about your allergy. Many restaurants put butter (which comes from milk) on steaks and other food after they've been grilled or prepared to add extra flavor, but you can't see it after it melts.

- Some ingredients seem to contain milk products or derivatives but actually don't. These are safe to eat if you have a lactose allergy: cocoa butter, cream of tartar, and calcium lactate.

A lot of my friends talk about gluten and say they're allergic to it. What is it?

These days, there's a whole lot of buzz surrounding the word *gluten*—and, no, it has nothing to do with exercises to tone your butt muscles. It has to do with the issue of intolerance, allergies, and diseases associated with *gluten, the substance found in wheat, rye, oats, and barley. (It's the doughy stuff that holds it all together).* The difference between an allergy and an intolerance is that an allergy can cause inflammatory reactions in the skin, mouth, and lungs, while an intolerance does not involve the immune system and manifests itself more in symptoms of discomfort such as gas, diarrhea, and abdominal pain. (Celiac disease, by the way, is permanent intolerance to the chemicals associated with wheat protein.) Besides the symptoms and discomfort, the problem is that these conditions alter the lining of the intestines, potentially making it difficult to absorb important vitamins and nutrients.

If you suffer from one of these issues, you need to know how to manage the nutritional limitations that may affect how and what you eat. Here are some tips:

◉ You may know the main foods that contain gluten: wheat, rye, oats, barley, and all their derivatives, such as bran, pasta, couscous, and orzo. But you may not know some of the more stealthy foods that contain gluten, such as beer, artificial flavors, candy, lunch meats, Communion wafers, soy sauce, and lipstick. Luckily, some grains are gluten free. They include chia, buckwheat, flax, corn, quinoa, rice, and soy.

◉ Spend some time searching online for gluten-free brands and products. Since online info isn't always accurate, check the labels of everything you drop into your cart. Under-the-radar, red-flag words include *modified, hydrogenated,* and *natural flavors* (as in, they may contain flavors from wheat).

◉ Whether you're eating out or at a party, don't be shy about letting your host and server know about your allergy or intolerance. They may be able to accommodate you, but it's always best to plan ahead and carry along a "safe" snack.

Some good gluten-free foods:

Fresh fruits	Popcorn
Peanut butter	Dried beans, lentils, and peas
Unflavored milk	
Eggs	100 percent fruit juice
Canned salmon, tuna, and chicken	Most yogurts
	Plain nuts and seeds

Fresh vegetables	Spices and herbs
Coffee and tea	Plain brown rice
Tofu	Pudding
Cocoa	Fresh pork and poultry
White or sweet potato	Canola and olive oil
Jell-O	Fresh fish or seafood
Corn	

My grandparents always seem to be talking about fiber. Why is it so good for you?

Most important, fiber helps keep digested food bulky and soft so that it moves easily through the colon. Found solely in plant foods, fiber is largely indigestible and passes through the digestive tract intact. *It contains no calories but makes you feel full, which helps control overeating.* There are really three kinds of fiber—you probably know two kinds: insoluble and soluble—but soluble has a subtype called gel soluble (whole oats and psyllium are the two common forms) that actually binds bile salts and lowers lousy LDL (low-density lipoprotein) cholesterol levels. All three kinds are good for you. Insoluble fiber doesn't easily dissolve in water and is not broken down by intestinal bacteria. It's found in grapefruit, oranges, grapes, raisins, dried fruit, sweet potatoes, peas, and zucchini, but especially in whole wheat or whole grain bread. (Important: It has to be whole grain, not five- or six-grain, to have enough fiber.) Soluble fiber does dissolve in water; it regulates metabolism and digestion, and stabilizes blood glucose levels. It's mostly found in grains such as oats, barley, and rye, legumes such as beans, peas, and lentils, and some cereals. We recommend that teens get 25 to 35 grams of fiber a day. Start to increase slowly if you currently get less than this; you risk an increase in gas if you add too much too soon. Some people feel bloated when they start the gel form of soluble fiber—again, start slowly.

Here are some examples of high-fiber foods:

Lima beans (3 tablespoons)	13 grams
Buckwheat cereal (1 cup)	10 grams
Artichoke (1 large)	10 grams
Soybeans (½ cup)	10 grams
Psyllium husks (1 tablespoon)	8 grams
Almonds (24)	5 grams
Peanuts (30)	5.5 grams
Oatmeal (1 cup, instant)	3 to 4 grams
Cheerios (1 cup)	3 grams

The other thing you need to keep things moving is H_2O. Water works as a natural lubricant that helps everything slide through your system. Plus, it helps quell hunger, fights bad breath, and helps you avoid dry mouth.

What is irritable bowel syndrome?

IBS is a very common and frustrating condition because of the symptoms: bloating, cramping, pain. Some people experience constipation with irritable bowel syndrome, while others experience the opposite effect and develop diarrhea. And some people flip-flop between the two extremes, living in a world where one moment they couldn't poop if they tried and the next moment they couldn't stop it if they wanted to. *People with IBS experience some dysfunction of the immune and nervous systems that regulate the lining of the bowel* (called the epithelium), which controls the flow of fluids into and out of the intestines. When stuff moves too quickly from start to finish, the intestines can't absorb fluids from it (hence diarrhea). And when the last meal moves too slowly, the bowel absorbs too much fluid (hence constipation). People with IBS have abnormally low levels of serotonin, most of which is produced in your gut, not your brain. This causes all kinds of digestive problems and makes these people more susceptible to feeling pain when those problems arise. Some tips for easing the pain:

If you're suffering from IBS, eliminate foods that are high in saturated and trans fats as well as all fried foods, alcohol, caffeine, carbonated drinks, and gum. (Why gum? Swallowing air makes matters worse.) Instead substitute foods that are high in fiber, and don't forget to add loads of water.

Many people with the diagnosis of IBS actually have difficulty digesting milk (lactose intolerance) or sugar. There are some ways to test for the problem, but it is easier to simply avoid all milk and sugar (especially sodas) for a week and see if the symptoms go away. Then you can add back milk, but with Lactaid (a pill or chew that gives your body the missing lactase enzyme you may lack) before the milk or dairy product. Some people need varying amounts of Lactaid to be comfortable with different foods; try 1 to 5 Lactaid pills or chews if you are getting gassy or crampy with dairy products and see how you do. Then talk to your doctor to see if you need to be formally tested for lactose intolerance.

Eat slowly and regularly to avoid extreme excesses and deficits of food, which can be traumatic for your digestive system.

Probiotics are probably your best allies. The best (in spore form, so the stomach doesn't destroy them) come in small capsules at less than $10 a month. We like Culturelle, Digestive Advantage, and Sustenex, which decrease IBS symptoms. Some experts believe that one of the causes of the condition is a lack of good bacteria in the intestines.

I seem to have an extraordinary amount of gas. What causes all this gas?

There are two main sources for nature's rear-propulsion system. Flatus comes from the air we swallow (20 percent) and the digestion of foods by bacteria in our intestines (80 percent). We have trillions of bacteria in our intestines and five hundred species that are so lethal that any alone could kill us. *These bacteria love digesting sugars, fiber, or milk that we can't digest quickly.* The result is lots of gas made up of carbon dioxide, nitrogen, and methane (which is flammable). You can reduce swallowing air by avoiding carbonated beverages and cigarettes, by slowing down your speed of eating and drinking, and by not chewing gum. Sugar-free gum is a particular culprit, as the sorbitol it contains can cause not only gas but also abdominal pain and diarrhea.

How can I tell if I have a urinary tract infection?

This is simple: pain when you pee (dysuria), sense of urgency (Gotta go! Gotta go!), frequent urination, having to go at night (nocturia), and blood in the urine. Any or all of those symptoms warrant a visit to your doctor to get checked out. *UTIs can also mimic STIs; the symptoms may be similar or the same.* UTIs are easy to ID with a urine test and easy to treat with antibiotics. There's a home test available in drugstores that measures nitrites (the breakdown product of bacteria), so you can sometimes diagnose yourself.

UTIs are three to five times more common in girls than in guys, due mainly to anatomy. A girl's urethra, or the tube through which urine passes from the bladder, opens very near the opening of the vagina, and not so far from the anus. If a girl wipes from back to front rather than from front to back, she can transfer vaginal or anal bacteria to the urethra. Both the anus and vagina normally have bacteria living there, but the urethra is supposed to be clean. So when bacteria climb up the urethra to the bladder, white cells get recruited in the body to come fight off the invaders. In the course of the battle, some tissue gets inflamed, and you might notice blood in your urine or feel a burning sensation when you pee. Another common scenario is "honeymoon cystitis," or UTIs that happen after a person has had sex, as sexual activity brings vaginal bacteria closer to the urethra, where again, the little buggers can climb up to invade the bladder. If you're susceptible to UTIs, drink cranberry juice, as it acidifies your urine, making it inhospitable to UTI-causing bacteria. If you suspect that you have a UTI, see your doc immediately to get a culture, and he or she will prescribe antibiotics if it looks like a UTI. Don't try to just continue cranberry juice until your kidneys are floating.

What if I have blood in my urine?

The most common cause is a UTI, but other things can cause it too, like certain diseases or bleeding disorders. Trauma, such as a car accident or even overly strenuous exercise, can cause internal damage that leads to blood in the urine. *If you see blood in your urine after trauma, visit the doctor or emergency room.* You can also get red urine if you have eaten berries, beets, some vegetable dyes, and other foods. When in doubt, have your doctor test your urine.

What if my pee smells really strong?

A strong smell (and bright yellow urine) usually means you are running dry, or need to be drinking more fluids. *A fruity smell can be a sign of ketosis, which can happen in the context of diabetes,* when the blood sugar level is too high and the extra sugar is dumped into the urine by the kidneys. If you have to urinate urgently, frequently, and a notice a funny smell, get your urine checked immediately.

Why do girls pee more than guys?

Men have a larger bladder capacity; they tend to pee in larger volumes, while women have smaller bladders and therefore pee less volume but more often. This is not true of all guys or all girls; some girls have the bladder capacity of a camel (well, not literally, but they sure can hold it), while some guys have to go every hour. In general, guys' bladders tend to be bigger than girls', just not always.

Is there a proper way to wipe?

We prefer to use wet wipes for number two—they reduce irritation that can be found in the area if you wipe with rough toilet paper, and always wipe front to back. For number one, girls always need to wipe from front to back, to avoid passing germs from the rectal area to their genitals.

★ FANTASTIC FIVE: STEPS FOR SUCCESS ★

1. **Drink lots of water,** and if you are trying to gain weight, make that low-fat milk or 100 percent fruit juice. Fluids help speed your digestive system along, and they're also good for flushing your urinary system, too. Aim for eight to ten glasses a day.

2. **Add some more fiber to your diet** to help improve your digestive process. Oatmeal and beans are good choices.

3. **If you are having too many loose stools, try the BRAT diet** (bread, rice, applesauce, and toast, as well as oatmeal, psyllium husks, bananas, and yogurt). If you are having problems with constipation, try the CRAP diet (cherries, raisins, apricots, prunes) to loosen yourself up.

4. **Solo work:** Check your poop. It should come out in the shape of an S—that's a sign that you're eating good foods and the digestive system is running smoothly. If your poop comes out in pellets or anything other than that nice, long, colon-mimicking shape, it probably warrants some dietary changes, like adding more water and more fiber.

5. **Discussion:** Spend one day thinking about how your stomach feels after every meal. Write down what you ate and how you felt. Share with others and note patterns about what foods gave you energy and what foods made you feel blah.

What You Will Learn

- The number one health risk for teens is bad decisions

- The teen brain is not always developed enough to allow logic to overrule emotion

- The most common accidents and injuries

- Stay-safe strategies

19

Making Good Decisions

leep happens.

True, there are a lot of things about the world that we can't control: like other drivers, like the irrational assignments of a certain social studies teacher, like the fact that your dad insists on wearing black socks with sneakers to mow the lawn. We don't control everything about the way the world works. But [*bleep*] doesn't always have to happen. In fact, a lot of what happens in the world around you is controllable. That's right. A lot of the stuff we chalk up to "it was just an accident" actually stems from decisions that we make.

When you consider that the leading cause of serious injury and death among teens isn't some disease or so-called health problem but is actually accidents (and the decisions that may play a role in them), then you realize the importance of this chapter. In fact, accidental injuries rank as the second most common reason why teens end up in the ER, just behind respiratory problems. Avoiding such potentially life-threatening situations is not just about listening to your elders when we tell you to "buckle up" and "don't drink and drive." It's about understanding that the teenage brain might not yet be really equipped to handle some of life's big decisions.

Here we're going to tell you why that's so and what you can do about it.

The Biology of Accidents

Chances are, some adult—a parent, a coach, a teacher—has wondered aloud what in the world you were thinking. You made a decision or did something that just had no basis in logic—from an adult's perspective. Why did you leave the oven on? Or jump off the roof into the swimming pool? Or decide that it would be fun to play a game where you and your friends throw a basketball at each other's private parts and see who's last to flinch?

Stupid choices, perhaps, but the interesting thing is that you can blame it on your brain.

While the overall size of a nine-year-old's brain is comparable to the size of an adult's, its structure differs. It appears that different brain areas mature at different times. Specifically, the self-regulatory centers in the frontal lobe of the cerebral cortex (see diagram on page 350)—that is, the parts that tell you, *Hello!??!?! You could break something jumping off that roof!*—are the last to reach maturity, at around age twenty-four (even later for men than women). In addition to decision making, also known as executive function, the frontal lobe governs aggression, impulsivity, judgment, and your ability to control thoughts about the future. The effect? The adolescent brain is one with adult-level pleasure and sensation centers but without adult-level control. Explains a lot, doesn't it?

So what does that mean for teens? It means that many of you try to seek pleasure through the activation of such feel-good hormones as dopamine and serotonin even if it involves considerable risk. That's because the part of the brain that tells you to take it easy is less developed than the part of the brain that tells you to bring it on. (See figure 19.1.) In addition, what judgment you do have is extremely vulnerable to influence by peers and media, as well as by alcohol and drugs, which alter your brain chemistry and actually make you feel even more invincible than you already do.

That's no excuse, mind you, but more of an explanation of why teens sometimes get into trouble. (It also makes you wonder how your parents made it—many of us wonder that about ourselves too, and it's worth noting that many more of us died in auto accidents before seat belts and airbags were universally available.)

By "trouble," we're not talking just about taking physical risks, like riding a skateboard without a helmet; we're talking about getting into situations that breed bad decisions, that call for doing things that perhaps you know you shouldn't—whether it's having unsafe sex, or getting in the car with someone who's drinking, or emailing your ten closest friends a photo of yourself wearing nothing but your—.

Ahem. These bad decisions often occur when we choose to do something that has an immediate reward—a laugh, admiration of peers, an adrenaline rush—without considering the potential long-term risk.

It's interesting to look at this process from an evolutionary perspective. Our stone-age ancestors lived at a time when there was a reasonable chance of dying during the course of any given day. (Back then, hearing the greeting "Honey, I'm home!" really meant something.) So it was worth it for them to take risks that could lead to immediate pleasure-based rewards. Over thousands of years, our brains became wired to gravitate toward immediate gratification, which satisfied the primitive, emotional centers of our brain, even if it entailed a significant risk. The ability to delay gratification is a relatively late occurrence in human history, as it is controlled by the frontal lobe—the most recent part of our brains to evolve. While we're not saying that teens are less evolved than adults, it is true that until your frontal lobes are fully mature, the emotional centers of your brain can in many situations outmuscle the rational centers of your brain, leading you to seek pleasure without weighing the consequences.

Unfortunately, all this brain business doesn't get you off the hook. Do something that gets you and your buddies in trouble, and you can't run to the principal's office and blame it on your frontal lobe. The real trick is to learn a little more about deci-

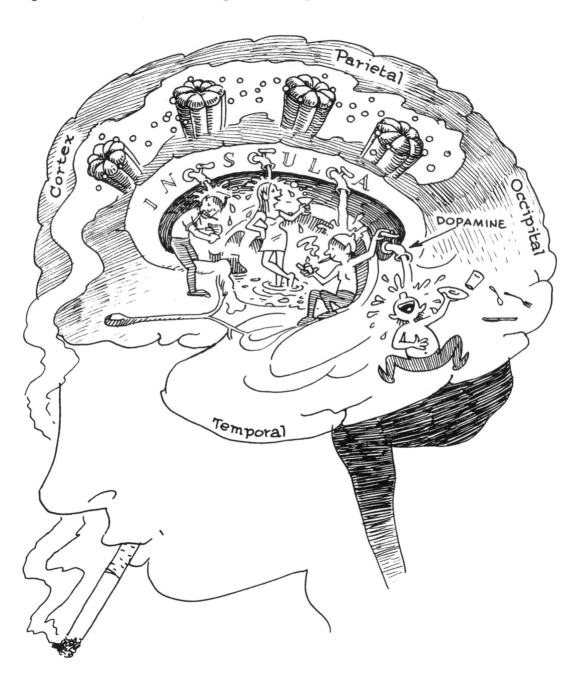

Figure 19.1 **Brain Drain** When you get addicted to something, some feel-good hormones create a craving that makes you want to continue the behavior.

sion making so that you can be aware of how it works biologically; that way, you can enjoy all that life has to offer—but in a safe and healthy way, where you'll "live to see another day."

So how do you do it? The answer ultimately leads back to something we talked about when we talked about sex. Remember the concepts of hot state and cold state from chapter 8? The hot state is "being in the heat of the moment," while the cold state is, say, nowhere near any trouble. It's easier for your brain to make rational decisions in a cold, unemotional state. Does that mean you're never going to go to a party or be alone with someone you like? Of course not! But what it does mean is that you'll anticipate those scenarios long before you find yourself in them and make the necessary preparations to ensure safe decisions, such as choose designated drivers in your group and make a pact to honor that designation (or don't attend parties where drinking occurs in the first place).

There's no doubt that today's teens face tough choices and find themselves in tough situations, many of which, unfortunately, come with a fair amount of risk—real risk. But we also believe that a "don't do this" and "don't do that" approach is about as effective as a cell phone with no service. For more info click on www.scenariosusa .org. The big lesson is here is to be aware of your environment and plan ahead so that your logic and smarts have a fighting chance in a battle with all of your emotions.

The YOU Qs
You Ask, We Answer, You Decide

Okay, I'll bite. How do you train your brain to be more logical?

Practice a bit of delayed gratification. Figure out how to *increase your reward if you don't go for the immediate gain*. That can mean thinking five steps ahead of the action in play. If I jump off the cliff into the water without checking first to make sure there are no rocks below, I might end up paralyzed and unable to walk, which would put a real damper on my lifestyle. But if I check first to see if there are no rocks, I can still be safe in jumping, and have the thrill of it, without putting myself at permanent risk. And I help out my friends whose frontal lobes are on overdrive and may not have the logic to make sure they check for themselves.

What are some of the most common injuries teens suffer?

Here are the top things that we treat in the ER, where, you'll remember, injuries are the second most common reason for teen visits:

Concussions and serious head trauma: Concussions occur in 1.1 million people a year, but even seeing stars from a minor head injury can lead to later memory loss. That's because your brain is floating in a sea of liquid; when your head stops suddenly, your brain bashes against your skull, potentially damaging the sheaths that protect your neurons. And those damaged neurons are what could make you occasionally forget your mother's birthday or the lyrics to the latest All-American Rejects song. Damage from repeated minor trauma, no matter how inconsequential it may seem at the time, can accumulate so that you suffer from mood changes and memory loss even twenty to forty years later.

Memory loss can occur when trauma disrupts blood flow or oxygen delivery to the brain, as can happen in boxing, football, and other sports where you can get your bell rung repeatedly. Bike accidents without a helmet are notorious for doing serious damage to brain cells, as are car accidents (the latter remains the number one cause of death in teens).

People who damage any part of their brain through a major accident can have some significant challenges learning how to compensate for lost gray matter (brain cells). Long-term behavior therapy involves rewiring their brains to function day by day. Many hospitals have special units where kids with traumatic brain injury (TBI) can go to rehab their brains. Some of the damage may be reversible (for instance, going from a coma to being able to speak, walk, return to school), but other faculties may or may not be recoverable, such as moving things from short-term memory to long-term memory. Many people with TBI go on to lead productive, healthy, happy lives, but with a lot of effort to get there; it's far easier to put on the helmet and make it a personal fashion statement than to wake up after a traumatic brain injury. So wear the helmet (and seat belt!) for protection, and take DHA every day (adult dose is 600 to 900 milligrams) to help improve your overall brain health.

Broken bones: The good news is that teen bones heal better than old folks' bones. If it is a "buckle fracture," or the kind that happens when you fall on a wrist extended to break your fall, it can be as simple as living in a cast for six weeks. Other fractures may be a bigger deal, as in a shattered pelvis from a car accident, which may involve months of casting and bed rest. Again, recoverable, but the missed school/life/activities make it a bummer.

Cuts that need stitches: It's best to get these taken care of immediately, as infection can settle in if you wait too long to get to the emergency room. (Not getting to the ER for, say, eight hours would definitely qualify as "too long.") Sutures are usually needed if the cut has jagged edges or is deep enough that it will not heal naturally in a useful way. Stitches have gotten sophisticated, with all sorts of medically safe forms, including dissolvable sutures and "skin glue" (no, not Elmer's or Super Glue used on skin). Not near an ER? Call 911 anyway if you or a friend or family member has a cut that looks serious.

What should I do if I do bump my head pretty badly?

Any type of head injury, no matter how minor it may seem, needs immediate attention, first from the training staff and/or emergency crew on hand (if you're at a sporting event, say) and then from a doctor. Even if there aren't immediate symptoms, all head injuries have to be monitored closely (so try not to get annoyed when your mom asks you how you're feeling for the fiftieth time—she's only doing her job). How do you know if you have a concussion after a head injury? Symptoms you might feel include headache, nausea and/or vomiting, dizziness, problems with balance, blurred vision or double vision, sensitivity to noise or light, feeling out of it or lethargic (sluggish), difficulty with short-term or long-term memory, and confusion. Other people may notice the following: You may look dazed or stunned, forget plays in sports, move clumsily, answer questions slowly, exhibit changes in personality or behavior, and have a hard time recalling events before and after the concussion.

We don't want to scare you, but head injuries are serious business. Sometimes even the best protection doesn't protect you adequately from concussions or brain injuries. If you don't remember the injury, you had a concussion, and you need evaluation and to refrain from any other risky endeavors for at least two weeks. After a concussion, you cannot go back to sports games or even practice for a whole week, lest you suffer what's called second impact syndrome, which can cause swelling, permanent brain damage, and even death. And if you have two concussions in a season, it is worth talking to your doctor to see if you can return to the sport that season or whether you need that delayed gratification we talked about above.

I know everybody is worried about teens driving. What's your advice for us?

The biggest rookie error is talking on the cell phone or playing with the iTouch, sound system, or other electronic gadget while driving. It is the equivalent to driving drunk. This gets back to brain biology: From ages fifteen to twenty-five, you are still hardwiring neural pathways—making brain superhighways, so to speak. By the time you are thirty or forty years old, you may be able to drive home without giving it a second thought; in fact, you may get home and not even realize you drove there, it is so automatic. At this point, however, driving still requires your full attention. Those pathways are not yet hardwired to function without conscious thought.

Using common sense also makes good sense. Clearly, drinking and driving don't mix, but marijuana and other recreational drugs also interfere with your nonhardwired brain pathways, affecting both your reflexes and your judgment. If your friend is supposed to drive but has had a few cocktails or used some other substance, you need to be able to get a different, safe ride home. Some families have a code phrase they use that the teen can text or call and say, such as, "I'm really worried about _____ [fill in dog's name, Grandma's name, family friend, or whomever]" and that means, "Come and get me, no questions asked—my ride home is not safe or the situation is not okay."

While you've been told about fifty million times not to drink and drive, do you really know why it's such a problem? Teen male drivers with a blood alcohol level of 0.5 to 1.0 (the equivalent of two or three drinks for full-grown women, three or four for full-grown men; it's significantly less for teens who haven't achieved adult stature) are eighteen times more likely than sober teen male drivers to be killed in a motor vehicle accident. Teenage female drivers with the same blood alcohol level are fifty-six times more likely to crash than sober teen female drivers. (That has more to do with the stronger effect of the same blood alcohol level in a female body than it does female driving skills!) And remember, accidents don't just injure and kill the driver—often passengers and innocent people in other cars are killed or maimed as well. One more thing: Don't drink and swim. Drownings account for 1,500 child and teen deaths a year. In the adolescent age group, where peer pressure is greatest, alcohol can play a role in getting your classmate to dive into the shallow end and end up unconscious at the bottom of the pool, unable to get back to the surface.

I want to get a motorcycle when I'm eighteen, but my parents are already all over me about it.

In the medical world, we actually changed the name from motorcycle to "donorcycle," meaning that *riders have a great chance of getting into an accident* and being in a position to give away their major organs as (deceased) donors. You can be a cool rider, but only if you wear a helmet. For every mile traveled, you have a fourteen times higher risk of death than if you were in a car. Think of your slower teen brain reflexes, combined with a higher likelihood of being in someone else's blind spot, since you are a smaller moving target for them to see, as well as having no protective frame like a car has.

What's the best solution to put in a wound?

Put nothing in a cut that you would not put in your eyes. If you do, you will kill millions of your loyal defender cells in order to knock off a few bacteria. *You can safely flush a wound with clean water or saline to remove any debris, such as pebbles, glass, and so on.* The exception is that if it's a puncture wound, applying hydrogen peroxide can help bubble infection out of the deep crevices. For puncture wounds, let nature run its course with scab formation, and the wound will heal most safely and quickly. If, after two to seven days, the wound is looking worse (swollen, angry red, oozing pus), see a doctor. Just make sure that you have had a tetanus shot in the last five years. (Note: Tetanus boosters are said to be good for ten years, but after five years, it's a good idea to get an update. Some pediatricians automatically give them to adolescents every five years, while others do not.) Not sure if you need stitches? It never hurts to get it checked. Immediately.

★ FANTASTIC FIVE: STEPS FOR SUCCESS ★

1. **Think before you jump.** Take a few moments to think ahead a few steps to see if that literal or metaphorical jump is something you really want to do. And if you're one of those people who can't help but think twenty steps ahead and that knowledge is paralyzing, think about how to take a calculated risk where the benefits outweigh the risks, in a healthy way.

2. **Practice driving in a parking lot in different kinds of weather**. If you have access to a climate with great snow, see what it feels like (in a place with no poles, other cars, or things to run into) to slam on your breaks versus gently pump them, how to turn into the curve in midslide, and other means of avoiding collision. Ditto for a rainstorm; see what it feels like to hydroplane and skid. Do not drink and drive, text and drive, or talk on a cell phone and drive. And don't ride shotgun with someone who does any of these things, either.

3. **Always wear a helmet** when you're biking, Rollerblading, skateboarding, skiing, snowboarding, or rock climbing.

4. **Learn to swim**. Drowning is a real risk, and we cannot guarantee you a life not exposed to a body of water. Besides, swimming is really fun!

5. **Discussion**. You are at a party, and your best friend is on her way to a really great buzz. She was supposed to drive you home. What can you do?

The YOU

We know, we know. Say the word *plan*, and it sounds like you've got to spend the next three weeks memorizing some formula for healthier living. But that's not the way we roll. We know that the only way you make changes in your life is to make them, well, easy to make.

We hope that you've enjoyed our candid discussion throughout the book, and we hope that you've learned quite a lot about how the body works—and what happens when it doesn't. Now, we'd like you to take matters into your own hands.

So what we'd like you to do is this: Take a look at our twenty-five most important health tips that you can and should adopt. (Remember, it takes only two to three weeks of practice to make something a habit.) Next to each one, mark the box that most applies to you:

🌀 I already do this.

🌀 I'm going to try to do this for two weeks.

🌀 I'm going to need some help to get this into my regular routine.

Now, of course, the closer you are to checking the first column of all the tips, the healthier you'll be, and the benefits are endless: more energy, higher self-esteem, better performance in all areas of your life, and overall more happiness as you move through these fun and sometimes challenging years.

We understand how complex your life is and that you have to balance many things. We don't expect you to make all the changes overnight, and we do expect some of them to be a little more difficult than others. So we hope that you—and your friends and classmates—take the opportunity to discuss the "why" behind the "what." Don't leave out the "how the heck you're going to do it," and you'll have created a cool network of friends who all have the same goal: making you as healthy and happy as you can be.

The Twenty-Five Top Health Tips for Teens

I DO THIS!	READY TO TRY IT FOR TWO WEEKS!	NEED SOME HELP!	THE TOP TIP FOR TEENS	YOUR NOTES
			Realize that you control what goes into your body.	
			Realize that it's never too late to start adopting healthy habits. You get a do-over.	
			Walk ten thousand steps a day (about five miles).	
			Have one buddy who shares your ideals about living a healthy lifestyle and who you're comfortable talking with about healthy habits.	

I DO THIS!	READY TO TRY IT FOR TWO WEEKS!	NEED SOME HELP!	THE TOP TIP FOR TEENS	YOUR NOTES
			Avoid known toxins such as tobacco, bisphenol A (BPA) in plastics, and toxins found in dry cleaning and some cosmetic products. That means stay away from formaldehyde (found in some Brazilian Blowouts, "smoking water," and embalming fluid).	
			Regularly avoid the major categories of unhealthy foods: saturated fats, trans fats, added sugar, added syrup, non–100 percent whole grains.	
			Eat cruciferous vegetables such as broccoli, cabbage, cauliflower, watercress, and arugula three times a week.	
			Take a multivitamin every day and get your recommended daily amount of calcium through food or supplements as well as vitamin D and omega-3 fats.	
			Floss and brush your teeth for at least two minutes twice a day.	

(continued on next page)

I DO THIS!	READY TO TRY IT FOR TWO WEEKS!	NEED SOME HELP!	THE TOP TIP FOR TEENS	YOUR NOTES
			Have your waist size equal less than half your height (in inches).	
			Sleep eight and a half to nine hours a night (in greater than ninety-minute blocks).	
			Do some kind of exercise nearly every day, including some form of resistance exercise and cardiovascular exercise.	
			Do one small (or big) form of stress management every day.	
			Have your vaccinations against major diseases up to date.	
			Commit to not texting and driving.	
			Have a passion. And do it as often as you can! Safely.	
			Protect your ears from noise louder than a lawn mower (including keeping your personal device on less than 70 percent of max when using earphones).	

I DO THIS!	READY TO TRY IT FOR TWO WEEKS!	NEED SOME HELP!	THE TOP TIP FOR TEENS	YOUR NOTES
			Keep your phone and other devices out of your hands (and away from your eyes) while driving (or walking, if you're in urban areas).	
			Find a mentor.	
			Practice smart internet safety, knowing that what you write or post can be saved forever, and be smart about who you communicate with.	
			Make sex a choice, not something that "just happens." And if you are considering becoming sexually active (whether you're a guy or a girl) remember to always carry a condom. And use a second method of contraception if you're having heterosexual sex.	
			Eliminate processed foods from your diet and substitute 100 percent whole wheat flour for white flour where you can.	
			Eat five servings of fruits and veggies per day.	

(continued on next page)

I DO THIS!	READY TO TRY IT FOR TWO WEEKS!	NEED SOME HELP!	THE TOP TIP FOR TEENS	YOUR NOTES
			Eat fruit but skip the juice unless you are specifically trying to gain weight.	
			Don't squeeze zits.	
			Wear a helmet when cycling, Rollerblading, skiing, snowboarding, skateboarding, or rock climbing and wear a seat belt whenever you're in a car.	

YOU Tools

If you've gone through this entire book, then hopefully you've come away with lots of great info, advice, and strategies for making your life healthier and happier. But the fun never ends! Here in our literary toolbox, we give you even more great info you can use. You'll find a teen-friendly workout, great and easy recipes that incorporate healthy foods, the lowdown on cosmetic surgery, and a final word about your rights regarding medical confidentiality. These tools are an essential part of your healthy-living plan, because they're exactly what they're named after: tools that will help you get the job done.

YOU Tool 1

Teen Fitness

You read about the basics of physical activity and fitness in chapters 4 and 5, and there's no doubt that fitness is a huge part of a healthy life—as a way not just to sculpt the outside of your body but also to keep the inside running smoothly. A fit body feels strong, energized, and ready to handle life's challenges. We believe that you don't need a gym or fancy equipment to work your muscles and your heart. In fact, you can use your own body weight as a gym—to challenge yourself and reap the rewards of a good workout in an easy, low-maintenance way. This workout, designed by trainer Joel Harper (www.fitpackdvd.com), works your entire body by strengthening and stretching your most important muscles—keeping in mind that a strong core will help you in your everyday (and athletic) life. Joel, who has designed the workout regimens in some of our other books, trains Olympic athletes, actors, musicians, kids—and Dr. Oz as well.

YOU Workout for Teens

1: Crisscross

Builds heart strength, helps improve coordination

With feet shoulder width apart and your hands on your waist, jump your feet into a crisscross position. Go back and forth, switching your feet from back to front. Do for thirty seconds. For a more advanced exercise, reach your arms out at shoulder height, palms up, and imagine you are holding glasses of water on your palms. As you crisscross, try not to move your hands, so that you don't spill the water.

2: Ground to Sky

Improves balance and strengthens every muscle

While balancing on one foot, reach down and touch the ground with both hands. Then reach up toward the sky while simultaneously swinging one foot up in front of you, ideally bringing your knee into line with your hip. Do ten times each leg.

3: Hamstring Hang

Stretches hamstrings and back

With your feet wider than shoulder width apart and your toes pointed forward, slowly drop your hands toward the ground between your feet. Hold for ten seconds. Walk your hands to your left foot and hold for ten seconds, then to your right foot and hold for ten seconds. Move back to the center for ten seconds. Really relax your neck and think about hanging down instead of reaching down. Take deep breaths the entire time.

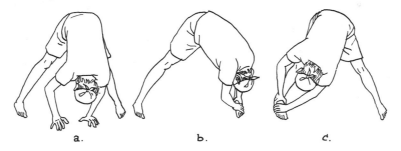

4: Armcopter

Stretches shoulders and gets the blood flowing in the arms

With your feet together, circle your arms five times. Try to clap your hands in front of your face. Your goal is to make circles as big as feels comfortable. Relax your shoulders and resist bobbing your neck; keep your head upright. Do twice.

5: Air Angels

Strengthens entire back

Lie face down on your stomach. Close your eyes and reach your arms above your head, your palms facing down. With your feet together, lift your legs off the ground and keep them there. Keeping your arms straight, reach your hands back toward your hips. Go back and forth twenty-five times, making an angel. For a more advanced exercise, move your legs as well. The higher you lift your knees and armpits, the harder it is.

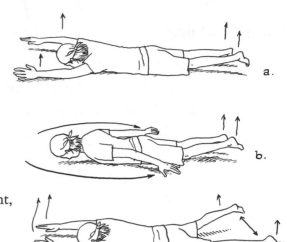

a.

b.

advanced

6: Triceps Push-ups

Works triceps and chest

While on your stomach, bring your hands underneath your shoulders, palms down and fingers spread. Kick your heels up so your legs are at right angles, and cross your ankles. Keeping a straight line between the top of your head and your knees, do twenty push-ups. Keep your elbows flush against your sides so that they rub against your shirt. Keep your abs tight. For a more advanced exercise, balance on your toes rather than on your knees.

a.

b.

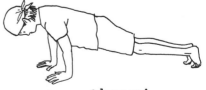

advanced

7: Donkey Kicks

Strengthens quadriceps and shoulders

While on all fours with your shoulders over your hands and your hips over your knees, lift your knees one inch off the ground. Now bounce and lift your feet one inch off the ground. Do twenty-five times. Try to float your feet off the ground, and make as little noise as possible. Do twenty-five times. For a more advanced exercise, try to kick your feet up behind you like a donkey while maintaining a soft landing.

8: Quad Bend

Stretches quads and knees

Kneel and position your feet and knees a little wider apart than your hips. Maintain a straight line with the outsides of your lower legs and point your toes directly behind you with the soles of your feet facing up. Drop your tailbone between your heels; lower yourself only as far as feels comfortable for your knees, or else drop all the way down and lie down on your back. Hold for thirty seconds. Scan your body and take deep breaths, releasing any tension.

a.

b.

9: Zigzag

Strengthens the entire core

a.

b.

side to side

Lie on your back with your legs bent and your feet flat on the ground. Interweave your fingers behind your head. Open your elbows to the side so you cannot see them. Lift your head off the ground and hold it there; maintain a relaxed neck. Lift your feet an inch off the ground and zigzag them out until they are almost straight. Go only as far out as you can keeping your lower back flat on the ground. Then zigzag them back toward your tailbone. Do twenty zigzags.

10: Back Bend

Stretches abs and chest

Kneel and place your palms on your back with your fingers pointing down. Looking up toward the ceiling, bring your elbows toward each other. To increase the stretch, gently press your hips forward. Take five deep chest breaths.

11: Break Dancing

Strengthens entire body; great for agility

Get into the "up" push-up position. Walk your feet around clockwise toward the outside of your left hand. When you get to your left hand, lift it off the ground and walk under it and put it back on the exact same spot. Keep walking your feet around in front of you until you get to your right hand. When you do, lift it off the ground and walk under it and put it on the exact same spot. Do five clockwise circles, then switch and do five counterclockwise. Focus on always having your middle finger pointed up and your elbows barely bent. For a more advanced exercise, do it faster.

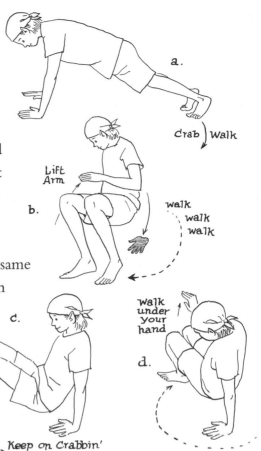

12: One-Foot Hop

Improves balance; strengthens legs; improves cardio

With your hands on your waist and balancing on one foot with your standing leg slightly bent, hop around in circles five times. Switch directions and do five more. Do twice. For a more advanced exercise, do a shoulder press on every hop. Resist looking down; look straight ahead.

13: Invisible Chair

Stretches hips and lower back and improves balance

Standing in place, lift your right ankle up on top of your left quad. With your hands on your waist, slowly lower your tailbone until you get a stretch in your hip. (For a more advanced exercise, straighten your arms above your head, palms facing inward, and bring your thumbs back as you squat lower.) Hold for twenty seconds and switch sides. Take long, deep breaths throughout the stretch.

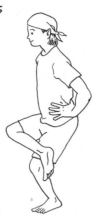

advanced

YOU Tool 2

Easy Recipes for Teens

We know that you've got enough on your plate when it comes to work, school, fun, and all of your other activities. But we also realize it's important to think about what's literally on your plate every day. Too many of us are falling into the trap of relying on high-calorie and non-nutritious convenience foods to get us through the day. But the fact is that nutrient-rich foods can taste great and be easy to make, and they provide so many more health options than overly processed foods. Many of these combos are really simple to make. For example:

Sandwich: Natural peanut butter, blueberries, and/or banana slices on 100 percent whole wheat bread

Salad: Favorite vegetables and lettuce topped with black beans and favorite lean meat (like chicken or turkey); sprinkle lightly with olive oil and lemon juice

Smoothies: Low-fat milk and/or low-fat yogurt, favorite fruit, and ice in a blender

Snacks: grapes on toothpicks frozen for a day or more in the fridge; fresh pea pods, cucumber slices, radishes, carrots, celery, beans, or other veggies with a healthy dip or salsa (we have each in the recipes that follow). You can also make homemade applesauce (peeled apple cut up into chunks or slices, 2 tablespoons water, and some cinnamon; microwave 2 to 3 minutes, check for softness/mushability, add another minute, recheck, until you get to the right consistency).

Burgers: Just sub in some beans (or even chopped veggies) for some of the lean ground meat

The options are endless (see more nutrition information in chapter 3).

But we also believe there's a lot of value in enjoying the process of preparing healthy foods—not only because it can be fun, but also because it teaches you a little something about making healthy eating a habit. So here we're offering up a few more fun and healthy recipes that will get you familiar with the kitchen. Make them with your family or friends, and enjoy the process of making healthy meals that everyone will enjoy because of how they taste—and how they make you feel.

JP's Chili Mac

6 (1 cup) servings

6 ounces uncooked elbow macaroni or short shape 100% whole wheat pasta

1 tablespoon canola oil

½ cup finely diced sweet onion

1 tablespoon minced fresh garlic

½ cup finely diced red pepper

½ cup finely diced green pepper

1 pound 99% lean ground turkey

¼ teaspoon dried thyme

½ teaspoon ground cumin

½ teaspoon ground black pepper

1 cup ketchup (less than 2 grams sugar per serving)

2 cups canned crushed tomatoes

1 teaspoon hot pepper sauce

1 tablespoon Dijon mustard

1 teaspoon sugar-free rice vinegar

1 teaspoon sugar

8 ounces shredded low-fat mozzarella

Cook the pasta according to the directions on the package. Drain and set aside.

Place the canola oil in large nonstick sauté pan on medium heat and tip it to coat the bottom of the pan. Add the onion and sauté until they are light golden. Add the garlic, sauté for one minute, then add the red and green pepper and sauté until the peppers are tender.

Add the ground turkey, breaking it into small pieces, and season with thyme, cumin, and black pepper. Stir the turkey frequently with a wooden spoon over medium heat and continue to break it into small pieces. When the turkey becomes firm and cooked, add the ketchup, tomatoes, hot pepper sauce, Dijon mustard, vinegar, and sugar. Stir until the ingredients are well mixed and cook them for 3 to 5 minutes more until they are heated through.

Add the cooked 100% whole wheat pasta and shredded mozzarella; mix and serve. If more time is available, before adding the mozzarella cheese, place the chili mac in a baking casserole, sprinkle the mozzarella cheese on top, and bake it in a preheated 350°F oven until the cheese is melted and bubbly (about 15 minutes) and serve.

WHAT'S IN IT FOR YOU

Calories (Kcal) 257 Fat (g) 9.6 Saturated fats (g) 3.8 Trans fatty acid (g) 0 Healthy fats (g) 5.8 Omega-3 fats (g) 0.2 Dietary fiber (g) 3.5 Carbohydrates (g) 33.4 Total sugars (g) 2.4 Protein (g) 21.7 Sodium (mg) 561 Calcium (mg) 221 Magnesium (mg) 16 Potassium (mg) 299 Iron (mg) 2.5

Amount/Serving		% DV		% DV
Total Fat 4.5 g		7%	Vitamin A	0%
Sat. Fat 2.5 g		13%	Vitamin C	0%
Trans Fat 0g				
Cholest.	10 mg	3%		
Sodium	700 mg	29%	Calcium	8%
Total Carb 38g		13%	Iron	8%
Dietary Fiber 1g		4%		
Sugars	7g			
Protein	6g			

Ingredients: Enriched Macaroni Product (wheat flour, glycerol monostearate, Niacin, Ferrous Sulfate (Iron), Thiamin Mononitrate (Vitamin B1), Riboflavin (Vitamin B2), Folic Acid, Cheese Sauce Mix (Whey, Corn Syrup Solids, Monterey Jack Cheese (Milk, Cheese Culture, Salt, Enzymes), Milkfat, Palm Oil, Sugar, Milk Protein Concentrate, Salt, Contains Less Than 2% of Cheddar Cheese (Milk, Cheese Culture, Salt, Enzymes, Skim Milk, Cellulose gum, Dried Buttermilk, Sodium Phosphate, Sodium Tripoly Phosphate, Citric Acid, Autolyzed Yeast, Torula Yeast, Guar Gum, Calcium Phosphate, Natural Flavor, Artificial Flavor, Yellow 5, Yellow 6, Cheese Culture, Enzymes, Celery Seed Oil), Modified Food Starch, Salt, Maltodextrin, Potassium Chloride, Acetylated Monoglycerides, Medium Chain Triglycerides, Apocarotenal (Color)

Mixed Bean Salad

8 (1 cup) servings

½ cup red wine vinegar

¼ cup canola oil

1 tablespoon plus 2 teaspoons sugar

½ teaspoon salt

¼ teaspoon ground black pepper

1 teaspoon powdered dry mustard

½ teaspoon garlic powder

¼ teaspoon paprika

2 tablespoons chopped fresh parsley

1½ cups canned cannellini beans, drained and rinsed

1½ cups canned red kidney beans, drained and rinsed

1½ cups canned black beans, drained and rinsed

1 cup finely diced celery

1 cup thawed frozen baby corn

½ cup finely diced onion

¼ cup finely diced green pepper

¼ cup finely diced red pepper

¼ cup finely diced yellow pepper

In a large mixing bowl, combine the vinegar, oil, sugar, salt, pepper, dry mustard, garlic powder, and paprika and whisk together. Add the remaining ingredients and mix well. Label, date, and refrigerate. Chill for about two hours before serving cold.

Note: This recipe is particularly good for a party and stores well in the refrigerator as a leftover—it tastes even better the next day!

Calories (Kcal) 220 Fat (g) 7.8 Saturated fats (g) 0.5 Trans fatty acid (g) 0.03 Healthy fats (g) 7.3 Omega-3 fats (g) 0.7 Dietary fiber (g) 8.3 Carbohydrates (g) 30.6 Total sugars (g) 5.4 Protein (g) 9 Sodium (mg) 579 Calcium (mg) 80 Magnesium (mg) 5 Potassium (mg) 218 Iron (mg) 2.5

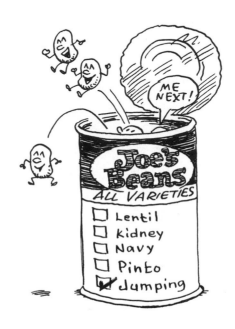

Rosemary Potatoes

4 (½ cup) servings

2 teaspoons chopped fresh rosemary

½ teaspoon salt

¼ teaspoon ground black pepper

1 tablespoon minced fresh garlic

1 tablespoon extra virgin olive oil

1 pound redskin potatoes, washed and cut into equal-sized wedges

Preheat oven to 375°F.

In a bowl, combine the first five ingredients; mix well. Add the potato wedges to the bowl, coating them evenly with the marinade. Spread the potatoes out on a nonstick baking sheet and bake for 30 minutes or until tender.

Note: If you're not a rosemary fan, you can substitute your favorite herb instead.

WHAT'S IN IT FOR YOU

Calories (Kcal) 115 Fat (g) 3.8 Saturated fats (g) 0.5 Trans fatty acid (g) 0 Healthy fats (g) 0.5 Omega-3 fats (g) 0.1 Dietary fiber (g) 1.9 Carbohydrates (g) 17.7 Total sugars (g) 1.4 Protein (g) 2 Sodium (mg) 291 Calcium (mg) 12.4 Magnesium (mg) 24 Potassium (mg) 487 Iron (mg) 0.8

Black Bean Soup

4 (1 cup) servings

1 15-ounce can black beans, drained and rinsed

1 tablespoon extra virgin olive oil

1 cup diced onion

2 teaspoons minced fresh garlic

½ teaspoon dried oregano

½ teaspoon paprika

¼ teaspoon cumin

2 cups water plus 1 tablespoon natural vegetable base,
   or 2 cups vegetable stock

1 tablespoon canned jalapeño chili peppers, finely chopped

2 tablespoons tomato paste

In medium pot, on medium heat, add the oil and sauté the onion until it is transparent. Add the garlic and sauté for two more minutes. Add the remaining ingredients; bring to a simmer and cook for 10 minutes. Turn off the heat, then remove the pot from the stove and stir the soup with a wooden spoon to mix well. Serve or allow the soup to cool, and then cover, label, date, and refrigerate.

WHAT'S IN IT FOR YOU

Calories (Kcal) 105 Fat (g) 3.3 Saturated fats (g) 0.5 Trans fatty acid (g) 0 Healthy fats (g) 2.8 Omega-3 fats (g) 0.02 Dietary fiber (g) 4.9 Carbohydrates (g) 17.5 Total sugars (g) 2.8 Protein (g) 4.3 Sodium (mg) 275 Calcium (mg) 43 Magnesium (mg) 8 Potassium (mg) 362 Iron (mg) 1.6

Aglio e Olio/Whole Wheat Angel Hair with Broccoli

4 (1½ cup) servings

1 bunch broccoli (8 ounces), cut into 2-inch pieces (3 cups),
    or 3 cups frozen florets

8 ounces 100% whole wheat capellini (angel hair) pasta

2 tablespoons extra virgin olive oil

2 cloves garlic, minced

2 tablespoons chopped fresh parsley or basil

½ teaspoon kosher salt

¼ teaspoon crushed red pepper flakes

Fill a large saucepan three-fourths full with water. Bring to a boil over high heat. Add the broccoli; reduce the heat and simmer until crisp-tender, about 4 minutes. Use a slotted spoon to transfer the broccoli to paper towels to drain. Add the pasta to the simmering water; cook until al dente (firm to the bite), 2 to 4 minutes. Drain the pasta in a colander. Wipe out the saucepan; place it over medium heat. Add the oil and garlic; sauté for 1 minute, or until the garlic just begins to brown. Add the broccoli, pasta, and remaining ingredients; toss well.

WHAT'S IN IT FOR YOU

Calories (Kcal) 306 Fat (g) 8.8 Saturated fats (g) 1 Trans fatty acid (g) 0 Healthy fats (g) 7.7 Omega-3 fats (g) 0.1 Dietary fiber (g) 5.8 Carbohydrates (g) 5.8 Total sugars (g) 3.3 Protein (g) 9.0 Sodium (mg) 318 Calcium (mg) 61 Magnesium (mg) 1 Potassium (mg) 404 Iron (mg) 2

Spicy, Crunchy, Garlic Broccoli and Cauliflower

4 (½ cup) servings

2 cups small cauliflower florets, fresh or frozen (4 ounces)

2 cups small broccoli florets, fresh or frozen (4 ounces)

2 tablespoons extra virgin olive oil

1 teaspoon minced fresh garlic

3 tablespoons fresh lemon juice

½ to 1 teaspoon crushed red pepper flakes, as desired

1 teaspoon dried oregano

1 teaspoon minced fresh parsley

½ teaspoon kosher salt

Cook the cauliflower and broccoli florets in a medium saucepan of simmering water for 2 minutes or until still crisp. Drain; rinse with cold water and drain well. Wrap them in paper towels and refrigerate.

Dry the same saucepan and add the oil and garlic. Sauté the garlic over low heat for 2 minutes or until it is softened. Add the blanched vegetables (the lightly cooked broccoli and cauliflower) and remaining ingredients to the oil and garlic and toss well. Serve at room temperature or reheat if you prefer it warm.

WHAT'S IN IT FOR YOU

Calories (Kcal) 96 Fat (g) 7.5 Saturated fats (g) 1.1 Trans fatty acid (g) 0 Healthy fats (g) 6 Omega-3 fats (g) 0.1 Dietary fiber (g) 2.5 Carbohydrates (g) 6.3 Total sugars (g) 1.4 Protein (g) 2.2 Sodium (mg) 266 Calcium (mg) 38 Magnesium (mg) 20 Potassium (mg) 306 Iron (mg) 0.8

"Soycado" Salsa

8 (⅓ cup) servings

2 teaspoons extra virgin olive oil

½ cup extra firm diced tofu (cut into ¼-inch cubes)

½ cup finely chopped sweet onion

1 teaspoon minced fresh garlic

1 teaspoon minced jalapeño pepper

1½ cups diced seeded tomatoes

½ cup minced fresh cilantro

¼ cup minced fresh parsley

2 tablespoons fresh lime juice

1 teaspoon kosher salt

¼ teaspoon ground black pepper

1 ripe avocado, peeled, seeded, and diced

Heat the oil in a large nonstick skillet over medium heat until it is hot. Add the tofu; sauté until lightly browned, about 3 minutes. Add the onion, garlic, and jalapeño; sauté for 2 minutes. Add the tomatoes; sauté until the tomatoes begin to soften. Turn off the heat; stir in the remaining ingredients except the avocado. Refrigerate for up to 3 days. Stir in the avocado just before serving. Serve with whole wheat pita bread or pita chips, baked corn chips, or raw fresh vegetables.

WHAT'S IN IT FOR YOU

Calories (Kcal) 80 Fat (g) 5.5 Saturated fats (g) 0.7 Trans fatty acid (g) 0 Healthy fats (g) 4.3 Omega-3 fats (g) 0.5 Dietary fiber (g) 2.4 Carbohydrates (g) 6.8 Total sugars (g) 2.8 Protein (g) 2.4 Sodium (mg) 239 Calcium (mg) 41 Magnesium (mg) 15 Potassium (mg) 259 Iron (mg) 0.9

Blueberry, Strawberry, Raspberry, and Oatmeal Crisp

6 (½ cup) servings

2 cups fresh or frozen blueberries

¾ cup fresh or frozen raspberries

½ cup quartered fresh or frozen strawberries

2 tablespoons agave nectar, divided

1½ teaspoons chia seeds

1½ teaspoons grated orange zest (the outermost orange-colored
  layer of the peel)

1 cup quick-cooking or old-fashioned oats

2 tablespoons whole wheat flour

½ teaspoon baking powder

½ teaspoon baking soda

¼ teaspoon kosher salt

3 tablespoons unsweetened almond milk

2 tablespoons canola oil

Preheat oven to 400°F. Mix the blueberries, raspberries, strawberries, 1 tablespoon of the agave nectar, the chia seeds, and orange zest in an 8- or 9-inch square baking dish.

Combine the oats, flour, baking powder, baking soda, and salt in a medium bowl; mix well. Combine the almond milk, oil, and remaining 1 tablespoon agave nectar in a small bowl. Add the liquid mixture to the oat mixture; stir with a fork until crumbly. Sprinkle the mixture over the fruit. Bake for 20 to 25 minutes or until the crisp is bubbly and the topping is golden brown. Let it stand for 15 minutes before serving.

WHAT'S IN IT FOR YOU

Calories (Kcal) 178 Fat (g) 6.5 Saturated fats (g) 0.4 Trans fatty acid (g) 0.02 Healthy fats (g) 5.9 Omega-3 fats (g) 1.1 Dietary fiber (g) 5 Carbohydrates (g) 28.5 Total sugars (g) 12.6 Protein (g) 3.3 Sodium (mg) 238 Calcium (mg) 44 Magnesium (mg) 15 Potassium (mg) 118 Iron (mg) 1.5

Lifestyle 180 Chocolate Banana Creamers

8 servings (2 banana slices each)

1 large (8-inch) ripe banana

16 small wooden skewers (preferably two-prong design)

3 ounces 72% dark bittersweet chocolate, chopped,
    or ¾ cup dark chocolate chips

Peel the banana and cut it crosswise into 16 slices; skewer each slice and place it on a waxed-paper-lined plate. Freeze for at least 1 hour.

Place the chocolate in a small saucepan. Cook over very low heat, stirring constantly with a wooden spoon, until the chocolate is almost completely melted. Remove the saucepan from the heat; stir until the chocolate is completely melted. Tip the saucepan to one side and dip each frozen banana slice in the chocolate so that it is completely covered. Scrape the bottom of the banana slice on the edge of the saucepan, letting the excess chocolate flow back into the saucepan. Place the chocolate-dipped banana slices back onto the waxed-paper-lined plate and freeze for at least 30 minutes before serving. Store in the freezer for up to 2 weeks.

Note: This recipe requires time to freeze, but the delayed gratification is well worth the wait!

WHAT'S IN IT FOR YOU

Calories (Kcal) 74 Fat (g) 4.4 Saturated fats (g) 2.7 Trans fatty acid (g) 0 Healthy fats (g) 1.7 Omega-3 fats (g) 0 Dietary fiber (g) 1.5 Carbohydrates (g) 9 Total sugars (g) 5 Protein (g) 1.3 Sodium (mg) 1 Calcium (mg) 8 Magnesium (mg) 5 Potassium (mg) 61 Iron (mg) 1

JP's Mac and Cheese

6 (1¼ cup) servings

6 ounces elbow macaroni, cavatappi, penne, or rotini 100% whole
    wheat pasta (2½ cups dry)

2 medium (14 ounces) sweet potatoes, peeled and diced (½-inch cubes),
    or 14 ounces canned sweet potatoes (no added sugar)

2 cups unsweetened almond milk

6 ounces extra firm silken tofu

1 teaspoon Dijon mustard

¼ teaspoon ground black pepper

⅛ teaspoon nutmeg

⅛ teaspoon cayenne pepper

4 ounces low-fat shredded mozzarella cheese

Preheat oven to 350°F. Cook the pasta according to the package directions, omitting the salt. Meanwhile, combine the sweet potatoes and almond milk in a medium saucepan. Bring to a boil over high heat. Reduce the heat; simmer, uncovered, until the potatoes are very tender, about 20 minutes. Drain the potatoes, reserving the milk. If the milk measures less than 1½ cups, add additional milk to equal 1½ cups. Puree the sweet potatoes and all of the remaining ingredients except the cheese in a blender until smooth or mash by hand with wooden spoon, the back of a fork, or a wire whisk.

    Toss the pasta with the sweet potato sauce and cheese; transfer to an 8- or 9-inch baking dish. Cover with foil; bake for 35 to 40 minutes, or until heated through.

WHAT'S IN IT FOR YOU

Calories (Kcal) 240 Fat (g) 7 Saturated fats (g) 3 Trans fatty acid (g) 0 Healthy fats (g) 3.5 Omega-3 fats (g) 0.1 Dietary fiber (g) 5.2 Carbohydrates (g) 36 Total sugars (g) 3.7 Protein (g) 12 Sodium (mg) 270 Calcium (mg) 242 Magnesium (mg) 53 Potassium (mg) 366 Iron (mg) 1.7

JP's Kale Kakes

Makes 24 (½ ounce) servings

1 cup toasted walnuts

1½ cups golden raisins

2 ounces whole wheat cakes (10 squares)

¼ teaspoon ground cinnamon

½ teaspoon turmeric

1 ounce dried kale*

1 tablespoon vanilla

2 tablespoons orange juice

Preheat oven to 300°F.

Place the walnuts in a food processor and pulse until fine. Add the raisins and pulse until the mixture becomes sticky. Add the wheat cakes and pulse until fine and the mixture is loose. Add the cinnamon, turmeric, and dried kale and pulse until the mixture is fine and still fluffy. Add the vanilla and orange juice and process until the mixture is gummy/sticky.

Transfer the contents of the food processor into a bowl and knead for one minute to combine the ingredients into a large ball. Break off ½-ounce portions, flatten them to ⅜-inch thick rounds, then place them on a parchment-paper-covered baking sheet and bake for 20 minutes. Remove and cool on a rack for 20 minutes. Serve or store in a covered container.

Note: Impress your friends by bringing this into school as a snack!

WHAT'S IN IT FOR YOU

Calories (Kcal) 231 Fat (g) 9.7 Saturated fats (g) 0.9 Trans fatty acid (g) 0 Healthy fats (g) 8.8 Omega-3 fats (g) 1.4 Dietary fiber (g) 2.8 Carbohydrates (g) 33 Total sugars (g) 23 Protein (g) 4.3 Sodium (mg) 35 Calcium (mg) 50 Magnesium (mg) 29 Potassium (mg) 374 Iron (mg) 1.6

* Dried kale procedure: Preheat oven to 300°F. Wash four ounces of raw kale with the thick center rib removed; shake off excess water, place the leaves on a rack over a sheet pan, and allow them to dry in the oven for 25 to 30 minutes until the kale is crisp but not brown.

Tofu Mousse

Makes 12 (⅓ cup) servings

12 ounces extra firm tofu

2 medium bananas

Grated zest (the outermost orange-color peel) from one orange

Juice from one orange

2 ounces baking chocolate

2 ounces cocoa powder

2 teaspoons vanilla extract

1 tablespoon plus 2 teaspoons sugar

Place the tofu in a food processor; process until creamy. Add the bananas, orange zest, and juice and process until smooth. Melt the chocolate according to the package directions. Add the chocolate and remaining ingredients to the banana mixture; process until smooth. Transfer the contents of the food processor to individual dishes or a large bowl; cover and refrigerate at least 30 minutes before serving.

WHAT'S IN IT FOR YOU

Calories (Kcal) 79 Fat (g) 3.6 Saturated fats (g) 1.4 Trans fatty acid (g) 0 Healthy fats (g) 2.2 Omega-3 fats (g) 0.1 Dietary fiber (g) 1.9 Carbohydrates (g) 9.7 Total sugars (g) 4.5 Protein (g) 3.2 Sodium (mg) 0.3 Calcium (mg) 49 Magnesium (mg) 5 Potassium (mg) 108 Iron (mg) 1.4

"Soyesto" Green Beans

4 (⅔ cup) servings

1 clove garlic, peeled

½ cup thawed frozen shelled edamame beans

⅓ cup chopped walnuts, toasted

⅓ cup chopped pecans, toasted

¼ cup packed fresh basil leaves

¼ cup packed fresh parsley leaves (no stems)

¼ cup packed fresh spinach leaves or ¼ cup frozen spinach, well drained and squeezed to remove excess moisture. You may use 2 tablespoons additional basil and parsley instead of the spinach.

½ teaspoon kosher salt

¼ cup extra virgin olive oil

12 ounces fresh or frozen green beans, trimmed (3½ cups)

With the motor running, drop the garlic through the feed tube of a food processor; process until minced. Add the edamame, walnuts, pecans, basil, parsley, spinach, and salt; process until the mixture is minced. With the motor running, gradually pour in the oil until it is well blended.

Cook the green beans in simmering water until just tender, about 5 minutes. Drain; return to the same pot and toss with ½ cup of the "soyesto" (the sauce from the food processor). Refrigerate the remaining ½ cup "soyesto"—it's great tossed with hot cooked pasta or stirred into soup.

WHAT'S IN IT FOR YOU

Calories (Kcal) 156 Fat (g) 13 Saturated fats (g) 1.5 Trans fatty acid (g) 0 Healthy fats (g) 11 Omega-3 fats (g) 0.5 Dietary fiber (g) 2.6 Carbohydrates (g) 5.9 Total sugars (g) 2.2 Protein (g) 3.3 Sodium (mg) 110 Calcium (mg) 36 Magnesium (mg) 11 Potassium (mg) 44 Iron (mg) 0.8

Sweet Potato Hummus

6 (⅓ cup) servings

2 cloves garlic, peeled

1 15-ounce can cooked sweet potatoes, drained

1 4-ounce jar roasted red peppers, packed in water, drained

3 tablespoons fresh lemon juice

½ teaspoon ground cumin

¼ to ½ teaspoon cayenne pepper, as desired

¼ teaspoon kosher salt

1 tablespoon chopped fresh parsley

With the motor running, drop the garlic cloves through the feed tube of a food processor; process until minced. Add the remaining ingredients except the parsley; puree until smooth. Transfer the hummus to a serving bowl; refrigerate for at least 1 hour. Garnish the hummus with the parsley just before serving. Serve with baked pita chips or raw vegetables.

WHAT'S IN IT FOR YOU

Calories (Kcal) 93 Fat (g) 0.2 Saturated Fat (g) 0.04 Trans fatty acid (g) 0 Healthy fats (g) 0.2 Omega-3 fats (g) 0.1 Dietary fiber (g) 1.5 Carbohydrates (g) 19.5 Total sugars (g) 3.8 Protein (g) 2 Sodium (mg) 308 Calcium (mg) 27 Magnesium (mg) 17 Potassium (mg) 241 Zinc (mg) 0.2 Iron (mg) 0.9

Caramelized Onion, Chive, Zucchini, and Potato Pancakes with Broccoli

6 pancakes

3 teaspoons extra virgin olive oil, divided

½ cup finely diced sweet onion

¼ cup whole wheat flour

1½ teaspoons baking powder

½ teaspoon kosher salt

1 large Idaho (baking) potato (10 ounces), peeled and diced (2 cups)

1½ tablespoons low-fat milk

½ cup grated zucchini (1 small zucchini), squeezed dry

1 tablespoon chopped fresh chives

1 10-ounce package frozen broccoli spears (6 large spears),
   cooked according to package directions

Heat 1 teaspoon of the oil in a 12-inch nonstick skillet over medium heat. Add the onion; sauté until golden brown, 5 to 6 minutes. Set aside to cool.

Meanwhile, combine the flour, baking powder, and salt in a medium bowl. Puree the potatoes with milk in a blender, scraping down the sides of the blender occasionally. Add the flour mixture; blend until smooth. Pour the mixture back into the bowl; fold in the cooked onion, zucchini, and chives.

Heat 1 teaspoon of the remaining oil in the same skillet over medium heat until it is hot. Drop the potato mixture by heaping ¼ cupfuls into the hot oil in three mounds. Press the mixture flat with a large spatula to form 5-inch pancakes. Cook for 3 to 4 minutes per side, or until golden brown and cooked through. Repeat with the remaining oil and potato mixture (or use 2 skillets at one time). To serve, wrap one warm potato pancake around each broccoli spear.

Note: The pancakes may be made ahead and reheated in the oven or toaster oven. If you like ketchup with your fries, wait till you try it with these potato pancakes!

Calories (Kcal) 92 Fat (g) 1.8 Saturated fats (g) 0.3 Trans fatty acid (g) 0 Healthy fats (g) 1.3 Omega-3 fats (g) 0.2 Dietary fiber (g) 2.7 Carbohydrates (g) 16 Total sugars (g) 1.6 Protein (g) 3 Sodium (mg) 318 Calcium (mg) 51 Magnesium (mg) 21 Potassium (mg) 270 Iron (mg) 0.7

JP's More Broccoli, Please

6 (½ cup) servings

1 small sweet potato (7 ounces), peeled and diced (½-inch cubes) (1¾ cups)

1 cup unsweetened almond milk

3 ounces extra firm silken tofu

½ teaspoon salt

¼ teaspoon Dijon mustard

⅛ teaspoon ground black pepper

⅛ teaspoon ground nutmeg

Pinch of cayenne pepper

1 tablespoon canola oil

1 teaspoon minced fresh garlic

4 cups small broccoli florets, fresh or frozen

½ cup chopped walnuts, toasted

½ cup finely diced red bell pepper

Combine the sweet potato and almond milk in a small saucepan. Bring to a boil over high heat. Reduce heat; simmer until the potatoes are very tender, about 20 minutes. Strain the potato, reserving the milk. Measure the milk, and if there is less than ¾ cup, add additional almond milk to measure ¾ cup. Place the sweet potato and milk in a blender with the tofu, ¼ teaspoon of the salt, the mustard, pepper, nutmeg, and cayenne pepper. Blend until smooth. Transfer the mixture back to the small saucepan.

Heat the oil in a large nonstick skillet over medium heat. Add the garlic; sauté 1 minute. Add the broccoli, walnuts, red pepper, and remaining ¼ teaspoon salt. Stir-fry the mixture for 5 to 6 minutes or until the vegetables are crisp-tender. Heat the sweet potato sauce over medium heat until hot. Serve the broccoli with the sweet potato sauce.

Note: Be creative and serve this wonderful "cheeseless" cheese sauce on top of any of your favorite vegetables or use it in recipes for nachos, quesadillas, tuna melts, au gratin potatoes, or any creation where you add cheese!

Calories (Kcal) 146 Fat (g) 9.7 Saturated fats (g) 0.9 Trans fatty acid (g) 0.01 Healthy fats (g) 8.8 Omega-3 fats (g) 1.2 Dietary fiber (g) 3.6 Carbohydrates (g) 12 Total sugars (g) 2.3 Protein (g) 4.8 Sodium (mg) 73 Calcium (mg) 82 Magnesium (mg) 44 Potassium (mg) 392 Iron (mg) 1.2

RB's Vegetarian Chili

Makes 15 (1 cup) servings

2 tablespoons canola oil

1 large yellow onion, chopped

4 smashed cloves fresh garlic

1 cup diced carrots

2 large green peppers, roughly chopped

2 jalapeño peppers, seeded and diced

2 medium zucchini, sliced and diced

1 8-ounce bag frozen corn (or 1 cup fresh)

1 8-ounce can tomato paste

1 16-ounce can Muir fire-roasted tomatoes, drained (juice reserved) and chopped

4 to 5 tablespoons chili powder, or more to taste

2 to 3 tablespoons ground cumin

2 to 3 bay leaves

2 tablespoons dried oregano

Freshly ground pepper (about 15 grinds)

2 chopped chipotle peppers in adobo sauce (these come in a can and can be found in the ethnic section of the grocery store)

3 15-ounce cans of red and/or black beans, drained and rinsed

1 cup vegetable stock

In a large heavy pot, heat the oil over medium-high heat. Add the onion, garlic, and carrots; sauté until translucent. Add the peppers (except the chipotle), zucchini, and corn; sauté for five minutes, stirring occasionally. Add the tomato paste, chopped tomatoes, and tomato juice. Then add the chili powder, cumin, bay leaves, oregano, and pepper. Stir well. Add the chopped chipotle peppers and beans. Stir well. Add the vegetable stock until liquid covers all of the ingredients in the pot. Bring to a boil, then reduce heat to medium low. Simmer for a half hour, stirring occasionally. Remove from heat, adjust the seasonings to taste, and remove the bay leaves.

Serve with chopped avocado and fresh lime juice.

Note: This chili is always best the second day. It also goes well with fried or poached eggs for brunch.

WHAT'S IN IT FOR YOU

Calories (Kcal) 163 Fat (g) 3.3 Saturated fats (g) 0.3 Trans fatty acid (g) 0.01 Healthy fats (g) 2.9 Omega-3 fats (g) 0.2 Dietary fiber (g) 7.8 Carbohydrates (g) 27 Total sugars (g) 5.7 Protein (g) 7.5 Sodium (mg) 431 Calcium (mg) 88 Magnesium (mg) 19 Potassium (mg) 309 Iron (mg) 2.9

White Bean Dip

Makes 4 (½ cup) servings

4 cloves fresh garlic, minced

Dill, rosemary, or any other herb you like

1 tablespoon olive oil

1 15-ounce can cannellini beans

Sauté the garlic and dill (or other herb) in the olive oil for a few minutes. Add the white beans (undrained) and heat, mashing them with the back of a wooden spoon. When thickened to the consistency of a paste (in 10 to 15 minutes), remove from heat. Serve warm or cold as a dip with fresh veggies, on top of grilled chicken, as the spread for a "gourmet" sandwich, or as a great filling in a 100 percent whole grain tortilla wrap with vegetables. The bean dip can be refrigerated for 3 to 5 days.

WHAT'S IN IT FOR YOU

Calories (Kcal) 119 Fat (g) 4.4 Saturated fats (g) 0.5 Trans fatty acid (g) 0 Healthy fats (g) 3.8 Omega-3 fat (g) 0.03 Dietary fiber (g) 4.2 Carbohydrates (g) 15 Total sugars (g) 0.9 Protein (g) 5 Sodium (mg) 34 Calcium (mg) 40 Magnesium (mg) 51 Potassium (mg) 223 Iron (mg) 1.5

YOU Tool 3

Cosmetic Surgery and Teens

At one point or another, many teens and adults want to be magically transformed into a different shape. A smaller or straighter nose, bigger (or smaller) breasts, less fat. Plastic surgery can help you breathe easier if your nose isn't aligned right, reduce back pain if your breasts are so large that your back constantly hurts, and instill confidence if you have a physical flaw that impacts your self-esteem. *But* it's not a miraculous cure-all, cannot guarantee instant popularity or sex appeal, does not always achieve the desired results, and should not be a substitute for feeling good about yourself from the inside out.

Who should get plastic surgery? People with a deviated septum (crooked inside of the nose) who can't breathe easily can benefit from a brand new nose. Laser surgery can help with birthmarks such as port-wine stains: purple, flat birthmarks that can be quite large and prominent. People with chronic back pain due to a seriously large set of breasts may be better able to enjoy sports, fit into clothes, and so forth after a breast reduction. And plastic surgery may be of great benefit to those who feel the psychological weight of one isolated perceived defect.

Here are the most common cosmetic surgeries undergone by teens. Please do not do these procedures on yourself; and if you think you are going to have your younger sister do any of these, don't risk it. Please discuss these with a qualified plastic surgeon for the particular procedure (qualified is board certified who can prove to you she has already done more than fifty of these a year for at least five years).

Male breast reduction: It is normal for adolescent guys to have a brief time, somewhere between ages eleven and fourteen years, when their breasts grow just a bit. This can be so embarrassing that guys may refuse to take off their T-shirt for gym or to swim without a shirt. Most of the time, this breast growth is transient, going away within a year or two of when it started. Some guys, however, do get stuck with breast tissue moving beyond the nipple line that plans to be there for the duration. This kind of breast tissue can be removed surgically under general anesthesia and usually leads to a cosmetically pleasing result. Guys with gynecomastia often worry that they're "turning into a girl"; ironically, the real cause of that extra breast tissue may be a surge of testosterone. Other causes of gynecomastia include use of marijuana or steroids (not the kind you use for asthma; we're talking about the kind used by weight lifters who artificially try to achieve that carved look). Obesity can also cause enlarged breasts, but in this case, it is fatty tissue, not real breast tissue. Cosmetic surgery will remove only the breast tissue; the fat you are stuck with unless you follow our exercise plan and start eating healthier (see chapters 3 and 4).

Breast implants: Implants are placed either in front of or behind your pectoralis (chest wall) muscle in this two-hour surgery, which is best performed with general anesthesia. The newest technique, in which the muscle is actually cut through to let the implant hang more naturally, makes it harder for women to flex their pecs. Unless you're headed for the Olympics, this won't hurt your athletic performance. One of the main problems with breast augmentations is that implants distort X-ray mammograms (something to think about down the line), meaning that you'll require annual MRIs to check for breast cancer. You need to consult with a doc and determine whether your breasts are finished growing and developing—as some women's breasts can grow into their early twenties (especially if they start puberty at fourteen and it takes up to eight additional years for breast development to be complete).

Rhinoplasty: It sounds like a procedure performed on zoo animals, but nose jobs are serious business. This two-to three-hour procedure can be done with you either awake or asleep. The doc will sculpt the cartilage and bones in your nose, making you look like . . . yourself, but hopefully without that hump. The noses of today are much more conservative than your mother's rhinoplasty, but even so, 15 percent of people who have their noses operated on have to go under the knife for a touch-up. Don't expect your insurance to cover rhinoplasty; it's usually cosmetic.

If you think you need plastic surgery, you should be able to spell out your reasons pretty clearly to both your parents and your doctor. The plastic surgeon may require you to discuss the surgery with a psychologist—not to see if you're crazy but to make sure that this will be a useful procedure for you, rather than leaving you with scars but otherwise still not happy with yourself. If plastic surgery is truly for cosmetics only, then most insurance companies won't pay for it. So, if you feel that plastic surgery must be part of your future, start saving now.

YOU Tool 4
Medical Confidentiality

As a teen, you have legal rights regarding medical confidentiality. These vary from state to state. Some terms you should know:

Confidentiality: The most essential right is to confidentiality—a legal term that means that unless you give explicit permission, your doctor cannot disclose information about you and certain health topics unless it is life threatening to you or to someone else.★ A doctor might phrase it as such: "With your parent out of the room, everything we talk about is confidential, meaning I will not share with your parents anything you say unless it is life threatening or dangerous." The clinician will usually

---

★ To tell you how seriously hospitals treat the electronic medical record confidentiality, think about Gabby Giffords, the Arizona congresswoman who was shot in Tucson in January 2011. A few hospital employees who were not caring for the victims of the shooting looked at their records. All three were fired and will have a tough time being hired by anyone. Similarly, two Cleveland Clinic employees not involved in the care of a famous basketball player looked at his medical records. Both were fired. We take these matters seriously.

then ask all the personal questions, including questions about risk-taking behavior— sex and drugs and rock and roll (well, maybe not about the latter). Admitting that you smoke cigarettes should not just get you the "don't smoke" sermon; an expert physician can also help you figure out if you are addicted, and ideally help you stop before you are.

In all fifty states, teens have the right to seek confidential diagnosis and treatment for STIs (though some states allow physicians to contact a minor's parents), and some states allow for minors to consent for contraceptive services. (See chapter 8.)

Informed consent: To give informed consent means that you (1) have been given adequate information about the risks, benefits, and alternatives to make a decision about a proposed medical intervention and (2) are mentally capable of making an educated decision. Clearly, people who are profoundly developmentally challenged or mentally ill are not able to give informed consent; young children are also not capable of giving informed consent. Teens are often considered old enough; where the law does not specifically prescribe an age of consent (for instance, with regard to sex), the decision is made on a case-by-case basis.

State-by-state variations in consent laws are most common around teen sex and pregnancy issues. See www.cahl.org/web/ for state-by-state info.

Minors: What is a minor? Someone under eighteen? Not necessarily. An emancipated minor is a "mature minor" able and allowed to give consent to certain procedures. Emancipated minors may include those who are married, in jail, enlisted in the armed services, or who have shown proof of self-sufficiency (living on their own without a parent, paying all bills, and so forth). These individuals can legally consent to all medical care and treatment, including rehabilitation from drug and alcohol abuse, diagnosis and treatment of STIs, prevention of pregnancy, and mental health care. Adolescents can also give consent for the treatment of a medical emergency, including severe abdominal pain.

The mature minor doctrine was developed in the latter half of the twentieth century in response to the civil rights movement, with the thought that adolescents also deserved certain rights. It was felt in those years that many teens were deprived of needed medical services because they would rather not receive care than have to tell their parents. Many states passed laws that gave the treating physician the ability to determine who is a mature minor. This was a landmark for teens, as it took the decision for certain medical treatments out of the hands of legislators, judges, committees, or psychiatrists. This mature minor doctrine has withstood numerous court challenges.

HIPAA: Many teens invoke "HIPAA" without actually understanding what the Health Insurance Portability and Accountability Act actually means. The HIPAA privacy rule creates new regulations guaranteeing adult patients' medical records be kept confidential in certain states. HIPAA does not provide confidentiality protections for adolescents on a national level, but it does not remove any state-level protections that exist. So if a state law allows a teen to consent to confidential care, under HIPAA the information about this care cannot be shared with anyone, including a parent, without the teen's consent. So before invoking HIPAA, you need to know exactly what the laws are in your state.

Acknowledgments

From the YOU Docs—Mike Roizen and Mehmet Oz

A few years ago, we wrote *YOU: The Owner's Manual,* which taught people about the inner workings of their bodies—and how to keep it running strong. We learned that lots of kids (and teachers) were using the book to share the coolest revelations about the maturing body. But you know what? There's a big difference between an adult's body and the teen body, between adult health mysteries and *teen* health mysteries, between adult health questions and teen questions. So we pulled together the team to craft a customized Owner's Manual that every soon-to-be-adult can use.

For the first time, pediatrician Dr. Ellen Rome joins us on the cover and has been an inspiration for both this and the prior book on parenting. She contributes life-changing insights to every chapter in this book and helped generate the overall approach to getting the attention of teens. The practical experiences she collects while working with adolescents at the Cleveland Clinic helped us share the essence of her unique specialty with our readers.

Ted Spiker culled together the best ideas from our adult and teen consultants to generate an uplifting, edgy text that thrills readers which insights spiced with humor. Professor Spiker (at the University of Florida) knows how to communicate with his classroom and used those gifts to help write this work. He has crafted an elegant and comprehensive compilation of the most important issues plaguing teens.

Linda Kahn's meticulous attention to detail improves the quality of every book we author. She shares her mothering wisdom thoughtfully as she educates the doctors quite a bit about health. She continued to provide profound criticisms of our work and help us revise the text into the fabulous final result by commenting on both the content and the style. She keeps us focused on our readers.

Gary Hallgren's visually arresting medical cartoons have brought alive every one of our books, and we modified many and added plenty more to keep teens engaged in the current work. We love his childlike enthusiasm, which is perfectly matched to our audience this time around.

Craig Wynett offers high-level concepts that allow us to offer knowledge through unique metaphors. Craig transforms doctrinal discussions into profoundly insightful meetings on how to change our reader's minds so they act on what we teach.

Joel Harper has created high quality YOU Workouts for all age groups and offers several options for all ages in the current book.

Zoe Oz, my sixteen-year-old daughter, recruited numerous friends to test-drive all the chapters of the book and reminded us that teens think about life very differently than adults. Few of our original lighthearted jokes impressed her, but with her contributions and Ted's nimble writing, we found a happy (and playful) middle ground.

We want to specially thank our many readers, including the leadership of our children's health education foundation healthcorps.org, led by Michelle Bouchard and Rob Roberts. Their editorial contributions and classroom-tested tools improved our effort. Finally, our agent Candice Fuhrman brought reality to many of crazy brainstorming sessions and kept us on target for teens and their parents.

Thanks to our friends in the publishing world who have so passionately supported this material designed for a younger readership. Dominick Anfuso and Martha Levin (along with Carolyn Reidy) have been our partners at Free Press (Simon & Schuster) for books and other endeavors and we are most appreciative. The superb team of Maura O'Brien, Jill Siegel, Carisa Hays, Suzanne Donahue, Claire Kelley, Laura Cooke, and Leah Miller are always seeking solutions to our many needs in the print and digital world and have dedicated themselves to making our books the best possible experience for teen readers.

Most of the recipes came from the Lifestyle 180 team of master chef Jim Perko, nutritionist Kristin Kirkpatrick, and former medical director Elizabeth Ricanati.

These Lifestyle 180 recipes are based on guidelines for YOU healthy foods, and were tested for love of taste and texture and ease of creation by teens.

We are indebted to our close partners at RealAge.com, including Val Weaver, Keith Roach, Carl Peck, Axel Goetz, Diane Lange, Susan Seliger, Greg Zegras, and Meredith Wade, and at YouBeauty.com, including Steve Lindseth and Laura Kenney. And we thank our wonderful friends at *Good Morning America* including Patty Neger and all the anchors who make waking up early to discuss health a lot of fun.

Thanks to all of our friends at *The Dr. Oz Show,* especially executive producers Mindy Moore Borman and Amy Chiaro, as well as Lori Rich, Donna O'Sullivan, Diane Amato, Tina Tung, Tim Sullivan, and all the great production team who make our day-to-day lives so much fun.

Thanks to the Oprah radio team, including Ximena Lavender, Corny Koehl, and Katherine Kelly. The Sharecare and Doctor Oz web team with Jeff Arnold, Dawn Whaley, Justin Ferrero, Michael Bloom, Samantha Lazarus and Angela Bruno have kept us digital.

Our books contain so broad a range of topics that we are compelled to ask advice from many world experts who selflessly share their insights in the true academic tradition. We list them all here without details of their contributions in order to save space for the actual book, but we deeply appreciate your dedication to your specialties and willingness to sacrifice your time in helping craft the most scientifically accurate book on adolescent health possible.

Kandi Amelon, Ivorie Anthony, Lisa Arnson, Christina Vernon Ayers, David L. Bell, MD, BK Boreyko, David Bronson, MD, John Campodonico, Regina Chandler, Kay Cherian, Glen Copeland, MD, Liz Dickinson, Courtney Dunlop, Erinne Dyer, Tanya Edwards, MD, Elizabeth Fiordalis, Lee Fleisher, MD, Emily Fox, Larry Friedman, Phillip Friedman, Joe Galuski, Gary Ginsberg, Susan Goldberg, Ian Gomar, Cindy Hundorfean, Paul Katz, Paul Keckley, Dennis Kenny, Eric Klein, MD, Richard Lang, MD, Jessica Leslie, Deb Lonzer, MD, Heather Lowry, Marsha Lowry, Paul Matsen, John Mauldin, Holly Miller, MD, Anthony Miniaci, MD, Anita Misra-Hebert, MD, Marleyna Mohler, Cindy Moore, Tom Morledge, MD, Steve Nissen, MD, Steve Oates, Bill Peacock, Jim Perko, Arthur Perry, MD, Susan Petre, Charise Petrovitch, MD, Larry Pollock, Anne Marie Prince, Heidi Roizen, Steven Ross, Raul

Seballos, MD, Eileen Scheil, Emma Steinberg, Zack Wasserman, Marta Worwag, Jim Young, MD.

From Mehmet Oz

Dr. Oz thanks his colleagues in Surgery for their continued support, including Dr. Craig Smith, Dr. Yoshifuma Naka, Dr. Mike Argenziano, Dr. Henry Spotnitz, Dr. Allan Stewart, and Dr. Mat Williams. The physician assistants, especially Laura Altman and Tom Cosola, the nurses in the OR and floor, and our spectacular ICU team always care meticulously for my patients. Our divisional administrator Diane Amato offered unique insights to books and life and has graced our efforts as my chief of staff at *The Dr. Oz Show,* and Lidia Nieves kept me on time and on target as I combined a life of heart surgery with media. Thanks to the dedicated staff at New York-Presbyterian Hospital, including Herb Pardes, Steve Corwin, Bob Kelly, David Feinberg, Bryan Dotson, Alicia Park, and Myrna Manners for their heartfelt advice. Thanks to the inspired Harpo leadership of Oprah Winfrey, Erik Logan, Sheri Salata, Harriet Seitler, and Doug Pattison and the Sony team led by Steve Mosko and John Weiser.

My parents, Mustafa and Suna Oz, taught me how to raise a tough teen as they struggled to parent their mischievous children. My parents-in-law, Gerald and Emily Jane Lemole, led by example while bringing all six of my brother- and sister-in-laws through the teen years. Lisa, my wife of a quarter century, has changed my life for the better in every way and raised four rambunctious teens and pre-teens. Her own *New York Times* number one book *Us* taught us all how to live in relationship. Daphne and Arabella helped review design and tonal elements and helped their sister and my coauthor Zoe keep up with my many demands on her time so we could keep this newest YOU book on schedule.

From Michael Roizen

Dr. Roizen wants to thank his administrative assistant, Beth Grubb, who made this work possible. And to thank many of the staff at the Cleveland Clinic and physicians elsewhere who answered numerous questions. Many of the Clinic's Wellness Institute staff and associates made scientific contributions and constructive criticisms, and allowed the time to complete this work. Cleveland Clinic CEO Toby Cosgrove has said that while the clinic will continue to be one of, if not the best, in illness care, wellness is what the clinic will do for every employee and person we touch. I am fortunate to work with such a talented and creative group who helped our thought processes as Dr. Martin Harris, Dr. Joe Hahn, and clinicians and leaders that span the gamut from inner-city schoolteachers to executive coaches.

Our family was fully engaged—with Jeff as our MD, PhD research associate, and Jennifer and Nancy as critical readers. I also want to thank Sukie Miller, Diane Reverend, and others for encouraging and critiquing the concepts. Having a great partner to ablate stress daily is clearly a magnificent way to help life and even writing be better—thank you, Nancy.

From Ellen Rome

From the moment Drs. Mike Roizen and Mehmet Oz approached me to collaborate on this book, I have been energized, enthused, and forever learning from their ability to make complex medical concepts easily digestible to multiple readerships. Now, we bring their YOU style to teens, with the shared hope of improving the health and wellness of young people worldwide. Thank you both for this golden opportunity!

I sincerely thank all of my brilliant colleagues who patiently answered my questions and emails. At the Cleveland Clinic Children's Hospital, outstanding pediatric gastroenterologist Dr. Barb Kaplan taught me about probiotics and other topics to keep me most up-to-date. My general pediatrics colleagues, Drs. Elaine Schulte, Laura Gillespie, Allison Brindle, Kim Giuliano, Skyler Kalady, and Mike Macknin continually were role models for dispensing sound advice and evidence-based best practices. Dr. Johanna Goldfarb, who serves as an infectious disease expert in her day job, has given me outstanding practical pearls for parenting a teen, as well as lending her own daughter Rosa to be a favorite babysitter for many years. Thanks to Drs. Allison Vidimos, chair of Dermatology at the Cleveland Clinic, and her star resident, Dr. Ed Galiczynski, for their expert advice on shaving, razor burn, and other teen dermatologic emergencies. I would also like to thank my mentors in adolescent medicine who continue to inspire me, including Drs. Hoover Adger and Alain Joffe, who helped me discover the joys of adolescent medicine at Johns Hopkins. To Drs.

Jean Emans, Estherann Grace, Liz Woods, Bob Masland (still cheering us on from the Great Beyond), Norm Spack, Joan Mansfield, and many others at Children's Hospital, Boston, thank you, thank you, thank you! I live by your words and teachings today. And to Drs. Richard MacKenzie, Marianne Felice, David Kaplan, and so many others, your pearls of wisdom are interspersed throughout the book. There are many more inspiring adolescent medicine docs to thank for their wisdom, and I wish I could list all of you!

It has been a pleasure and an honor to work with Linda Kahn, whose wisdom, humor, and ability to cut to the chase kept us at our best. Gary Hallgren's illustrations helped our ideas come alive, with his artful subtlety hopefully not lost on this readership. Ted's ability to "Spikerize" the text kept us laughing and learning how to get a message across without being too medically dry. I hope our teen readers appreciate and enjoy his style!

Most important, many thanks to my family for putting up with me through the many Sunday seven a.m. calls, the weekend and evening hours writing, and the humor that sustained me throughout. Our nanny, Christine Vargo, continues to amaze me with her wisdom, sparkle, and ability to keep the fun in our family day by day. Thanks to my father, Dr. Leonard P. Rome, whose amazing role modeling has been transformative, and who remains the best pediatrician I have ever known. His spirit lives on every time I watch our children at their best. I thank my mother, Nancy Rome, for her ongoing parenting pearls, which still keep me on track at home and elsewhere, for modeling how to keep multiple balls in the air with ease and grace, and whose unconditional positive regard has always been a source of strength and support for me. She is part of the family fabric that weaves us together, literally and figuratively (yes, she sews buttons, too!). To my brother, Peter Rome, thanks for being the best big brother an adolescent girl could wish for back when, and for sharing your own pearls of wisdom along the way. He and Sara Snow raised two amazing children, Lisa and David Rome, who have made it through adolescence with style! Lisa Rome, in particular, helped with many edits of this book, and now is pursuing a career in our Cleveland Clinic Wellness Institute as a writer and web guru—ever an inspiration for her archaic, e-challenged Auntie El! To Martha Rome, we'll try to get you meeting Oprah yet! And especially thanks to my own children, Andrew (thirteen) and Katherine (eleven), who read over my shoulder, shaped some of my ideas, kept me on track, and helped to make the recipes a little more kid-friendly. Saving the best for last, I thank my soul mate, best friend, and partner in parenting, husband Fred. His sense of humor keeps me sane, and his wisdom and intuitive people sense makes for some great dinner conversation and parenting moments at home. We're in early adolescence: the best is yet to come!

From Ted Spiker

To my sons, Alex and Thad: As you soon enter your teen years, I'm looking forward to seeing all of the opportunities that are ahead of you. I want you to enjoy, learn from, and be inspired by every adventure you take. To my wife, Liz: thank you for your passion, love, support, and always steering our boys in the right direction. I'm also appreciative of my entire family (Alex and Thad's grandparents, aunts, uncles, and cousins), friends, the whole YOU team, my colleagues and students at the University of Florida, and all the various magazine editors I've worked with over the years.

From Craig Wynett

To my sons, Ryan and Jim:

To say that your teenage years provided me with a wide range of learning experiences would be an understatement. I learned much more from you than you have from me. Particularly, how important it is to have a significant voice in what you did and how you did it.

To my sixteen-year-old niece, Lindsay, and my fourteen-year-old nephew, Ben:

It is hard to imagine a pair of more perfect teens. But just in case, I am sending you two copies of the book.

From Zoe Oz

I would like to thank my dear friends Kara Byron, Haley Brescia, Rachel Kupelian, who have always offered a helping hand and guidance, not only with this book, but also in life. To my mentors: Matthew Larrowe and Peter Bograd, who have refused to give up on me countless times when I have come close to doing so myself. And to my beloved family, to whom I owe the world and then some.

From Linda G. Kahn

Once again, thanks to Drs. Mehmet Oz and Mike Roizen for including me in yet another challenging and engaging project. Thanks also to Drs. Bruce Armstrong, David Bell, and Marina Catallozzi at Columbia University's Mailman School of Public Health for sparking my academic interest in adolescent health and providing insight into the physical, emotional, social, and cognitive issues facing teens today. To Dr. Ellen Rome, Craig Wynett, and Ted Spiker—talk about a Dream Team! And, of course, to my husband, Rob, and our three endlessly fascinating children, Elliot, Eva, and Leda—who will be needing the advice in this book all too soon.

From Gary Hallgren

To my daughter, Annabel, who belied the common wisdom that the teen years are hard on parents. Congratulations and welcome to adulthood. You're a love.

Index

stomach
thinking about, 344
ulcers of, 331
upset, 336–37
waste and, 332, 335, 336–37
See also abdomen
strains, knee, 98
Strattera, 183
strength exercises, 88, 101, 367, 368, 370, 371, 372, 373
stress
addiction and, 202, 239, 240, 242, 244
anger and, 201
antidotes to, 196, 198
asthma and, 319
balancing school, work, social life and, 200
benefits of, 190–91
biology of, 190–95, 197
brain and, 172, 180, 194, 196, 198, 227
breathing and, 317, 325
chronic, 190–91, 193
coping strategies and, 192, 201, 202
crying and, 229, 230
cutting/self-mutilation and, 234
diet/food and, 55, 191, 194, 200, 201, 202, 203
eating disorders and, 62, 67
emotions and, 201, 202
energy and, 190, 193, 194
evolution and, 190–91
examples of, 189–90
exercise and, 194, 198, 199, 201, 202
Fantastic Five about, 202–3
gender and, 198
hair and, 36
hanging out as antidote to, 196–98
headaches and, 199–200
health impact of, 192–95
hormones and, 192, 194, 196, 198, 229

identifying your, 203–5
identity and, 268, 270
immune system and, 306
jaws and, 30
kinds of, 191–92
low-level, 191
major life events and, 192
management of, 194–95, 196, 198, 202–3, 233, 240, 308, 362
menstruation and, 125
mood and, 194, 231, 234
nails and, 44
NUTs, 191–92, 203
ongoing low-level, 191
of parents, 288
preventing sickness and, 308
relationships and, 278, 283, 293
relaxation techniques and, 326
sex and, 268
skin care and, 20
sleep and, 191, 194, 200, 209
STIs and, 158
weight and, 194
YOU Plan and, 362
You Qs about, 196–202
stress fractures, 66
stretch marks, 16
stretching exercises, 90, 102, 105, 106, 199, 367, 369, 371, 372, 374
strokes, 164
subcutaneous tissue, 6, 8
sugars
biology of hunger and, 50–51, 53, 54, 55
brain and, 173
energy and, 61
as food felon, 56
heart and, 81
muscles and, 104
PCOS and, 129
sleep and, 210
stress and, 192, 203
teeth and, 28

waste and, 331, 334, 336, 341, 343
YOU Plan and, 361
See also blood sugar; glucose
suicide, 225, 226, 228, 231, 233, 234, 235, 291
sun
hair and, 25, 46
immune system and, 306
scars and, 17
skin and, 5, 5*n*, 6, 7, 10, 12, 14–15, 20
sunblockers, 12, 14–15, 17, 20
supplements, vitamin/mineral, 19, 142, 184, 200, 230, 335, 361. *See also specific supplement*
support systems, 192, 225, 270
surgery. *See type of surgery*
Sustenex, 308, 341
sweat glands, 6, 8
sweating: excess, 18–19
Sweet Potato Hummus (recipe), 392
swelling
of breasts, 121
causes of, 102–3
endometriosis and, 129
head injuries and, 354
immune system and, 304
in joints, 98
treatment for, 102–3, 106, 141
swimming, 33, 77, 91–92, 160, 355, 357
swine flu, 312
synapses, 174, 175, 208–9
synovial fluid, 98
syphilis, 140
systemic infections, 301, 303

T cells, 301, 303, 309
T-shirts, sun and, 15
Tamiflu (oseltamivir), 305
tampons, 125–26, 160
tanning beds, 16
tapeworm, 306
taste, sense of, 41, 331

Whole Wheat Angel Hair with
Broccoli (recipe), 282
whooping cough (pertussis), 311
wiping: and body waste, 344
wisdom teeth, 42
Woods, Tiger, 261
wounds: treatment for, 356
wrinkles, 5, 6, 7, 10, 14, 19, 28,
30, 77, 240, 243
wryneck, 88
www.cahl.org, 404
www.collegeboard.com, 218
www.davidlynchfoundation
.org, 202
www.ec-help.org, 165
www.fitpackdvd.com, 367
www.glsen.org, 269
www.itgetsbetter.org, 269
www.iwannaknow.org, 156
www.lambda.org, 269
www.morethansound.net, 273
www.scenariosusa.org, 351
www.sexetc.org, 154
www.suicideprevention
lifeline.org, 233
www.youbeauty.com, 19, 112

X-rays, 115, 401–2

yeast infections, 126
yoga, 89, 322
yogurt, 308, 309, 338, 344
YOU Activity
about brain, 185–86

emotional intelligence test as,
270, 271–74
food diary as, 71–72
YOU Plan, 359–64
YOU Qs
about addiction, 241–50
about allergies and asthma,
321–25
about body waste, 336–44
about bones, 86–92
about brain, 178–84
about breasts, 119–22
about breath/breathing,
321–25
about carbohydrates, 56–70
about decision making,
352–56
about diet, 56–70
about exercise, 86–92
about fats, 56–70
about female biology, 119–29
about food, 56–70
about hair, 32–38
about hunger, 56–70
about identity, 265–70
about immune system, 307–11
about joints, 102–5
about male anatomy, 138–43
about menstruation, 122–29
about mood, 229–34
about muscles, 86–92, 102–5
about nails, 43–44
about physical fitness, 86–92,
102–5

about protein, 56–70
about relationships, 285–93
about sex/sexual intercourse,
155–66
about skin, 11–19
about sleep, 214–18
about stress, 196–202
about teeth, 38–42
about waste, 336–44
about weight, 56–70
YOU Test, for skin, 20–21
YOU Tool
importance of, 365
See also specific YOU Tool
YOU Tool 1, exercises, 86, 92,
367–74
YOU Tool 2, recipes, 375–99
YOU Tool 3, cosmetic surgery,
400–402
YOU Tool 4, medical
confidentiality, 403–5

Zigzag (exercise), 372
zinc, 41, 309, 310
zinc oxide, 17
zinc pyrithione, 34
Zithromax, 156
Zmax, 156
Zoloft (sertraline), 231
Zovirax (acyclovir), 158
Zyban, 247, 249, 250
Zyban (exercise), 372
Zyrtec (cetirizine),
324

About the Authors

MICHAEL F. ROIZEN, MD, is a *New York Times* bestselling author and co-founder and originator of the very popular RealAge.com website. He is chief wellness officer of the Cleveland Clinic, chair of its Wellness Institute, and chief medical consultant to *The Dr. Oz Show* and chief medical expert for sharecare.com.

MEHMET C. OZ, MD, is also a *New York Times* bestselling author and the Emmy award–winning host of *The Dr. Oz Show*. He is professor and vice chairman of surgery at New York Presbyterian Columbia University and the medical director of the Integrated Medicine Center and the director of the Heart Institute.

ELLEN ROME, MD, MPH, is head of adolescent medicine at the Cleveland Clinic Children's Hospital. She is a board-certified pediatrician who is among the first in the country to also be board certified in adolescent medicine. Dr. Rome received her undergraduate degree from Yale University, her medical degree from Case Western Reserve University's School of Medicine, and her master's of public health from Harvard's School of Public Health.